1985

WOMEN
Like Us

WOMEN
Like Us

What Is Happening
to the Women of
the Harvard Business School,
Class of '75—
the Women Who Had the
First Chance to
Make It to the Top

by
Liz Roman Gallese

William Morrow and Company, Inc.
New York

Grateful acknowledgment is made to the Procter & Gamble Company for permission to quote from their Sales Management recruiting brochure.

Quotations from "Some Precepts from a Bunkhouse Philosopher" by Benjamin Stein, reprinted by permission of *The Wall Street Journal,* copyright © June 11, 1976 by Dow Jones & Company, Inc. All rights reserved.

Library of Congress Cataloging in Publication Data

Gallese, Liz Roman.
    Women like us.

    1. Harvard University. Graduate School of
Business Administration.   2. Master of business
administration degree—United States.   3. Women
executives—United States.   I. Title.
HF1134.H4G35   1985   658.4'09'088042   84-19095
ISBN 0-688-02176-X

Printed in the United States of America

In loving memory of my mother,
        Almerinda Rose Roman,
And to my father,
        Edward Walter Roman

Acknowledgments

This book couldn't have been written without the assistance of a number of people on, appropriately enough, the two great fronts of my own life, the professional and the personal. On the professional side, I am deeply grateful to my former colleagues and superiors at my previous place of business, *The Wall Street Journal.* No young journalist could have received better guidance or training than that provided by such a dedicated and talented staff of reporters and editors—the finest, I'm convinced, in the profession. While the people to whom I am indebted at *The Journal* are too numerous to mention, I would like to say a special thank you to William M. Carley and Neil Ulman, two of my five former bureau chiefs, for their faith in me and for their support.

More recently, I am grateful to the people who believed they could turn a strictly objective newspaper reporter into a writer of books, a profession that, I feel, demands so much more in terms of formulating and shaping one's own ideas. I am indebted especially to Harold T. Miller, who first believed I could be an author and who encouraged me to get on with a project; to my agent, Roslyn Targ, who never lost faith in me even at the darkest

7

moments; and most particularly, to my editor at William Morrow & Company, Pat Golbitz, whose brilliance and inspiration shine through the pages of this book. Finally, I would like to thank David Treharne who knew from way back that I would someday be a writer.

On the personal front, I owe an untold debt of gratitude to my father and my late mother, to whom this book is dedicated, to the other member of my family of origin, my sister, Christine Roman, and to the members of my extended family. They were the first to teach me the importance of balancing family and career and to hold me to the task on both fronts. In that department, I am also grateful to the family of which I am a part today—to my husband, Paul, and my daughter, Amy Elizabeth—who provided that critical day-to-day support. They were the ones to bear the brunt of the price that a project such as this demands, and to see me through with compassion, humor, and love.

The point at which the personal and professional converge comes with my thank yous to Regina M. Collinsgru, owner of Letter Perfect Office Services, and to her marvelous staff, who transcribed hours of taped interviews and typed and retyped the many drafts of this book; and to the three individuals—in particular, Margaret Adams—who provided my daughter with the conscientious and loving care without which I couldn't have researched or written it. These individuals started out as professional associates and, to my happy surprise, have become cherished friends.

Finally, at that point at the edge of the personal and the professional, I am most grateful to the women of the class of 1975 at the Harvard Business School, who shared with me their highest aspirations and deepest concerns with respect to both aspects of their lives. Without their support and faith in me, this book couldn't have been written. I can only hope that the results affirm their confidence, not only for women like us, but for the generations of women to come whose futures will hold places in both the nation's institutions and its families.

CONTENTS

ACKNOWLEDGMENTS   7

NOTE TO THE READER   10

PROLOGUE: Women Like Us   13

1 The Ticket   21

2 "But I'm Not Typical . . ."   65

3 SUZANNE: The Making of a Female Chief
        Executive Officer   83

4 PHOEBE: The Antithesis of the Corporate Woman   111

5 MARY PAT: Femininity and Fit   135

6 TESS: The Fight for Control   165

7 MARTHA: Femininity, Overexpectations,
        and the Loss of Control   191

8 HOLLY: Unspoken Perceptions   211

9 How Ambitious Would You Say You Are?   231

EPILOGUE: The Score   247

Note to the Reader

To protect the privacy of those interviewed for this work, certain changes have been made respecting names, background and present situations. While these changes do not affect the substance of this book, the reader is accordingly cautioned against speculating as to the identity of particular interviewees.

There are a number of things you have to possess to reach the top rung. A modicum of ability helps, but what really counts is persistence, luck, the willingness to take risks, and an enormous desire to become rich and famous.

All of these things can be controlled—even luck. Luck can be controlled only partially, but I learned how it could be controlled even that much from a book by Joan Didion. In the book a character says, "You can't win if you're not at the table," by which he meant that you could not win at craps unless you were at the craps table. The secret of being lucky is to give yourself enough chances to be lucky—to roll the dice enough times to make your point, even if you don't roll seven on the first roll. You may crap out a number of times, and each time hurts. But you keep rolling. . . .

That means—if you want to be a writer, you must write and show your writings to people who can publish them, even if those people are insulting and cruel, as they will be; if you want to be a politician, you must go out and speak before people who will fall asleep in front of your very eyes and will treat you as if you were a piece of furniture; if you want to be an actor, you must audition in front of men and women with smug faces and glazed eyes who will treat you like a piece of meat, and so it goes.

But while all those things are happening to you, you will be at the table, and you cannot win if you're not at the table. And eventually, if you have even a modicum of talent, you will make your point, even if the bet is small at first. . . .

—BENJAMIN STEIN,

"Some Precepts from a Bunkhouse Philosopher"

Prologue:

WOMEN
Like Us

This is the story of the women of the class of 1975 at the Harvard Business School. It is the story of one tiny fragment—an "elite," if you will—of a generation of women who, for the first time, have had the opportunity to advance in the country's corporations and professional associations. It is the story of a group of women who were among the first to have had a chance in the world—for money, for power—and of what happens when they do.

Like so many stories, this one began as a personal saga. Six years ago, in the fall of 1978, when I was a staff reporter for *The Wall Street Journal,* I came face-to-face with a dilemma that led me to raise some fundamental questions about the women of my generation, those of us who had gone to work in the 1970's and who were then in our early thirties.

Simply put, the dilemma was this: I had worked in the Boston news bureau of *The Journal* for eight years, and I was told that I would have to relocate if I wanted to get ahead. I was offered a position in New York, a post that could have led to bigger jobs with the paper. But my husband, Paul, had opened his own law practice and had begun to settle into the Boston area.

The dilemma wasn't simple, I soon began to discover. For beneath the straightforward question of, Shall I accept the job or not? lay a host of unanswered questions about my personal and professional future. Personally, the questions centered around my marriage and whether or not it was strong enough to be sustained given my desire to advance on the job. There was the question of whether or not Paul and I should have children, given what we both hoped to achieve in our careers.

Professionally, the questions were equally complex. I wondered about the importance of the job that was offered to me and where it might lead. I was told that management was eager to advance women. But women had been on the staff for a dozen years by then, and not one was even a bureau manager, the lowest-level management position. The first woman bureau manager, in fact, wouldn't be named until three years later, in the fall of 1981.

Just as critically, the questions about both of these phases of my life overlapped and entwined. I realized that I would have said a firm yes to the job if I had been single or divorced. But with Paul's career to be considered, was the job I was being offered not only important, but important *enough*, to accept?

Furthermore, I could see that I would have to make my decision based on the logistics of the situation as they were, not as I would have liked them to be. In my fantasies, I could envision a job that, say, allowed me to work at home two days a week so that I could commute to New York and still maintain a marriage. But this job was five days a week, eight hours a day, in an office two hundred miles away from home.

In the wake of confronting my own dilemma—and I decided finally to turn down the job and remain in Boston—I began to question the set of assumptions that appeared to be growing up around the women of my generation: that we were advancing fast and far in the country's companies and professional firms and doing so, if we so chose, without sacrificing husbands and children. There was even a name for us: We were the "superwomen" whose goal was to "have it all." And in the course of my questioning, I began to suspect that the reality for women like us was far more complex than that pretty image would make it seem.

So it was that I decided to write this book about the women of Harvard. In trying to ascertain the reality behind the image, I wanted to pursue my quest in microcosm, through the eyes of a single group of women. And I wanted to focus on a group that, more than any other single group, would have *the* credential for success: the coveted master of business administration, or M.B.A. degree, from the country's most prestigious graduate school of business.

I chose the class of 1975 very particularly, because that was the first class at the Business School to be fully 10 percent women, and thus, I felt, the first whose members would embrace the tenets of my generation. Women were first accepted as degree candidates at the Business School in the fall of 1963, and until a decade later, comprised no more than a scant handful of any one class. I also felt that by 1981, the year I interviewed them, the women of this class would have been out of school long enough to be able to speak from experience about their professional and personal lives.

In researching this book, I decided to proceed simply as a reporter. Without using questionnaires or statistical data of any kind, I merely contacted each of the eighty-eight women who had been enrolled in the fall of 1973—seventy-eight of whom graduated with the class two years later, four of whom graduated the following year after a year off to work or study, and six of whom dropped out or flunked out and never graduated.

I asked each woman for an interview on a confidential basis, which meant that I agreed never to reveal her name or business affiliation, and in whatever writing I did, to alter details that would identify her. At the interviews, which took place over drinks or dinner at restaurants or on weekday evenings or weekend afternoons in their homes, I kept my questions as open-ended as possible. I asked each woman simply to tell me her story: Who are you? Where did you come from? Why did you go to the Business School? What did you find when you got there? What has your life been like since? What are your dreams for the future?

Then, when patterns began to emerge about who these women were and what their lives were like, I chose six women whose stories each said something different to me about what it is like to be a woman in business today. I interviewed each of those women a second time in greater depth, and whenever possible, I talked to the men in their lives.

In some respects, I was surprised by their enthusiasm for the project. Of the eighty-eight women I contacted, fully eighty-two agreed to talk to me, and of the remaining six, only four actually declined. The other two couldn't accommodate me at a mutually convenient time. They were candid to a degree that I wouldn't have expected, even given my assurances of confidentiality, and in some cases, they were extraordinarily generous. Some had me to breakfast or dinner at their homes or insisted on picking up the restaurant check. One woman who lived and worked in the Midwest invited me to stay at her home, and when we finished our interview, took me on a grand tour of her community; another in the Pacific Northwest made my hotel reservations and treated me to a day's outing at a famous resort in her area.

I knew they were curious about my project, of course, especially since I alone had access to the type of information that would put their own stories into perspective. Then, too, by telling them that they were vying for one of six places in my book, I had set up a contest that would appeal to what I had supposed would be common to all of them, their competitiveness. Indeed, one woman who had been especially reluctant—she refused to discuss her personal life, snapping when I appealed to her sense of friendship, "I don't consider you a friend"—nonetheless conceded that she would cooperate further if asked. "It would be nice for my ego to know that I was one of the six selected," she explained. But in the final analysis, I attributed their candor to the fact that they, too, sensed a dichotomy between the reality of their lives and the image that had emerged.

The reality, as I see it, can be found in the stories of the six women who appear as the central figures in this book, and from the comments and observations of the women who knew those six at the Business School and who appear as minor characters. (Crucially, none of the characters, either major or minor, is a composite.)

The reality can be found in part in the story of Suzanne Sheehan, the provincial woman from Texas who, I felt, stood the best chance of making it to the top of a major American corporation

—and in what there was about her that made me feel that way. It can be found in the story of Phoebe Holstrom, who shared many of Suzanne's characteristics but nonetheless struck me as least likely to achieve such a position. It can be found in the story of Mary Pat Horner, who brought an emotional dimension to the job that virtually guaranteed that she would fail in American business. It can be found in the story of Tess Beckett, who won the fight for control over that same issue; and in the story of Martha Davis, who did not. Ultimately, the reality can be found, in the story of Holly Lane Pfeiffer, who wouldn't sacrifice what was innately hers as a woman for success in her career.

At various points along the way in researching and writing this book, I found it tempting to compare the women of the class of 1975 with the successful businessmen I had met and interviewed as a staff reporter for *The Wall Street Journal*—men who currently hold senior positions in the country's corporations and professional firms. After all, in many respects the women of my generation were just grappling with the types of questions successful men have always had to deal with—specifically, that the pursuit of money and power often comes at the expense of personal relationships.

But the attempt at comparison proved to be a two-edged sword. While the story of the women of Harvard was indeed the story of ambition in women—who had it, who didn't, and why the difference—the fact remained that it was difficult to compare these women to the men I knew. First of all, women were just beginning to seek access to the environment in which the struggle for power is played out, the milieu of management, and for the most part, they found it to be as alien as it is natural to men. Unlike the professions in which women have always been more likely to enter, the milieu of management rewards, not so much excellence at a particular task, but the pursuit of sheer power; not so much the results of any one individual's effort, but an individual's ability to relate to others up and down a chain of command. Indeed, the very point of management becomes not the product but the process, the struggle for that next rung on the ladder. And the manager's source of satisfaction comes not from within himself but from how he is perceived by others, his superiors, peers, and subordinates.

On the other hand, it was virtually impossible for me *not* to compare the women of the class to successful men. In entering the race for money and power in a milieu that had been all but closed to them, women were signaling their readiness to play by the rules set by such men and, even more critical, their willingness to be judged by those men. For corporations are not democracies, and in the years ahead, the men who are currently in positions of power will be the single most important determinant of whether or not women are allowed access to the senior positions in the country's institutions.

If the women of my generation were the first to be seeking access to positions of power in the nation's corporations and professional firms, they won't be the last. Women comprise a fourth of the places in the graduate business schools, a third in the medical schools, and up to half in the law schools. That is up from less than five percent a decade earlier, a fourfold increase in the short span of a decade.

And so in a broader sense, the story of the women of the class of 1975 at Harvard is the harbinger of what is to come—for women, for men, and for institutions. In considering this, I sometimes think back to a remark I made to my boss when I turned down the job in New York. It was late in the afternoon in December, and we were sipping Cokes in the windowless cafeteria of *The Journal*'s New York office.

"Let me tell you why I turned it down," I began. "I would have taken it, but . . ."

Into my mind flashed the bitter fights Paul and I had had; the points we had thrashed over again and again: that accepting the offer would have meant we both would have had to pull up stakes for something that may or may not have worked out for me alone, for something that indeed may or may not have been the opportunity it was purported to be.

So it was easy for me to avoid the whole truth: that I was afraid to take a chance. Afraid that I would fail. Afraid that my husband would leave. That, in fact, I wasn't as ambitious as I would have liked to believe. It was easy for me to finish the sentence with a half truth.

"Paul has to find a *job*," I said.

"I can see that," my boss said. "I can see why it would be a problem for you."

"It is more than a problem," I said. "I see it as the challenge of this generation."

That it is. Never have I believed it more than after talking to the women of the class of 1975 at the Harvard Business School. It has been their challenge. They're meeting it. This is their story.

1.

The Ticket

SUZANNE

It was a warm Wednesday evening in May 1981, and I hurried into Il Monello, a northern Italian restaurant on New York's Upper East Side between Seventy-sixth and Seventy-seventh streets. I was nine months pregnant and I couldn't walk as fast as I would have liked, so I was late. I had taken the local subway from midtown and gotten off at Seventy-seventh Street, the closest stop. But I still hadn't made it. It was past 7:30 P.M., the time I had arranged to meet Suzanne Sheehan, thirty-five years old and director of planning for a Fortune 100 company. One of the biggest: $6 billion in annual sales.

When I walked into the restaurant, Suzanne Sheehan hadn't arrived yet. A waiter ushered me to a table by the wall toward the center of the room. There I slipped a sixty-minute cassette into my tape recorder; checked the red light that meant, when it was on, that I was recording; pulled out a slim notebook—and waited for Suzanne.

I had called Suzanne a week earlier, when I first arrived in New

York, and I hadn't suspected from the telephone conversation that this interview would be any different from all of the others. We had set a date for Wednesday, May 20. Then she had called to say that she could make it a week earlier, May 13, and we had changed it. Nothing out of the ordinary, except for one slight clue. Two nights before our meeting, on May 11, I had had dinner in the same restaurant with another young woman, Claire Jacobsen, who had roomed with Suzanne years earlier, when they were both students at the Harvard Business School.

"Suzanne was my best friend, and we still keep in touch," Claire had said, emphasizing the word *best* in her soft tone of voice. Then she had added simply, as if sharing a secret, "You will enjoy meeting her."

A few minutes before 8:00 P.M., the same waiter ushered an ordinary-looking woman to my table. She appeared to be a bit disheveled: She was wearing a simple tan poplin summer suit, a wrinkled white cotton blouse, and pumps with rundown stacked heels. Of average height and just a touch too plump, she had brushed her short black hair behind her ears, as if to hide the fact that it needed to be trimmed. She had big brown eyes, a full mouth, and a small nose that seemed to be too slender for her coarse face—because, she would explain later, she had gotten it fixed. She had spent the first thousand dollars she earned in business the summer after her graduation from the Business School for the nose job she had always wanted.

Without smiling, she slipped into the chair at right angles to me and held out her hand. "I'm Suzanne Sheehan," she said. We shook hands silently, ordered some wine, and I launched into an explanation of my project, which by that time I had boiled down to a standard pitch. "Tell me your story," I said. "Who are you? Where did you come from? Why did you go to the Harvard Business School? What did you find when you got there? What has your life been like since?"

Before I even had a chance to flick on my tape recorder, Suzanne began talking, without smiling, in a rapid-fire, high-pitched monotone. She spoke matter-of-factly, as if reciting a speech. It was as if she knew what I would ask and had rehearsed her answers. She looked straight ahead, at the back wall of the restaurant. She didn't seem to think it was necessary to meet my eyes.

"I went to the company I'm with now immediately after the Business School. I chose this company very particularly, because I wanted to go to work where I would be the only M.B.A. in the department or in the company coming in right then. I was twenty-nine years old, and I did not want to join as a member of the class of 1975. Claire [Jacobsen], for example, went to an investment-banking firm, where they hire lots of M.B.A.'s. There's always the danger in going to a bank or an investment-banking firm of becoming one of the 'class of . . .' and I, because I was older, wanted to be considered more senior than the class of 1975. So I went into a situation where I would be the only M.B.A. and I would be treated totally as an individual. As a twenty-nine-year-old professional who had worked before. My work before, by the way, was as a pediatric nurse for six years."

"I had heard, yes," I interjected, trying to tease her about it. "Claire was telling me on Monday night that you came out, diapers in hand, onward to the Harvard Business School."

Suzanne wasn't amused. "It just happened that I caught that line," she said briskly, glancing at me for the first time, a touch of annoyance in her eyes. "It was one of the things one did after college. I didn't get married to the guy I was going with for many years. I left Austin, Texas, hopefully with a postponed wedding, and I came to Boston. And I just didn't go back. I sent the ring back in February. I left in June, sent the ring back in February. And once I got on the airplane, I had my first drink, my first airplane ride. I was twenty-two years old and I never turned around. And I didn't really even know that I wanted to move away from Austin. It was a sort of immediate thing of getting away from Austin, of getting away from having babies, and you know, just car, apartment, kids. I was just getting away a little bit and I didn't think I was getting away for good. But I did get away for good."

Suzanne paused and glanced again at the back wall of the restaurant. The spools of the cassette were spinning, and I felt relieved. The interview had come dangerously close to having come to a complete halt. I had obviously misjudged her sense of humor. But now she was sliding comfortably into the spell of self-revelation, and she continued with her story. Fifteen minutes into the first side of my sixty-minute tape, she was relating the events of her past so rapidly that I began jotting down key words in my notebook as points of reference: hometown—Alvin, Texas; University of Texas at Austin—class of 1967; pediatric nurse—Boston Lying-In Hospital, 1967 to 1973; party girl—razor thin, always on a diet; boyfriend—Butch. She seemed to be enjoying herself now; she began punctuating her story with amusing anecdotes.

She laughed when she told me that she tried to get a clerical job in a bank in Boston, after having worked for years at the Boston Lying-In Hospital. "Going to work in one of those tall buildings with a view. It looked great! I was just dying to work there. And they rejected me because they said, 'You know, we said typing was only ten percent of the job, but it's maybe a little bit more, and you don't type at a-all!'"

So she decided to go to the Harvard Business School, and the summer before she enrolled, she received a reading list of business books from a campus group called the Women's Student Association. She read every one of them. "They were great books, jillions of books." When I asked her how many there were, she brightened, and I thought she was going to laugh again. "Fifteen, twenty," she said. "But I had the summer. Just going to the Cape. Going to Martha's Vineyard. Having a great time!" she added hastily, as if she didn't want me to think of her as the type who would read all twenty books on a suggested list.

She told me about her career at the Fortune 100 company: how she had started as an analyst in the department of planning at a time when the company was diversifying from its mainstay products that weren't growing; how she became assistant to the director of planning, a title she held for three years and by the end of that period loathed to such an extent that she was "ready to kill"; how she was offered a promotion to direct the company's planning department in the Far East only to have it snatched away from her at the last minute because the company had political debts to pay to another person; how finally, finally, she was able to shed that horrid title—assistant to the director of planning—and be named a director in her own right; how, when it came right down to it, she wanted to go into senior management. She wanted to be an executive vice-president, then president, then chief executive officer "of some big thing." Only she didn't go around saying that, "because I may not think I am going to get promoted that far, no matter what I do."

As the interview progressed, I found myself laughing at the moments in her story that she punctuated with laughter, even if I didn't find the anecdotes particularly funny. At several points, I found myself actually imitating her distinctive laughter and her mannerisms, throwing back my head and looking at the back wall and laughing in a rapid-fire staccato that wasn't laughter at all. I often find myself imitating people who impress me. It was clear that Suzanne had, and that both pleased and annoyed me. I became suddenly envious of this disheveled woman and somewhat self-conscious of my swollen belly, nine months pregnant as I was.

"I don't really have this desire to get big and have babies," Suzanne said, slowly and deliberately, when I asked her, as I did all of the women I spoke to, about children. Her voice trailed off, her placid expression metamorphosed into a frown. She was single. There was no one in particular, only "sexual arrangements," she said. It was as if she had more important things planned for herself in the world: She wanted to make it into senior management, to become an executive vice-president, then president, then chief executive officer.

As I listened to Suzanne, I began to realize what there was about this interview that made it so unusual, different from all of the rest. I began to realize why Suzanne was special. She, alone among all of the women who had graduated from the Harvard Business School in the class of 1975, told me that she wanted to be the chief executive officer of a major American corporation.

For the previous nine months, since September 1980, I had been researching this book about the women of the class of 1975 at the Business School. My objective was to find out what had happened to them in the six years since their graduation. By the time I talked to Suzanne at Il Monello in New York, I had interviewed about two thirds of the eighty-eight women who had been enrolled in the class in the fall of 1973. I had gone to New York in May to finish the interviews, to talk to the women who were working in New York. These women comprised about a third of the group, by far the largest segment.

What had struck me about the women I had talked to up to that point was that very few seemed to be planning careers the way men do. Most of the men who graduate from the Harvard Business School join a big company and work their way up a ladder, striving for power and money and prestige, many of them aiming for the ultimate goal of chief executive officer. Another large number invest in or start their own companies.

As I talked to Suzanne, I thought back to all of the interviews I had had since the previous September. The faces of the women flashed before me, seated as they had been across the table from me in restaurants from Boston to San Francisco, from Miami to Calgary. There were the women who had husbands and children, who worked part-time or full-time at administrative jobs in colleges or nonprofit organizations, who spoke of "balanced lives." There were the women who were married or single or divorced —it didn't matter—who always seemed to be working, working, working, in consulting firms or companies, without having any idea what it was they were working for. There were those who seemed to have goals, but who, consciously or subconsciously, seemed to stop short of wanting to advance into senior positions. There were a few who drove themselves beyond that point, but who chose consulting firms rather than corporations, because they were convinced they stood a better chance of "making it" in consulting. Then there were a few—but more than I would have guessed—who had done the unthinkable: They simply had dropped out. Unemployed, they spent their days tending to homes and, in some cases, children, not really questioning, as perhaps they should have, why they had gone to the Harvard Business School in the first place.

What struck me about Suzanne, therefore, when I talked to her on that warm May evening, was that she alone wanted what it had become possible only recently for women to aspire to: the position at the pinnacle of power in a major American corporation, chief executive officer. I was fascinated. Like all of the other women in the class, she had been one of a privileged minority. She had had the benefit of an education at the most select graduate business school in the country, and she had, by some fortuitous stroke, come of age when, for the first time, opportunities were opening to women. She was poised to take fullest advantage of those opportunities, and none of the others were. I wanted to find out why. In short, who was Suzanne Sheehan, and why was she so different?

It was late by the time my interview with Suzanne ended, and the restaurant was practically empty. We slid out of our seats, made our way through the door, and walked up Second Avenue to the corner of Eighty-second Street, where I was staying at a friend's apartment. As we walked, Suzanne glanced at my belly. "When are you due?" she asked.

"End of this month," I replied. End of May—that had been my stock response for the previous nine months. I was actually due June 1, but I always said, "End of May," so that people would think I was further along than I was and marvel at how little weight I had gained.

"You should have seen Holly when she was pregnant," Suzanne continued, oblivious to my response. "She had a forty-eight -inch waist. Chuck measured it. He couldn't believe what he had done to her." Suzanne laughed and asked, "Did you meet Holly? I suppose you did if you've already been to Dallas. When did you see her?"

I had indeed met Holly Lane Pfeiffer, the previous December. We had had dinner at The Ritz-Carlton Hotel in Chicago, and I remembered her particularly well because of all the women I had interviewed I was most impressed and charmed with her. She had been in Chicago overnight, on her way home to Dallas from a business meeting in New York, and we had met in the hotel's elegant thirteenth-floor lobby. She had rushed up to me and stood squarely in front of me, as if making a statement. She was a tall woman with short, straight blond hair pinned back at her temples with silver barrettes; a pair of round tortoise-shell glasses lent an air of authority to her delicate oval face. She was slim as a reed, I had noted, despite her three pregnancies, so slim that she appeared to be all angles. Her cheekbones, elbows, knees looked like the jagged edges of a rock.

Throughout the interview, I had found myself making mental notes. Holly Lane Pfeiffer seemed to be doing it all, and I would soon be called upon to do the same. I could learn from her. After the Business School, she had joined a major corporation in New York as assistant to a powerful vice-president for finance. It was the kind of job companies save for the best M.B.A.'s, those they put on the "fast track." She had quit in less than a year, however, to move to Dallas and marry Chuck Pfeiffer, a classmate of hers at the Business School, surprising all of her friends when she did, Suzanne included. But she had landed a job in Dallas, in a big but rather unimportant unit of a giant New York–based company. She had had, as she put it, a "bunch of babies," but she had kept right on working and being promoted. She was making her mark in what companies call materials management, the job of buying all the mundane things companies need to conduct their daily business, everything from pencils and paper to shipping cartons and computers. Now she wanted to transfer to headquarters in New York, to get back on, as she said, "the fast track."

I had asked Holly about her children, how she managed. She had told me that she had taken six weeks off to have her first child, but had cut that time in half for both her second and third. She had hired a housekeeper to live in her home and care for her children. There had been crises at first: The weekend before she went back to work after her first child was born, she still hadn't found a housekeeper, and she had been desperate. An agency she had contacted sent a short, squat Greek woman who showed up at her doorstep with a suitcase. Chuck was away somewhere on a business trip. "Look, I wasn't really looking for a live in," Holly had told her. "And I'm going to have to discuss this with my husband when he gets home. But as long as you're here, and I need a warm body . . ." The arrangement had worked well, and now, Holly had told me, she wouldn't have it any other way. She had to have someone living in, she had explained, because there were some nights that she simply had to stay late at the office, or other nights, like that night we talked, when both she and Chuck were away on business trips.

I had winced slightly at the thought of my own unborn child, four months along at that point and not even a slight bulge, being left alone with a housekeeper while my husband and I whisked off to the far corners of the country on business trips. I remember feeling slightly relieved: I wouldn't have to worry about *that* for months. But Holly had laughed, her nose crinkling like a little accordion, her eyes narrowing into slits. She had a distinctive laughter that was both genuine and infectious.

"I think I had a lot of very mixed emotions with my first child," she had said, "but what happens is that you go to work and you come home . . . you feel really good. It feels good to work, it feels productive. Then you get into the car and you feel guilty, thinking, 'I had a great time. But my poor kid. I haven't thought about my kid all day.' And then you get home and there's your kid, alive"—at this point, Holly had held up her hands and wiggled her fingers in an effort to imitate the gestures of her children—"saying, 'ha, ha, ha' and 'goo, goo, gah, gah.' Happy! Having a great time! So what the heck?"

She had laughed again, and so had I, as much in relief as for any other reason, for the subject we had been discussing, we both knew, was a hot potato for women like us. That evening in Chicago, just before we had parted at the elevators in the lobby of The Ritz, I had asked Holly one final question, a bit impulsively. "Why do you do it anyway?" She had looked at me and said, honestly, I thought, "Oh, ego, I suppose. Why does anyone do it? To see if you can really do it, to see if you are as good as you think you are. . . ."

Turning now to Suzanne, as we walked along Second Avenue, I said, "Yes, I met Holly. In December. At The Ritz in Chicago." Suzanne nodded, the smile fading from her lips.

Throughout the interview at Il Monello, Suzanne had talked freely about the women who were her friends at the Business School, in that same rapid, high-pitched monotone. Her first year, she had shared a suite in Chase Hall with three other women. She and Holly Lane had been roommates; across the hall, Claire Jacobsen roomed with a much younger woman, Connie Paulsen, who like Suzanne, was from the South. The second year, Suzanne, Holly, and Claire had rented a townhouse on Beacon Hill in Boston. The townhouse had belonged to a young divorcée, who had left all of her things, so it was beautifully appointed. The divorcée had left her silver and her china and her furniture; she had left all of her books in the tiny library on the first floor.

The three women had asked Connie to join them, but Connie had gotten married over the summer to a second-year student she had met the first day of school and, it seemed to Suzanne, clung to for the rest of the year. So they invited a fourth woman, Elizabeth Conner, whom Holly knew only slightly because Elizabeth had beaten her out for a job with a major consulting firm that summer, to join them in the house on Beacon Hill.

"Elizabeth's a hard one for me, actually," Suzanne had said at one point during our interview. She had said this rather wistfully, which seemed out of character for her. "Elizabeth is interesting and bright, and I've seen her a couple of times when she's in town, I've tried to. The last time it was Sunday morning. She was working, so she joined me for an hour and went back to work, and I didn't feel much communication with her." Suzanne's voice had trailed off.

I smiled to myself as Suzanne spoke. I had interviewed Elizabeth Conner the previous December, on my way home from Chicago to Boston, just after I had met with Holly at The Ritz. I had made a special effort to stop over in Philadelphia to talk to Elizabeth, whom I had tried to contact several times that fall but never had been able to reach. She worked for a major international foundation and traveled four fifths of her time, trips that lasted for weeks and often took her out of the country.

So that Friday evening in December, I had gone to her office, where we had agreed to meet. It was past 5:00 P.M., the building was deserted, and when I opened the door, she wasn't there. Something told me she wouldn't be coming, so I called her home. She answered the phone; she was sick, she said. She would have to cancel the interview. Then she mentioned that she planned to work the following day, a Saturday. Not that sick, I had thought to myself, so I had pressed her to keep our appointment.

"I can't believe you're pressuring me like this," she had said angrily. And I had thought to myself, Oh God, a fight! It's curtains for this one.

We tussled a bit on the telephone, and then finally, she had agreed to meet me for brunch the following morning, at a small hotel in a recently renovated neighborhood of the city. I had arrived early that morning and was seated on a small velvet sofa in the lobby when I spotted her. She breezed through the revolving door, charged right past me, and instinctively I knew that it was she. She had appeared as stately as the foundation for which she worked. She had long legs, short brown hair with ends that jutted out, as if she couldn't be bothered putting them in place, and a head that she kept pointed upward. She had reminded me of a dart, whisking its way to the bull's-eye of a dartboard, oblivious to everything around her.

At brunch, Elizabeth had mentioned the house on Beacon Hill and her three roommates, and thinking about that now as Suzanne spoke, I could see why Suzanne seemed intimidated by Elizabeth. Elizabeth hadn't been able to remember any of her roommates' names. "There was . . ." she had said, and then, "Oh God, I'm terrible at names, which is embarrassing." But she hadn't been embarrassed. "There was . . . Suzanne what's-her-face," she had said, finally, clearly dismissing Suzanne as unimportant and not worth remembering.

As Suzanne and I walked along Second Avenue on this May evening in New York, therefore, I felt a pang of sympathy for her. She had obviously liked Elizabeth very much and couldn't understand why Elizabeth hadn't returned the friendship. For a moment, she was silent, reminiscing, I supposed, about Elizabeth. Then she started talking once again about her roommate Holly Lane.

"Holly's a very interesting case, I think," Suzanne began. "She had a very rural New England classical family life—a farm life almost, in Manchester, Vermont. And she went to Wellesley College—her mother is very cultured. And then she went off to Asia, and she came back. She has a lot of life and warmth, and she's charming. She can charm the pants off anyone, and she just fell in love with this guy, Chuck Pfeiffer, who was the class rogue. He did unbelievable things. Their relationship at the Business School was unbelievably stormy; it was one for the record books. And suddenly, she just calmed down. . . ."

Suzanne told me that she had seen Holly in Dallas the previous October, for the first time in three years. She had stayed with Holly and Chuck and the three children at their home in suburban Richardson, and her impression was that Holly had changed from their days at the Business School.

"She's much more—well, she's cut her hair. She used to have wild hair—fluffy, wild hair. She used to dress in a much more appealing—" Suzanne caught herself, then continued. "She's a young suburban wife and mother with a very good job, and she's very motivated, and I think she can do extremely well. But she's changed to me because I would have thought she would have kept more of her—well, her flair."

Suzanne spoke about her roommate, not sadly, but in a detached sort of way, as if she wasn't surprised that Holly had, to her way of thinking, changed. "My image of Holly was that she could be one of the best of us, that she would sail right to the top. But she's made certain compromises because of moving to Dallas and the kids and Chuck. As I talk to her more, I see that she's still . . . it's still there. We have conversations sometimes that can get fairly bitter about the chances of this or that happening in our companies. So I do see the same energy and interest. But my image of her at the Business School was of someone who was just going to be like a little lawnmower, whereas she's done a lot of things, and her personal demeanor has changed."

Suzanne sighed. "Maybe I'm seeing the more organized side of Holly, which I didn't see at the Business School. But then we were living together in the house off campus. She was more flamboyant. She was in love with Chuck and they were happy—dancing! Now, well, there are the kids, there's a big house, there's a housekeeper. It's tough. She could be picking a growth company to be in, but she's not doing that. She's picking a life-style that will work for her when she's got a four-year-old child, a two-year-old child, and a one-year-old child."

We had reached the corner of Eighty-second Street by then. I asked Suzanne for her business card, and she explained that she didn't have one. She had just changed pocketbooks, because her other pocketbook had fallen into the sink in her apartment near the United Nations. All of the stuff in her pocketbook had spilled into the sink and gotten wet. "If I have a card, it will be a shot in the dark," Suzanne said, fidgeting through her small leather shoulder bag.

"That's okay," I said. I pulled out my notebook and wrote down her title and her telephone number at work. I suppose I knew even then that I would want to talk again to the woman who, in my opinion, stood the best chance of becoming the chief executive officer of a major American company.

PHOEBE

The Friday before I met Suzanne Sheehan at Il Monello, I was seated at the small, white built-in desk in my friend's apartment on the corner of Eighty-second Street and Second Avenue. I was placing calls, setting up dinner dates with the women in New York I had yet to interview. I dialed the number of one of the country's most prestigious national consulting firms, and I was put through to Phoebe Holstrom, thirty years old and a managing director.

I introduced myself, and as I had done with all of the others, I explained my project to Phoebe. I asked her if she would like to get together to talk about her experiences in business. To my surprise, she began to talk as if she had known me all of her life, as if we were good friends.

"There were two women at the Business School who hated me, absolutely hated me," she said. Those were the first words out of her mouth, the moment after I had introduced myself on the telephone. "Alexis Drake and Pauline Adams. They were in my section, section six. Did you talk to them?"

I had talked to Alexis the previous December in California. I had spent a day at her home on a hillside in Palo Alto, where she had all sorts of free time to talk to me because she was unemployed. I remembered her now, as Phoebe spoke, as a small woman with a tight little figure, large breasts, and a mane of curly chestnut-brown hair. I remembered her particularly well because she had explained, so poignantly and honestly, why she couldn't bring herself to find a job, even though she was a graduate of the Harvard Business School. The reason, she had said to me, was that she wanted her husband to support her and she wanted a family.

Without waiting for my response, Phoebe continued. "Alexis was the brightest of the three of us—Baker Scholar, the school's highest honor. One of only two women in the class who were. I wasn't as bright and I did well, and she hated me for that." Phoebe paused. "But Alexis never got out of the Boston/Cambridge student milieu and she never will. She lived in New York the summer between years at the Business School and she called me. For her to have done that, she must have been really depressed."

Then Phoebe began talking about Pauline Adams, whom I hadn't yet interviewed but whom I had met briefly. Pauline recently had been named a vice-president of a major New York–based insurance company where she had worked since her graduation from the Business School. I had met her the previous fall, at a panel discussion for women in business, where she had been sitting like a paper doll at the head table. She was a tall, gaunt woman with a long nose that cast a shadow across her upper lip; dressed in a tailored suit, she wore her shoulder-length hair straight and simple. I listened to her speak, methodically, about her job at the insurance company, and I approached her afterward about my project. "It doesn't do anything for one's career to talk about these things," she had said, and I had let the subject drop, figuring that I would try to convince her to cooperate at a later date, in private.

"Pauline was a good friend of a friend of mine at work," Phoebe was saying, "and she told this friend that she feels uncomfortable in my presence because her husband is attracted to me. She wouldn't let me near her husband, she told my friend. Pauline and her husband came to a dinner party at my apartment our first year in New York and he—he is so stupid—he came into the kitchen and made a pass at me."

Phoebe paused, then abruptly changed the subject. She began speaking more philosophically about women in business. "Women in business don't compete as women. They 'neuterize' themselves. They are becoming more like men professionally, who are equally "neuterized.' I don't consider myself to be a neuter. People like to work with attractive people. I've never had anyone compromise me or put me in a difficult position."

I was beginning to wonder what she was talking about when, seizing an opportunity to put a word in edgewise, I suggested that we get together. We agreed to meet that very afternoon for drinks in the lobby of the Berkshire Place hotel on Fifty-second Street between Fifth and Madison avenues. It was Phoebe's suggestion, and it was lovely. The afternoon was sunny and warm, and I walked to the hotel from the subway stop at Fifty-ninth Street. She wasn't there when I arrived at four o'clock, so I sank into a deep-cushioned sofa in the corner, waiting for her and observing the sights and sounds: the little bar and pastry shelf in the far corner, the fresh flowers on the end tables, the white walls that looked like cool marble.

Then, shortly after four, Phoebe arrived. She whirled into the lobby, which was slowly filling with people coming for Friday-afternoon cocktails before dinner or the theater, and she headed for the sofa where I was seated. She introduced herself, shook my hand, and settled into a high-back chair across from me so that I had to look up at her.

Looking at her, I began to have a sense of what she had been alluding to on the telephone. She was, at age thirty, one of the youngest women I had interviewed, but she appeared, oddly, both young and old at the same time. A short, slight woman who, at first glance, resembled a waif, she had a tiny face with freckles on her nose, a little mouth that curled up at the edge making her smile seem like a sneer, and long dark hair that flowed like ribbons down her back. She was, I thought, so inappropriately dressed for business that one could have felt embarrassed for her. She was wearing a black voile dress with a flowing calf-length skirt and brightly colored striped canvas sandals with ties wrapped up her legs.

But I wasn't embarrassed for her. Rather, she made me feel dowdy and self-conscious, seated matronly as I was on the sofa in my navy-blue maternity skirt, pin-striped top, and navy-blue blazer that together, I hoped, looked like a smart suit.

Not too far into the interview, she glanced at my ensemble and, apparently referring to the point she had begun to make on the telephone, she said, "I am *not* the navy-blue business-suit type!" And I remember being taken aback by the comment. "I'm lucky I have anything to wear at this point," I retorted, clearly flustered.

People had told me about Phoebe Holstrom—here a clue, there a clue—ever since I had begun to work on this project the previous fall. But it wasn't until January, on a night in Boston that was as raw and cold as this afternoon in May was sunny and warm, that I first became intrigued with the prospect of meeting her. I was interviewing a woman named Karen Muller, a thirty-seven-year-old divorcée who had been Phoebe's best friend at the Business School. I remembered Karen particularly well, because like Phoebe, she had agreed to meet with me immediately, the night after I called. I remembered wondering why she had shown so little discretion. She apparently hadn't bothered to check my references, nor had she made me believe she would by putting me off for a few days.

We had met for dinner at Casa Mexico, a Mexican restaurant located in a basement in Harvard Square in Cambridge. She was wearing a cotton turtleneck that she had pulled haphazardly over corduroy jeans, trying, it seemed, to hide a prominent spare tire. We were seated toward the middle of the small room, and she ordered nothing but a bowl of avocado soup which she barely touched. She had a cold, she had explained. But every so often, she would pull up her thick torso from the slump into which it had settled, raise her forearm like a baton, and hold out her wine glass to signal the waiter. "Another glass of wine, please," she would say, almost begging. By the end of the evening, she was slurring her words and speaking even more freely than she had at first— and she had been particularly candid.

At dinner, Karen had immediately launched into the problems she was having on the job, in her position as managing director of a small consulting firm in Cambridge. She was at a point in her career, she felt, where what mattered was the right home in the right suburb, the right spouse, the right clubs. She had none of these things, and she had failed twice to be made a vice-president.

She had been equally candid about her personal life. At one point in the interview, she told me in straightforward narrative, as if reciting the date of her birth or her graduation from high school or college, about one event in her life that to me was so startling I couldn't put it out of my mind. When she was twenty-two years old, she had given birth to a daughter who had died a few days later. Now, at thirty-seven, she was planning carefully for the day, sometime that year, when she would be artificially inseminated. "Your body wants to be pregnant," she said, emphasizing the word _wants._ "Your body craves it."

Karen and I hadn't talked about the Business School until late in the interview, and it was then that she first mentioned Phoebe. She hesitated when she spoke about her. "There was a difference in perceptions about Phoebe, and I don't want to get into it," she had said. "People didn't like her very much. They thought she was very power hungry and ambitious. But I didn't see her that way at all. I liked her."

When I asked her why she had liked Phoebe, Karen had alluded to Phoebe's ability to move in and out of different social circles, to feel equally at home at a celebrity ball at The Plaza and at a heroin party in Harlem. She was evasive about Phoebe beyond that statement, and I didn't press. Mentally, however, I had put Phoebe Holstrom on the list of people for whom I should keep a special watch.

Seated across the glass coffee table from me, on the straight chair so that she was looking down at me, Phoebe Holstrom explained why so many people disliked her at the Business School. She wasn't one of them, she confided. She may have looked like a little girl, a waif, but she wasn't leading a student life. She flew to New York every weekend to see the man she had been with since she was eighteen years old, a Venezuelan who had graduated from the Business School a few years earlier.

Then, too, she knew how to play what she called the Harvard Business School game, and people resented her for that. She was always late for class, and she was never prepared. Yet she did better than most of the people who spent their weekends grinding in the library. She made the Century Club second year, for God's sake.

"Do you know what that is?" she asked, and when I confessed that I didn't, after having spent practically a year on the research for this project, she explained that it is a campus club so secret that most people don't even know it exists, so exclusive that only a few dozen first-year students are asked to join every year. "Those who have a broad range of interests—politics, religion, the arts, those who are destined for leadership at the very top," she said.

Then Phoebe gave me an example of her ability to play the Business School game. She told me that once, when she was called on in class and wasn't prepared, she had said, straight out to the professor, "I haven't read the case. I don't think I want to waste everyone's time." But she had said it in a way that had amused rather than angered him. He had grinned and said, "Well, then, we'll look forward to hearing from you tomorrow." But she hadn't prepared for class the next day either, because she knew he wouldn't call on her the day he said he would. Three days out, when she figured he would finally get around to calling on her, she had been ready for him. She had stood up from her seat and talked for an hour straight, rather than the usual fifteen minutes.

The case had concerned J. M. Smucker & Co., the maker of jams and jellies, and the issue had been whether the company should bring out a line of ketchup in wide-brimmed jars. Phoebe had argued that the company should not, even though wide-brimmed jars would be easier to use. "My contention was that part of the whole schtick of ketchup is the bottle. Pounding the bottle! People aren't gonna . . . you don't dish out ketchup, that's not what it's all about!"

She said she had the professor pacing back and forth, scribbling on the blackboard, and saying, "Yes! Yes!" When she sat down, there was nothing else to be said. There was literally no discussion. "That was probably the first time I spoke in class. And I would hypothesize that it was resented that I had managed, very nicely, not in a nasty way, to let the professor know that I didn't want to be played with like an idiot student called upon and taken to task."

She had connections, Phoebe continued, and a lot of people at the Business School hadn't liked that either. She had gotten her job at the consulting company because she had happened to be at the New York Yacht Club for dinner with Johnny Carellas, her Venezuelan boyfriend, and had met a man who knew a partner at the firm. The man had suggested that she get in touch with that partner who eventually hired her.

"Johnny used to say, 'People are always sort of attracted to you because you always walk into something like you own it,'" Phoebe explained. "It's funny. I'm very short, in fact. Whenever I happen to have my shoes off, people who've known me for years are amazed to see how short I am. Johnny used to say, 'You just walk tall. You walk as though you're in charge. Or you walk as though this is your kind of place, even if you've never been here before.'"

Phoebe had a way of speaking that could only be described as direct and pointed. Her voice was hard, insistent. If I closed my eyes and forgot the voile dress, I would have felt I was hearing the voice of a street urchin peddling dope, a movie magnate closing a deal. She would make her point, support it, then push on; make another point, support it, push on. So that as people swarmed in and crowded the lobby of the Berkshire Place, I was oblivious to all of that. I was entranced with the details of the life of Phoebe Holstrom.

She was telling me about the consulting company. She was only a kid when she got there; barely twenty-three, she looked nineteen. And everyone in national consulting at that time was much older, at least twenty-nine. But it was the same story: She left work at 6:00 P.M.; she never worked weekends; she had a whole life outside of the office. Yet it was she who was approached by the chief executive officer of one of the biggest Fortune 500 companies, a firm that was in deep, deep trouble. He wanted her, Phoebe, who wasn't even a partner, to lead the team that would help the firm get back on its feet.

Then there was the incident the previous December, when a dear friend and one of the senior partners at the consulting firm had called her into his office and begged her, "Do you want to be a partner?" And she had said, as she had said so many times before, that no, she didn't want to be a partner. "'Just say the word, Phoebe. What can we do to make you say the word?' he said to me."

The lobby was hot and crowded by then, and cigarette smoke was swirling around us. Phoebe set her lips together firmly and shut her eyes. She was about to make another point. "It wasn't me, mind you," she was explaining. It was Johnny, whom she had been with all of those years, who had made her wise to the ways of the world.

She began to talk about Johnny: how she had met him the summer she was eighteen and was working in an antipoverty program in Mayor John Lindsay's administration in New York; how he had gone to Brown University a decade earlier, worked in business, then gotten his M.B.A. at the Harvard Business School; how he had convinced her that she should too, because a degree from the Business School would give her "the widest range of options for [her] life"; how he had been married when she met him; how he had left his wife and two children to marry her, in May 1975, a month before she graduated from the Business School.

At that point in the interview, she shut her eyes even tighter and placed a pointed finger on her cheek. *"Shut that thing off,"* she commanded, and I obeyed.

While the spools of the cassette were still, Phoebe told me about her marriage to Johnny, what had gone wrong, and why she had decided, finally, to leave him. That had been three years before, and there had been times since the annulment—Johnny was a Latin American Catholic and couldn't conceive of divorce—that had been painful. He had been such a nice guy—"the nicest guy in the world!" she said.

But gradually, she had begun dating again, so that now there was the Jewish businessman whose family owned a chain of men's clothing stores, the Italian duke who saw his wife and four children in Venice for the Christmas holidays, and Will who owned the ranch in Nevada. She smiled and let out a little sigh when she spoke about Will.

My mind was spinning, and I tried to take stock. From one perspective, there wasn't anything unusual about her. She had grown up in Greenwich, Connecticut, in an upper-middle-class family; she had attended the public high school where she had been, she said, a bit of a femme fatale—she dated the boys and knew how to give them "the old dump." She had been Miss Greenwich in the Junior Miss contest her senior year; she had graduated from Connecticut College, the only school her father would let her attend if she wanted to live away from home, which she had wanted.

But there was another side to Phoebe Holstrom which I tried to consider. She had grown up biculturally. Her family had spent summers in Jamaica, and there, as a young teen-ager, she had had her first sexual experience with a black man twenty-five years her senior. Then, from the age of eighteen, she had been with Johnny, who was ten years older than she. And her best friend at the Business School had been Karen Muller, a divorcée seven years her senior. In summary, she seemed old beyond her years. "The child-woman," she called herself.

Images immediately came to my mind, a jumble of images I had gathered throughout the course of the year from people who had known Phoebe or who had known of her: Phoebe on the cover of a major national magazine, in a satin dress with spaghetti straps, tippling champagne with a young film director; Phoebe featured in an article in another national publication about the top ten New York businesswomen under age thirty-five; Phoebe easing her way from a reception at The Plaza to a heroin party in Harlem.

Looking at her, her face small and waiflike, her body enveloped in a sea of black voile, I thought that she appeared hard, used, and used up. I thought about all she had told me, about her career at the consulting company, about her marriage to Johnny and why it had gone wrong, about the men she was dating now.

There were a lot of things about her story that seemed unbelievable, that I doubted, but that didn't matter. What mattered was that I was in awe of her. If I had felt dowdy and self-conscious when she made the remark about the navy-blue suit, gazing directly at my outfit, I felt even more so after having heard her story. I always had considered myself a woman of the world—I had spent a year interviewing for and researching this project, after all; I had been a reporter for eleven years, traveling throughout the country, finding stories. But my experiences paled beside hers. It wasn't that I was intimidated by her. I was fascinated by her. I envisioned myself as her friend, sort of a straight man for her, the alter ego for a person who lived on a grand scale and who had had experiences of which I could only dream.

It was nearly 7:30 P.M., and Phoebe had to go. I had just one last question for her. "You have done so much in the first thirty years of your life. What else is there? What will you do to fill up the next thirty?" I asked.

She told me that she wasn't sure, but that she had some ideas. She said she wanted to live a "more settled" life, in one place, with one man. She could see herself with Will, running the ranch in Nevada. She had this vision: She would bring troubled kids from New York to the ranch, straighten them out.

I raised an eyebrow, and she smiled. "I always want something better. I always want to know the things I don't know," she said, as if to convince me of her sincerity. "I mean, I'm curious. I like to answer things for myself. I'm sure I just set up challenges for myself. I just like to see if it can be done."

She had a date. She was going roller-skating with the Italian duke, and she was late. We made our way out of the side door of the lobby of the Berkshire Place. Outside, the May evening was soft and warm. We walked to the curb, on the corner of Fifty-second and Madison, and I started to hail a taxi. Phoebe turned to me, as if to try, once more, to convince me.

"I roller-skate; why do I do that? I like to see if I can do it. I like to fly; I love the feeling of flying. It's tremendously free. They laugh at me at the roller rink. They say, 'Everybody in the roller disco knows you, because you are out there in your own world,' and I do, I skate all the time."

She turned and started walking uptown. As I raised my hand, signaling a cab to take me back to my friend's apartment, I watched her, a tiny figure enveloped in a swirl of black voile and long hair, as she made her way up to the roller rink, where she could be free.

MARY PAT

Wednesday, May 20, my last day in New York. I was walking across town from the Hotel Algonquin on West Forty-fourth

Street, where I had met friends for drinks, to Zapata's, a little Mexican restaurant on Fifty-third Street between First and Second avenues. Ordinarily, I could have walked the distance with no trouble because I am a great walker; it's my favorite form of exercise, and I do it with ease. But well into the ninth month of my pregnancy, I was beginning to feel the strain. It was a sultry day, sunny and hot, so by the time I reached Zapata's, I was tired. I was anxious to be done with this last interview in New York and be on my way home.

I was planning to meet a woman named Mary Pat Horner, and I had been looking forward to this interview. Like Phoebe, I had heard about Mary Pat from so many of the others; she, it seemed, had been practically a legend on campus. She also had been difficult to locate. When I started my research the previous fall, I wrote down the names of the women in the class on long sheets of yellow paper. I sorted them geographically: those who lived in Boston or New York or on the West Coast. On a separate sheet, I wrote down the names of the ones I couldn't find, and she had been on that list.

The last affiliation the Business School had for Mary Pat had been as product manager for a large consumer-products concern in suburban New York. But when I called the company, I was told that she had left, that they didn't have a forwarding address. Throughout that fall, whenever I ran across people who had known her, I would ask them where I could find her. There had been smiles and winks when I mentioned her name, and sometimes peels of laughter. "I'm not surprised she left the consumer-products company," one woman said. "I didn't think she was cut out for a corporate job, for the rigid structure of the corporation. She was sort of a free spirit."

The smiles and winks were tinged with respect for Mary Pat, however. The previous December, when I had been in California, I had talked to a young woman who had lived on the same floor as Mary Pat in McCulloch Hall the first year at the Business School. Over rich coffee and croissants with strawberry jam in a Berkeley coffeehouse, the young woman, Esther Micholov Boron, had brushed back her long blond hair with a sweep of her graceful arm. She had told me there were some things about Mary Pat that one had to respect, no matter how much one made fun of her. "She came from a far different background than most of us," Esther had said. "She didn't go to a fancy college. She went to local schools and put herself through, she was so smart. She worked for a steel company in Pittsburgh for a year before going to the Business School."

Everyone who had known Mary Pat gave me suggestions about where she might have gone after the consumer-products company. At one point in California, I was told she had joined a firm in San Francisco. That day, I spent hours placing coins in a pay phone, tracing leads. I wanted to find her before I left, if she were in California, which she was not.

But it wasn't until I talked to Karen Muller, on that cold night in Cambridge, that I was finally given the name of someone who knew where she was. The man, a classmate at the Business School, had been a friend of Karen's too. The revelation had occurred when I had asked Karen if she had known Mary Pat. "Mary Pat Horner? Oh sure," Karen had said, in the same flat tone of voice she used to discuss the death of her daughter. "She used to dance on tables. She dressed up as a Playboy Bunny and danced on the tables of the Pub." There was that little snickering smile, and I pressed Karen, "Why? Why do people snicker?"

Karen was only too happy to tell me why she thought so. "Mary Pat was the perfect example of someone with every mental attribute who was plunked down in a situation she didn't understand socially or politically. I mean, dressing up like a Playboy Bunny and dancing on tables isn't something one does at the Harvard Business School, and she had no idea that it wasn't!"

Karen sighed, then put in the qualifier. "But mention her intellect and everyone would be intimidated. They were just glad she preferred dancing on tables to smashing people in the section." Karen shook her head. "The day everything clicks for Mary Pat will be the day she goes straight to the top."

The friend Karen suggested knew precisely where Mary Pat had gone; she recently had joined a major bank in New York. He gave me her direct-dial number. A quick call and there she was, on the line after all of those months. I was surprised by the tone of her voice. For someone who was said to have been a free spirit, she sounded distant and frightened. It wouldn't have been any trouble to meet me in the city in the past, she said, but now she was living in the suburbs, in Larchmont, New York, with someone, and he wanted her home. The only day she would be able to meet me was Wednesday, May 20, and it would have to be early, 5:00 P.M.

It was 5:00 P.M. at Zapata's, and she hadn't arrived. I was ushered to a tiny table wedged into a far corner near the kitchen, with a surface almost too small for my notebook and tape recorder. I was told by a waiter that Mary Pat's secretary had called; she would be late. I glanced around the near-empty restaurant. Artificial lighting mingled with the sunlight streaming through the storefront window, giving the room a reddish-gold patina. The effect was garish; it was as if there should have been a pinball machine in the corner.

Nearly an hour later, Mary Pat arrived. She walked toward the table, a tall, thin woman with long, straight auburn hair parted severely in the middle, and slightly protruding teeth. Wearing a plain navy-blue suit, part polyester, and a man-tailored shirt, she appeared elongated, like a figure stretched lengthwise in a fun-house mirror. She smiled quizzically as she approached my table, and in a fit of panic, she told me she was out of cigarettes.

From that point on, she did all of the talking. There was nothing I needed to say. She ordered a Dry Sack on the rocks, and when that one was empty, she ordered another. Every so often, she would jump up from the table and say, "I really need to find some cigarettes," and when there was none to be found, she would sit back down again and resume her story.

"For women to be successful and be my age, they had to have started out as overachievers," she began, "because back in 1966, when I was getting out of high school, they were telling girls you might become a teacher so you'll have something to fall back on when you get married. I mean, for me to be here today, I couldn't have been in the middle of the bell-shaped curve of the women in my age group.

"I'm thirty-two and I'm not married. I have a college degree and a graduate degree and six years of business experience and . . . I wouldn't be here if there hadn't been something different about me in the first place. So that I really began to question what it is that makes an overachiever and at what point do you begin to question what the heck it is you're overachieving *for*. And that was the question I've been thinking about ever since you made the phone call."

As she talked, I took stock, and I could see what Esther Micholov Boron had meant when she said that Mary Pat had come from a far different background. She was from Allentown, Pennsylvania, a grimy mill town on the New Jersey border, from a family of eight children; her father was a state trooper for the Commonwealth of Pennsylvania, who earned $6,000 a year when Mary Pat was growing up.

"It seems to me there is a self-selection process. Not self-selection," she said, correcting herself, "but a genetic selection of people who have a compulsion to achieve. I think many women my age, at my level or higher, had to have been overachievers, because it simply wasn't going to happen to them. They didn't grow up like . . ." She paused, for, she would soon explain, she had no idea how the others grew up. "Well, many of them might have, but I certainly didn't grow up in a culture that says, 'You have a career ahead of you. You can be a doctor, a lawyer, or an Indian chief.' People told me that maybe a waitress was a good job. I mean, tips were pretty good, you get to wear a cute outfit. My father used to tell me, 'Go down to the good restaurants, down there.' "

Mary Pat stopped herself. She looked at me plaintively, and with a sense of disbelief about what she was telling me. "I was not going to talk about this tonight," she said, curling her right hand into a fist and placing it on the table, deliberately. "I mean, I was not going to talk about this."

But the words came, a catharsis almost. For, as she explained, she had tried all of the things that were supposed to be solutions and none of them worked. There was the career, for example. Back in Allentown, when she graduated from high school and found a job as a waitress just as her father had suggested and then as a statistical clerk for the telephone company, she knew those jobs weren't the answer. She would have to go to college to learn a skill so that she could find the type of job that would bring in the kind of money she wanted. She would have to go to college "to save myself from the mediocrity that befell women who didn't have college degrees."

But now, with a college degree—Penn State, top of her class, and a Harvard M.B.A.—she had had three jobs in the short span of six years. There had been two partings, the second more bitter than the first. Now that she had been at the bank for a year, marketing a brand-new type of credit card the bank was introducing, just as she had marketed sugar at the consumer-products company and processed meats for her second employer, she was already seeing signs of trouble on the job.

She tried to explain what she meant by signs of trouble, but she could not. She had always performed exceptionally well. At the processed-meats concern, for example, she had been the only group product manager who brought her business in on budget, in one of the worst years for the meat-packing business, and there had been no kudos. She had, in fact, been asked to leave, or was it that she approached her boss and said, "You and I both know that the company wants me out. Let's make a deal," which was really the same thing. But it had confused Mary Pat. Why had this happened to her? Why was it happening again?

At the processed-meats concern, she had become involved with a fifty-year-old married man and a senior executive at the company, which was, she said, "about as self-destructive a thing I could do," both for her career and her personal life. But she couldn't help herself. When he left his wife, she agreed to live with him. She was still living with him; he was the man who had made it difficult for her to meet me for dinner in the city.

When Mary Pat spoke about the man she was living with, she spoke about her involvement as the symbol of all that was wrong with her life. The signs of distress were easy to pinpoint: six moves in nine years, count them—Allentown, University Park, Pittsburgh, Boston, New York, Larchmont; emotional dislocation; the overwhelming feeling of loneliness making that climb up the ladder at some company, all by herself.

"All of this for the sake of my so-called career ambitions," she exclaimed. Then she sighed. "I used to sit there in New York, in my empty apartment that overlooked the Hudson River. I used to say, 'What the hell am I doing here?' Going to work everyday for a company. They paid me a lot of money, but the place was crazy. And I'd sit there and I'd say to myself, 'I could die tonight and I would lie here. No one comes here. This is a life-style? My little closet? This is absolutely stupid! Is this what I drove myself through four years of college and two years at the Business School for, to find my closet on the Hudson River? With my wall-to-wall carpeting. And my stereo.' I used to sit there and say to myself, 'You must be out of your mind! This was at the end of that struggle. This was it. I mean, c'mon! There's got be more to life than this.' So that's when I got involved with Lloyd."

Click. My tape recorder shut itself off, and I slipped in another cassette. The sixth. This was one of my longest interviews, and though I was mesmerized by Mary Pat's story and by her desperation, I was getting tired of listening. I was also anxious to leave: I had planned to join my friends for another round of drinks on this my last night in New York.

I sensed that Mary Pat wanted to continue. She had begun to talk about Lloyd Whitmore, the man she was involved with, and I had picked up signs, during the interview, that she now felt he wasn't the answer she was looking for either. Before she resumed what had become a monologue, however, I stopped her. "Excuse me for a minute," I said. "I have to call some friends to break a date."

The interview came to an abrupt halt. The spell had been broken, the moment I spoke, signaling my presence; it was as if she suddenly realized she was speaking to someone.

I stood up from my seat. Mary Pat's jaw dropped. A look of surprise swept across her face. "Oh, you're pregnant," she said. "I didn't realize . . ." Her voice trailed off, as if she felt she would have to say something like, "Isn't that wonderful," and knew that she could not. I grimaced and didn't respond.

When I returned from making my call, Mary Pat was in a rush to leave. A chauffeured car from the bank was waiting outside of Zapata's to drive her back to the suburbs, where she lived with Lloyd.

There wasn't much more I could ask her, except for one question: "Are you happy?" She answered as she hurriedly rose from her seat, anxious to leave. "That's a funny question," she said, "because if you had asked me that question two weeks ago, the night you called, I would have said no. But something has happened to me in those two weeks to make me believe that I will be happier in the future than I have been in the past." She pulled herself up to her full height, and just before she whirled around on her heels and made her way out, she said, "I have found God."

I was left sitting there, in a state of shock. I was thinking about Mary Pat and how sorry I was for her. I was thinking about Karen Muller and what she had told me about Mary Pat—how she had dressed up as a Playboy Bunny and danced on the tables of the Pub. I realized that I hadn't remembered to ask her about that, even though we had talked for all of those many hours.

I was thinking about myself, how disappointed I was that I wouldn't be meeting my friends. I had been looking forward to seeing them. God only knew when I would see them again, considering all that lay before me. Yet I felt comfortable making my way out of the restaurant into the rainy New York night, knowing that unlike Mary Pat Horner, I would be safe and warm tomorrow, on my way home to have my baby.

TESS

It was a hot summer night, six weeks to the day since I had left New York, four weeks since the birth of my daughter. I was sitting across the table from Tess Beckett in an elegant continental restaurant in the basement of a Boston townhouse. The restaurant was nearly empty on this Thursday before the long Fourth of July weekend. The air conditioning was barely working; I was conscious of its halting whir, background music in a restaurant too sophisticated for Muzak.

I was studying Tess as she talked. She had small gray eyes that looked right at me, a thin upper lip that widened periodically into a brief smile, and short, straight sandy-colored hair that fell from her crown to her forehead, giving her the appearance of Buster Brown or an abbess of an order of cloistered nuns. She was heavy-set, but she carried her weight well, dressed as she was in a short-sleeved oxford shirt and a straight skirt, a tailored blazer on her arm.

She was as firm about her opinions as her appearance would suggest. She made her points in crisp declarative sentences, or by asking simple questions that she would punctuate with her own answers. Her major point was that things weren't so bad for her, a professional woman, part of a group that she considered an "elite." She had her job, the "neat and fun job" of sales manager for a small start-up computer company that was bringing out what many considered one of the decade's hottest products: a personal computer that would sell for around five hundred dollars.

She had gotten in on the ground floor. Four of the brightest engineers from some of the finest computer companies along Route 128, the beltway that rings Boston, had founded the new company a year before. She had written to them, and they had hired her; she had built a solid reputation selling computers for a major manufacturer for four years. She was given a respectable salary, a stake in the new concern, and options to buy a bigger share. All this, and hope for a bright future: "The title of vice-president—sales—by next year, which has been promised to me," she said in a hushed voice.

At thirty-five, moreover, she had her husband, Kevin, whom she loved, and a five-year-old son, Chris. She had a beautiful home in a fine suburb and "fun" things to do on weekends: taking Chris to the renovated Faneuil Hall marketplace in Boston, having friends over for dinner parties, tending to her big vegetable garden.

"For me at least, I think I've had some unique opportunities. I think I have a lot of neat and fun things ahead of me, and I'm kind of pleased about my life. Is it perfect? No. Do I face problems a man wouldn't face? Absolutely yes. Do I have to cope with them? Yes, because there is no alternative, right? Do I feel better about my life because I do? Yes. Do I work harder at relation-ships, be they personal or professional? Certainly. But so what?"

I studied Tess Beckett again. I wasn't impressed with her in the way I had been with Suzanne Sheehan, knowing immediately that

I had met someone who could make it to the apex of American business, nor was I fascinated as I had been with Phoebe Holstrom. I wasn't horrified or saddened as I had been listening to Mary Pat Horner. My emotions about Tess weren't as intense. But there was something about her, her dogged persistence, that made me want to listen. She was, after all, out there, on the road for the better part of her long work week, hustling a product that hadn't even come to market for a firm that was barely out of its infancy. She was doing that while tending to a husband, a preschool child, and a home in the suburbs.

I had first heard about Tess from two women I had interviewed earlier in the year, Maureen Graham and Polly Drascovitch. They had been in her section at Harvard, and both had insisted that I talk to her.

I had interviewed Maureen on a Saturday afternoon the previous November. She had been one of the first women I talked to, so I had been surprised to find her unemployed and comfortably settled in a country colonial, circa 1919, in the seacoast village of Falmouth on Cape Cod. She was walking up the steps of her home when I first saw her, a woman of medium height with short, wavy blond hair and a sad look in her blue eyes. She was carrying an infant in a Snugli strapped to her stomach and, in her left arm, a bagful of groceries.

Maureen and I talked all afternoon. Her husband was away on a business trip; she told me that he was an investment banker who traveled frequently. She told me her story in between jumping up to feed or amuse her infant daughter, saying in a somewhat resigned tone of voice when she'd burp or spit up, "Oh, Cait-lin!"

She told me that she and her husband had both worked in New York until she insisted they return to Massachusetts, buy a home in the country, and start a family. She had found a job with a small local chain of children's clothing stores, but she had quit to have her baby. She had thought she would start looking for another job within a few months, a part-time job perhaps, but since having her baby she wasn't sure. "Having a baby is a little bit like falling in love," she said, which I could have understood if she had said that with enthusiasm and joy, but she did not.

She hadn't warmed to me, and it was only because I had pressed and pushed that I was able to find out as much as I did about her. At one point, as the late-autumn afternoon turned to dusk, I asked a question that I asked each of the women I interviewed: "Were you ever in therapy?" She said that she had been, and I pressed again: "Why?" Seated on the long couch in her upstairs sitting room, Maureen began to cry. "Because my husband," she began, then broke off sobbing, "had an affair—when we were in New York."

She had been equally cool to me earlier in the afternoon, when we had talked about the Harvard Business School. She had been scared and uncomfortable there, surrounded by men for the first time—she who had gone to a girls' boarding school and to Wheaton College. "To see myself at the Business School, I had to see myself as a man," she said, which she couldn't bring herself to do. Then, too, the work had been hard. She had cried over her first assignment in accounting, and when she wasn't able to solve the problem, she had gone to her professor for help. "I don't believe you asked me that," the professor had said angrily, and he had thrown her out of his office.

I asked Maureen about the other women in her section, and she ticked off the names, telling me, if she knew, what each was doing now. There weren't many who were building careers the way men do—who were, as she put it, "killers." Which was to be expected, she added, for the women she knew weren't ready to forfeit husbands and children for their careers. It was at that point that she had suggested I talk to Tess Beckett. It was funny, Maureen said. Tess had been even more afraid than she had been at the Business School—so afraid that she flunked out the first year. But now, Tess was one of the few who had that kind of commitment. "You should talk to Tess," Maureen had insisted. "She is more the type of woman you are looking for than I am."

I had talked to Polly Drascovitch five months later, in April, and she had said the same thing. Polly was a short, plain woman, two weeks away from the birth of her second child. We met for brunch at the posh Hyatt Regency hotel in Cambridge. Whereas I had chosen a smart maternity ensemble, a silk blouse and linen skirt, she was wearing a wrinkled corduroy maternity jumper over a plaid cotton shirt. Her brown hair was unwashed and stringy.

She had begun her story even before we were called for our table, anxious to get it over with so that she could go home to her family. She had gone to the Business School after having worked as a medical technician at the Tufts–New England Medical Center in Boston, where she had met her husband. He was a resident in dental surgery, destined for the hospital staff and for a teaching position at Tufts' School of Dental Medicine. He hadn't wanted her to go to the Business School, and she hadn't the year she married him. But she had changed her mind the following fall, in 1973, and decided to enroll.

Once her husband was named to the hospital staff, however, she had begun cutting back. After graduation, she had taken the job of controller at a privately held Boston-based company, a maker of deviled ham and other processed foods, and she had gotten to know the family very well. When she had her first child, she had been able to convince the family to let her work part-time. Now that she would have a second child, she planned to take off six months and then decide whether to return to work. She wanted time, she said, for family, for friends. She wanted to raise money for Bryn Mawr, her alma mater.

"The Junior Leaguer updated for the 1980's?" I suggested, and she replied, "Yes."

We had left the Hyatt late in the afternoon, far later than she had planned. She called her husband from a telephone in the lobby to tell him she was on her way home. Then we walked to the parking garage. Only then had she perked up and asked about my findings. I told her about one of the most surprising: that a large percentage of the women in her class weren't interested in climbing the corporate ladder, in the way it is supposed graduates of the Business School are. Then I mentioned another finding that also had surprised me: that those women who were ambitious for their careers were just as likely to be married and to have children as they were to be single or divorced. I suggested to Polly that those findings raised an intriguing question: Where does ambition in women—that kind of ambition—come from?

We had reached my car by then, a battered 1970 American

Motors Hornet. I rested my hand on the door and looked at her. She stopped and considered my question. Then, standing there, a silent figure about to make a statement, she had said, "The Harvard Business School, at least back then, accepted smart women without trying to ascertain how ambitious they were for careers. They'll be more careful in the future." Then she had added, "Be sure to talk to Tess."

I hadn't called Tess until the very end, and I had debated about calling her. Despite what Maureen and Polly had said, Tess hadn't graduated with the class of 1975. She had dropped out after her first year, then returned the following year to graduate with the class of 1976. I had to be consistent about whom to include as a member of the class of 1975. Finally I decided that anyone who had enrolled with the class in the fall of 1973 would be included. I had called Tess late in June, a few weeks after I had my baby, and we had set our date.

Looking at her now, seated across the table from me in the near-empty Boston restaurant, I could see her in relation to the women who had been her friends at the Business School, Maureen Graham and Polly Drascovitch. Considering her in that respect, I found her story to be incredible—the stuff of movies, of television specials, of thick books by born storytellers.

She was born Theresa Wocjski, and she had grown up in a tenement in Pawtucket, Rhode Island, the daughter of an alcoholic father who worked as a welder in the mills. She had one dream back then, to go to college. But she hadn't. She wasn't bright enough to win a scholarship and she didn't have the money to put herself through. She went to work first as a clerk in a furniture store, then as a secretary to the manager of a sweater mill. After that, she joined a computer company in Massachusetts, a maker of the small machines called minicomputers that were just beginning to hit the market. The company was so new and growing so fast that she knew she would have a future there.

Her gray eyes sparkled when she told me about those heady first days at the minicomputer company in the late 1960's: how she had been determined, just determined, to learn the computer business; how she had risen from secretary to marketing assistant by doing everything—writing brochures, putting together trade shows, convincing the prettiest secretaries to pose for promotional literature in front of machines people knew nothing about; how she had decided to get her associate degree at night at a local junior college with a long Indian name she couldn't even pronounce; how, determined to do that and work at the same time, she commuted eighty miles a day, from Pawtucket to Westboro to Providence, then back to Pawtucket.

She told me about how her life had accelerated after that. She married an executive at the company and returned to college full time. She enrolled in a state school, then transferred to a better school, then transferred again to the best: Smith. Then, in the spring of 1973, short six credits for the college degree she had always wanted, she decided she couldn't wait any longer. She reached back into her fantasies for a dream that had always existed there. Without finishing her college degree, she applied and decided to enroll at the Harvard Business School.

Tess was frank about what a degree from the Business School has meant for her marriage, and I was surprised she told me what she did. Few of the others had, even though I suspected the same was true for many of them. She told me that she was earning more money than her husband; that her career has flourished whereas his has stagnated; that partly because of this, her husband was more responsible than she for the care of five-year-old Chris. "I better tell you this before it comes out in the questioning," she said.

She was equally frank about the birth of her son, Chris, midway through her second year at the Business School. She smiled when I asked her about her son, poised with a ready response, a shade defensive about what she was about to say. "I do not like small children or barking dogs," she said quickly. Then, referring to his birth, she said, "I remember thinking in the hospital, when the doctor handed him to me, 'Is this all there is?' I expected to feel this gush, which never came."

I winced when Tess said that, thinking of the moment four weeks earlier when I had held my own newborn. I felt that what she said wasn't the whole truth, yet I knew there was perhaps more truth to it than I dared admit.

I asked Tess why she had dropped out of the Business School the first year, and why she had returned a year later. She told me that she dropped out because she wasn't doing well. She returned to the minicomputer company where she had been successful, then did a short stint at another computer concern, and finally joined a small firm that wrote software for computers—packages of instructions that permit computers to do specific tasks. But it had been a hard year, and throughout Tess had been confused about what she wanted out of life. So it wasn't surprising that the following July, when the software company went bankrupt and she lost her job and her husband wanted desperately to have a child, she had gotten pregnant.

She began to tell me why she returned to the Business School that very fall, to tackle what she had failed at before, when our waiter approached the table. "Excuse me, but you have to go," he said. I couldn't let the conversation end there. I asked her to give me a ride home so that we could continue. She agreed, and it was in the parking garage in the Prudential Center that she made a point that touched a raw nerve in me.

I asked her if there had been anything specific that made her say, "This is what I have to do. I have to go back to school."

She turned to me as we made our way to her car. "Well, yes, there was," she said. Then, starting slowly, she explained. "For me, being pregnant was really very difficult. I found it very threatening—physically, emotionally. And I thought, 'I'm almost thirty years old and I'm doing something because someone else said I should be doing this.' And that's a bummer. That is utterly absurd. Am I going to spend my life doing that, or am I going to take control of my life and decide that I am going to do what I want to do and not what someone else wants me to do? It hit me very clearly at that point and I said, 'There is no choice. I am going to do what I want to do, and I don't care what other people are telling me to do.'"

"So it was the pregnancy that prompted you to go back," I said, and Tess replied, "That's right."

I looked at Tess in astonishment and with a fresh set of questions in my mind. I felt an uneasy twinge of empathy as I considered my own newborn child at home with her father.

I had heard and read a lot about the problems of working mothers, their concern about handling both work and motherhood, their efforts to work things out with employers. I was familiar with the options: Some women cut back to part-time work; others stop working for a few years to give their children what they feel is the best start in life. But never had I heard the reverse: pregnancy as the lever that pushes one on, relentlessly, toward achievements that one hadn't mastered beforehand. Or had I?

Listening to Tess, I felt uncomfortable in the way one does when coming across something that cuts too close to home. For the previous ten months, the time it had taken me to research this project, I had carried and delivered my own first-born child. I had been so proud, so smug: See world, I seemed to be saying, I can do it all, more than I dared to think I could accomplish. I can handle a full-time job, an extracurricular project, while carrying my child. I had carried her across the country, in pursuit of something I was now beginning to question. Why was I doing this? What drove me on? What was I trying to prove and to whom?

Considering Tess, I asked myself why I had undertaken the project at a time, the only time in my life, when my first-born child would be a helpless infant, needing me more than she ever would. I felt guilty, and profoundly sad, and curious. I felt curious because what Tess Beckett seemed to be suggesting was that it isn't enough to consider this awesome issue of work and motherhood in terms of guilt.

Tess had deliberately returned to the Harvard Business School the year she planned to have her child. The issue for her hadn't been guilt; it had been fear of what would have happened had she chosen not to return. Likewise, I could now admit, I had made the deliberate, conscious decision to become pregnant the year I knew I would be working on this project. I would have been afraid of pregnancy had I not had something like this to do, and I wanted to find out why.

I had finished all but three of my first interviews when I talked to Tess Beckett. My plan was to choose, from the eighty-two women I had interviewed, some six to twelve who seemed to exemplify the most common patterns emerging from the lives of these women, then talk to each of the women in this smaller group at greater length. The task of whittling down my sample was the most difficult in the project; it consumed the rest of the summer of 1981 and even then, I wasn't entirely satisfied with the choices I made. But I had no question about Tess Beckett. Although she was one of the last women I interviewed, she was the first I called back in September, when I began the second interviews with the women I wanted to include in this book.

MARTHA

While Tess Beckett had been the first woman I called back, Martha Davis was the last. I had interviewed Martha the previous December, and I had been uncertain about her from the beginning.

I had met her in New York, where she had been on assignment for the prestigious venture-capital group she worked for, an arm of a major national bank, whose headquarters was in Boston. She worked out of the branch office in Chicago, because she and her husband, Luke Davis, had decided to move there in 1975 when she graduated from the Business School and he finished his residency in cardiology at the Massachusetts General Hospital.

We met for lunch at the Plaza on Central Park South, and my first impression was that Martha was every bit as chic and sophisticated as the spacious lobby of this world class hotel. She was a small woman, in her mid-thirties, with large dark brown eyes, milk-white skin, and short black hair sculpted stylishly in waves in a way that can best be described as "smart." She reminded me of a movie actress of a past era, a young Mary Pickford perhaps.

Martha was in the process of adopting a child when we met, she said, and I looked at her first with a sigh of relief. It would be months before I would have to consider the issues she was now facing, I thought. My second reaction to Martha was admiration tinged with envy. I wanted to look like she did. She appeared to be every inch the stylish young venture capitalist she was: She was wearing high black boots, a black crepe de chine skirt with folds that fell naturally from a bias cut, and a paper-thin V-neck over-blouse in a brilliant shade of turquoise. The blouse featured a tiny beaded collar. I remember being particularly struck by the little collar. I wanted to continue to dress with as much attention to detail when I added a child to my busy life on the job, to show that even though I had been reckless enough to do this to myself, I could be careful and particular about how I would execute my new status.

We sat at a table in the Palm Court that opens onto the hotel lobby. Martha looked at me with utmost sincerity and professional decorum, but with a distinct undercurrent of unease. She immediately informed me that she wanted to know a lot more about my project than I had described on the telephone.

"Liz, what are your major hypotheses or themes going into this project?" she began.

"None," I replied.

"You're trying to generate that?"

"That's right," I replied. "I've done enough work in the field to suspect that there are some problems. Some of the obvious ones like the transfer situation, the decision about children. But the more talking I do, the more I realize that those are just surface problems. I think there are a lot of other problems that just haven't come out in the writing that's been done so far. Also, I think there are a lot of rewards that haven't been emphasized."

My comment about the rewards caught Martha by surprise and seemed to put her in a better frame of mind. She smiled briefly, as if to indicate that we were now on the same wave length.

"That's interesting," she said. "The articles do concentrate on the problems."

"On the negative," I replied.

A certain rapport thus established with Martha, I felt somewhat more comfortable about proceeding with the body of the interview, which lasted for an hour and a half. For her part, without really relaxing completely in the face of my pointed questions and spinning tape recorder, Martha ever so cautiously began to open up.

Talking to Martha, I had a sense of being out of my element in every respect: not only because of her style and sophistication, but also because of her better-than-average credentials and the plethora of opportunities she had had. I remember thinking that had I such a collection of advantages, I would have been able to conquer the world.

I made a mental file card of her curriculum vitae: She was the daughter of a wealthy businessman, who was the president of a family-owned retail chain in the Midwest; she grew up in the fashionable suburb of Shaker Heights outside of Cleveland, attended a private day school in the Cleveland area, and then went east to Brandeis University near Boston, where she graduated in 1969 with a double major, statistics and economics. She worked for a Boston-based advertising firm for four years doing market research. Then in 1973, she entered the Business School and married Luke Davis, a Bostonian who had just finished medical school at Harvard and was beginning his residency at Mass General.

Seated across the table from me, a picture of composure now, Martha was discussing her career. "To me it never seemed unusual; I always wanted to have a professional career. My long-term interest is in the international sector, but more directly, shaping foreign economic structures—foreign trade, for example —and I had analyzed as far back as freshman year at Brandeis that I wanted to be an economist. So I decided pretty early. I really thought about it freshman year and decided two years later to work for a few years in research and then to go to the Harvard Business School. I wasn't interested in going anyplace else."

"What if you didn't get in?" I interjected.

"I assumed that I would," she said, with an air of abrupt self-confidence that in people less privileged or bright comes across as short.

She was equally composed about her role as wife in a dual-career marriage. When she and Luke were married, the year he got his medical degree, they made a conscious effort to avoid the kind of problems that seemed to plague so many other couples in their situation. There was never a problem with the housework, for example. She and Luke rented the extra bedroom in their apartment to a student in exchange for housekeeping services, such as cooking and cleaning. Any tasks the student couldn't handle, such as the household bills, they split equally.

As Martha spoke, I was beginning to feel overwhelmed, partly because she was far brighter and more sophisticated and accomplished than I. Had she been a mere mortal, like most of the other women I talked with, I might have been able to spot the problem sooner. As it was, I picked up on it when she told me that she and Luke had attended a conference on women in business at the University of Chicago the year they moved to that city to begin their careers.

One of the reasons she and Luke had attended the conference, Martha explained, was because they wanted help in coping with the issue that was troubling them: relocation. So there was a problem, I thought.

From that point on, I listened as Martha appeared to become more and more despondent, her composure slipping a notch or two with every point she made, her comments sounding increasingly defensive. She told me about what had happened after she graduated from the Business School and Luke finished his residency: how Luke had been emotionally committed to moving to Chicago—he had received an offer to do advanced work in cardiology from one of the country's most prestigious hospitals and felt duty bound to commit himself to the pioneering work that was being done there; how she had wanted to work in Boston but couldn't stop him from going to Chicago because, she admitted, there wasn't anything she felt as strongly about doing; how they had decided to compromise—she would take the job with the venture-capital group in the branch office of the Boston-based bank for a few years, then he would relocate for her; how two years had slipped into three, four, so that now it had been five years since they moved to Chicago.

"But we're going to move for me next year!" She was speaking almost plaintively now. She wanted to return to Boston, to work for a more important bank or for a foundation, part time perhaps —she would have a child to consider, of course—that dealt with "international economics." She seemed to be rambling, to be speaking as if she weren't really thinking.

"What will happen if you don't go?" I asked.

She looked at me desperately; her upper lip trembled and her dark eyes met mine. "I don't know, Liz," she said slowly. "It will be bleak . . . so bleak."

For a split second, I found myself shuddering with her. Then I regained my objectivity and asked her about her decision to adopt. She and Luke had begun the process seven months earlier, but she wasn't sure what she would do. She hadn't decided how long she would take off from work, or even if she wanted any time off at all. She had no idea, of course, how she would feel once the adoption became a reality, and she refused to be forced to make up her mind beforehand. She would have to make adequate child-care arrangements. "It's terribly important," she began, and I thought I was about to hear something profound, "that children not be allowed to watch television." She looked so somber and serious that it was as if she had said, "To play with the atom bomb."

She certainly could see herself working part time, and staying home full time wasn't totally out of the question either. She began to ramble again. "A lot would bother me about staying home full time however. You lose contacts. Nevertheless, if I can't sleep at night, if I'm torn with guilt . . ."

But I wasn't listening. I could think of only one thing: this bright, sophisticated, and accomplished woman, a woman who had graduated from Brandeis with a double major and who had easily made it through one of the best business schools in the country, speaking to me in that plaintive tone of voice: "Bleak . . . so bleak."

I had noticed this pattern, whatever it was—desperation, ennui, a sense of disappointment about what it is all about—among many of the women in the class of 1975 at the Harvard Business School, and I was intrigued. So many of them had emphasized that they had gone to the Business School for what they called "The Ticket."

I remembered how one woman put it, because she had said it best of all. "There was definitely a motivation on my part to get a credential that would open doors, which is how I view an M.B.A. Being very honest . . . I wanted the ticket, I wanted to get on the train. I figured that once I got on the train, I could decide where to get off. But if I couldn't get on, then I was stuck in the station. And I didn't want to be in this particular station anymore."

Yet these women seemed disappointed, and profoundly so. They seemed quietly surprised that their degree wasn't a ticket to nirvana, but rather to a way of life that could be as difficult as it was rewarding, that came with demands as well as privileges.

There was something else about the women who fit this pattern. They were reluctant to talk to me again, as if I had touched an exposed nerve. For example, I had approached Maureen Graham, the Falmouth woman with the sad eyes who had been Tess Beckett's friend at the Business School. She was certainly representative of this pattern, and she had declined to meet with me for a second interview. It was as if she took pleasure in turning me down. "I'm glad you found me so interesting," she said on the telephone, when I called her again, "but no, I don't want to cooperate." In another case, I had actually begun to interview the woman before she grew edgy and cut me off. "I don't want to continue this," she said.

Toward the end of the fall, when I had completed most of my second interviews, I found myself thinking about Martha Davis. I played back her tapes, and I noted the points that seemed to be emerging from her story that were significant for women in business: overexpectations for her career; the transfer problem; children as a way, perhaps, to avoid hard decisions about a career; ambivalence. The list kept growing.

I concluded that she was probably the best example of this pattern in women. I wondered how anyone that bright, that privileged, that accomplished could come to a point where she would confess to a complete stranger, "Bleak . . . so bleak."

So I called Martha Davis in December 1981, just before the Christmas holidays, and to my surprise, she agreed to be interviewed for a second time.

2.

"But I'm Not Typical . . ."

During the course of my research for this book, I deliberately put off a visit to the campus of the Harvard Business School until the very end. First, I was primarily interested in what had become of the women in the class of 1975 in the years since their graduation, rather than in who they had been as students at the Business School. Second, I wasn't sure that any visit to the campus in 1981 could give me a picture of what the school had been like in 1973.

I personally knew very little about the Harvard Business School. During my eleven years as a reporter in Boston for *The Wall Street Journal,* I had had occasion to visit the campus from time to time to interview professors and students for stories I was writing, but my association had been peripheral at best. Certainly, in the fall of 1973, when the women I was interviewing had enrolled, I had no knowledge of or involvement with the school.

I formed my first perceptions of the school, therefore, from talking to the eighty-two women in the class of 1975 six years after they had graduated, eight years after they had enrolled. Through their eyes and through the veil of hindsight, I had caught glimpses of what the world was like for them at the Business School in the mid—1970's. From patches of conversation, from comments about their colleagues and professors, I tried to piece together a picture of the way it was back then for them in their dormitories, in their sections, in the campus Pub where they would gather for coffee or beer.

I had formed a mental picture of Chase Hall, for example, where Suzanne Sheehan had roomed with Holly Lane that first year. I remembered what Suzanne told me about her first day at the Business School because I found it so amusing: how she had shown up the weekend before classes began, in skin-tight jeans and a halter—she had been dieting and she was razor thin, "thinner than I've ever been in my whole life!"; how she wore her black hair in a shag, the little tendrils winding down the nape of her neck and in front of her earlobes; how she arrived on campus with a ton of stuff left over from her bachelor-girl apartment in the Fenway. There was the big beauty-parlor hair dryer with the little reclining seat, for example. One of her sisters had given it to her, and she had had it for a long time until finally, years later in New York, a battery blew. She had put it out on Sixty-second Street and someone had taken it away immediately, probably realizing it was an antique.

Suzanne told me about how small and cramped her tiny room in Chase had been, one of four that comprised her so-called suite, two rooms each to a bath. There certainly wasn't enough closet space for all of her things. So when her roommate, Holly Lane, sailed in late with long, scraggly hair and a backpack, and there was nothing in Holly's backpack but a rug, Suzanne said to her, "What's this? Where are your clothes?" Then she asked Holly if she could use the closet in her room. "Oh, I don't care. I don't have much anyway," Holly said. She had nothing, Suzanne noted. She had been traveling throughout Asia for the previous five years, and she had just returned.

"Jesus, what an odd one!" Suzanne told me she thought that day, considering her long-haired roommate. And Holly, glancing at the hair dryer wedged into the corner of the tiny room, admitted that she thought to herself, "A beauty-parlor hair dryer at the Harvard Business School! Of all people, who's this one?"

From the women I talked to, I began to understand what it must have been like to be part of a section, the units into which the first-year class of eight hundred students is divided. These groups —there were ten of them that fall—operate autonomously, as schools within a school. Students in each section take all of their first-year classes together: three classes a day, five days a week, for the duration of the thirty-nine week school year. As a result, the groups become social units as well as collections of students in class together and, in a very real sense, simulate groups in the real business world: companies, banks, consulting firms.

Considering what sections are at the Business School, I could understand why Phoebe Holstrom thought that two women in section six, Alexis Drake and Pauline Adams, despised her to such an extent. It would have been different if Phoebe had been just a fellow student in an ordinary classroom. But as a person her section mates could observe closely every day over the course of the year, it seemed plausible that Alexis could have been jealous and Pauline scared of her. Alexis, the Baker Scholar, could see Phoebe impress her professors more than she ever could, even though Phoebe was nowhere near as bright; Pauline, the prim conservative insurance woman, could watch Phoebe charm the men as she had her professors and fear that Phoebe would take her husband away from her.

I remembered, too, how one woman had said that the people in her section were vicious and cold. That had bothered her even though she had no trouble holding her own. There had been a rumor about one of the other sections that year, she had explained, shuddering to think that that section could have been worse than her own. It was said that administrators had started an experimental section to pair older, experienced people with students right out of college, theorizing that the older students would help the younger ones and the younger students would bring a fresh perspective to the classroom. But apparently it hadn't happened that way. She had heard that the older students had kept to themselves and the younger ones had felt intimidated by their more experienced classmates. The atmosphere had deteriorated to such an extent that administrators had the experimental section studied to determine what had gone wrong and disbanded the group the following year. (A spokesperson for the Business

School acknowledged the existence of an experimental section in the fall of 1973, but said its purpose was for the faculty to test new ways to teach courses. A mix of older and younger students exists in all sections at the Business School, the spokesperson said, adding that that particular section was disbanded because the experiment had run its course.)

From my interviews, I felt as if I could be at home in the Pub, the campus snack shop and bar. I could envision this tiny Spartan room on the first floor of Gallatin, an office and dormitory building. The room was crammed with wooden tables and chairs that were old in a way that collectibles, rather than pieces of used furniture, are old. I could see the jukebox in the corner and hear the music blaring through the room. I could imagine how Mary Pat Horner climbed up on the table in her Playboy Bunny outfit and, amid the hooting and hollering, danced to the rhythm of a Beatles song.

Later that fall, I walked over to the Pub to see it for myself, and I was surprised to discover that the room was slick. There was a long polished-oak bar and a graceful winding staircase that led to a second-floor mezzanine. I had written these details into an earlier version of this book when describing the Pub in 1973. But a friend of mine who had worked at the Business School explained that they had been added later. In 1973, the Pub was just a plain little snack shop and bar stuck into the corner on the first floor of Gallatin.

In the middle of the summer of 1981, when I had finished all but one of my first interviews with the eighty-two women of the class of 1975, I decided to make a formal visit to the campus. I called the Harvard Business School public relations office. Explaining who I was, I asked for a guided tour. Independently and at random, I also called a handful of Business School professors. I asked them if they would meet with me for informal interviews regarding the role of women at the Business School and in business.

On a hot afternoon in early July, I met a young woman from the Business School public relations office who had been assigned to give me a tour of the campus. We met on the steps of Baker

Library, the massive red-brick building with white pillars that marks the physical center of the campus and dominates all else. From the steps of Baker Library, one can peer across the vast expanse of broad green lawn to the Charles River, which, like a physical and psychological barrier, separates the campus of the Harvard Business School from the campus of Harvard University. The Business School is located in Boston; across the river in Cambridge, the university makes its home.

The young woman, Mame McCallum, approached me. "Are you Liz?" she asked. When I nodded my head yes, she said, "Okay, we'll begin here, in Baker Library."

The first room she showed me was, appropriately enough, the Career Resources Room, located to the left on the first floor of Baker Library. This is, I found myself thinking, the culmination, what one does it all for. In the room, a small library unto itself, one had the world to choose from: There were hundreds of glossy annual reports from the biggest and most prestigious corporations in the country; there were slick promotional films produced by a handful of companies that are among the very biggest. Toward the back of the room, on shelves that surrounded a reading table, a number of corporations, investment-banking firms, consulting companies, and banks had left their brochures and literature, as a woman would drop a handkerchief in front of a man she wanted to attract.

I flipped through the brochures, and the one from Brown Brothers Harriman & Co. caught my eye. It was printed on glossy paper, and the writing was crafted in elegant script. Gracing its pages were bankers in three-piece suits, posing in front of famous buildings in cities such as London, Zurich, and New York. Such was the firm's way of telling its story, that of one of the world's most exclusive private banks, I thought to myself. I noticed the literature from Procter & Gamble, the powerhouse firm if one wanted a career in marketing. P & G products— Pampers, Tide, Duncan Hines cake mixes—were featured on the cover. Inside, the text posed these questions—"Why sales management? Why P & G?"—and then attempted to offer an answer. "In sales, success is determined by your own initiative and ability. The potential for personal satisfaction, advancement, and financial rewards is unexcelled by any other profession," the brochure said.

I took a handful of brochures from a number of companies and, like a kid in a candy store, I stuffed them into my tote bag, pretending they were for me. I pretended I had this type of future ahead of me, one in which companies beckoned me, sought me out, as it must have been for the women of the class of 1975.

Mame and I walked briefly through the rest of the rooms in Baker Library. The main reading room was on the second floor; a fixture from the old New York Stock Exchange was in the process of being reassembled, right there in the center of the room, to serve as its focal point. The other rooms included Kress, which housed rare books, and Aldrich, a tiny and warmly inviting recreational reading room tucked into the corner of the mezzanine like a snug hideaway on a rainy day.

Then Mame took me through the long corridor that linked Baker Library with Aldrich Hall, the main classroom building on campus. We walked up to the second floor of Aldrich, but it wouldn't have made any difference if we had stopped on the first floor or the third instead. The floors were identical. Mame pointed out the semicircular windows that jutted out at intervals along the corridor that surrounded each floor of Aldrich. In each, there was a window seat.

In those cubicles, which could be closed off by a pleated plastic door, students met with recruiters from companies during what is called recruiting season. That is the formal period of time from January to mid-April when recruiters from across the country swarm over the campus, in a mating dance. I tried to envision how it felt to be recruited, to be seated in a semicircular cubicle behind a plastic pleated door, facing a nameless individual who represented my tie to the future.

When we walked into a classroom, Mame flicked on the fluorescent lights. The room she had chosen, identical to each of the other classrooms in Aldrich Hall, was windowless. Like the cubicles with the window seats, the classroom was semicircular. Rows of long tables were arranged in concentric semicircles; they swept down to the focal point of the room, an elevated professor's podium, backed by a large blackboard. Mame pointed to the orange swivel chairs placed at intervals along the tables. "The chairs were just done over," she said.

Then she explained that the sections, the groups into which first-year classes are divided, took all of their classes together in rooms such as these. Students sat at the semicircular tables, their names prominently displayed in bold letters on desk-top placards.

The effect on me was claustrophobic. I had a new appreciation for what it would have been like for the students in Phoebe Holstrom's section, to take one dramatic example, to see her pull herself up slowly from her swivel chair and, with perfect composure, present her case for why J. M. Smucker & Co. shouldn't put ketchup in a wide-brimmed jar. "Pounding the bottle! Part of the whole schtick of ketchup is the bottle. You don't dish out ketchup, that's not what it's all about!"

The effect would have been different if Phoebe had been a student at any other business school, where students congregate weekly for the lessons that comprise their courses, oblivious to each other. But to take all of one's classes for so many hours a day in the same room, with the same people, the effect must have been . . . I was searching for the right word. "There's a gestalt about the whole thing," Joanne Segal, the Business School's director of research, told me later that afternoon. "The section is a social unit. It is unique and central to what the Harvard Business School experience is all about. It is what differentiates Harvard Business School graduates from those who got their M.B.A.'s at night."

The way students learn in the classrooms at Harvard is also different, Mame explained. There are no textbooks or lectures at the Harvard Business School. Rather, students are given thick hand-bound mimeographed sheets of paper containing "cases," which are the units of instruction at the Business School. Cases are slices of life, or more to the point, actual business problems, culled from the files of real American companies. Professors at the Business School are responsible for finding these cases: contacting companies, researching corporate problems, and using these problems to teach the specific principles of business in each of their courses.

In these cases, students are given only the facts that were available to the corporate executive who actually confronted the specific issue. Which may not be enough information, or which may be too much, the salient points buried beneath a hopeless morass of useless data. As in the real world, there is no one correct answer. There are any one of a number of possible solutions, each of them imperfect, some of them better than others. It is up to the students, individually and in conjunction with each other in the classroom setting, therefore, to come to grips with a question that becomes uppermost in their minds and that has become a cliché of the Business School experience: What would *you* do?

Mame switched off the fluorescent lights in the classroom. I watched them flicker out beneath the metal grating in the ceiling that shielded the bulbs, leaving the room in darkness. We walked out of Aldrich into the bright sunlight of the hot July afternoon, and I felt a short jolt of relief—and of freedom. The bright sunlight seemed to be a foil for the confinement of the windowless classroom we had left behind.

Later that afternoon, Mame took me through many of the other buildings on campus. We walked past the dormitories that line the banks of the Charles River. We climbed up and down the stairs of the little gray-brick building that houses the doctorate program, its rooms paneled with rich dark wood. We strolled past groups of middle-aged executives, seated in little circles on the broad lawns, at Harvard for any one of a number of programs for middle- and senior-level corporate executives.

As we toured, however, I kept thinking of the classroom Mame had shown me, how all encompassing it had seemed to me. It would be bad enough, I thought, to be a typical student in that room, being introduced to a system and method of teaching that, in fact, is a mirror of business itself. A perfectly controlled microcosm, a little laboratory. It would be bad enough to be a man, for whom the system was designed.

But I wondered what it must have been like for students who weren't typical, students like the women of the class of 1975. It may have seemed that, as 10 percent of the class, women were a significant presence in the fall of 1973, especially since the Business School hadn't even accepted women until the fall of 1963, a short decade before. Yet at 10 percent, the women of the class of 1975 were still a distinct minority. In a deeper sense, they were oddities in a culture completely alien to them, and I couldn't help but think that this must have had a significant effect on them.

In talking to Business School professors and administrators, informally and at random, I hoped to get another perspective on the issue of women at the Business School and in business. I had my own perceptions, of course, having just finished a year of interviews with the eighty-two women. But I wanted to see how my opinions would compare with those of people who had observed these women at another point in their lives, and who had since observed the increasing number of women who had enrolled in subsequent classes.

One of the first people I talked to was a young Navy man, himself a graduate of the Business School, who recently had been named director of the school's career development office. I met him in his second-floor office in the tiny gray-brick building across the lawn from Baker Library, and I remember not taking to him at first. I was put off by his clean-cut appearance and his close-cropped brown hair, which was a touch too militaristic for my taste.

I was also put off, that day in July, by what he was telling me. I asked him how Business School women were faring in the job market, and I felt that the answers he gave were too stereotypical, too pat. "There are differences between men and women when it comes to their approach to jobs," he began, and already I didn't like what he was saying. "There aren't many men who take paternity leave and many women do, for example. Not just maternity leave, but women are more likely to drop out for a while. The probability that a woman will drop out for several years is much higher than for a man."

He cited an article that had appeared that same morning on the front page of *The Wall Street Journal,* reporting that women managers taking maternity leaves were disrupting offices throughout the country. I had scoffed when I had read that article, but apparently people were taking it seriously.

"Read the article in your own newspaper," the career official challenged. "A lot of women put male bosses through the ringer. The problem for companies is a lack of continuity. Companies just don't know what women will do when they get pregnant, and that article heightened the problem."

Miffed, I tried to reason with the young man. I asked him how women compared academically with the men on campus. He readily admitted that the women were "very good," that their collective grade point average was, in fact, higher than the men's average.

So it isn't that, he was saying. The problem for women involves other issues. Work on the home front isn't equally shared. Women still generally earn less than men, even professional women. "Psychologically"—and at this point he picked up the issue of pregnancy again—"a woman goes through changes when it comes to pregnancy. There is a much stronger pull for women to drop out."

I tried another tack. "Then why do they go to the Harvard Business School to begin with?" I asked.

He had a ready answer. I would have suspected that he rehearsed it had it not been for his sincerity. "The rigors of the challenge," he said. "Then, too, people change their minds. Maybe they thought they could handle both career and family."

"Have you done a study of the female corporate dropout?" I asked. He shook his head no, and I asked him why not. "Maybe if we found that thirty percent of the women we graduate dropped out, we wouldn't like that," he said.

It was easy for me to dismiss the comments of the young career development officer as coming from someone who may have been programmed to think that way, who, if the truth be known, could have prejudices of which he himself wasn't fully aware. It was much more difficult, however, to say the same thing about the next person I interviewed. She was Regi Herzlinger, a professor of business administration and the first woman to have gotten tenure at the Business School.

Regi and I met for lunch in the faculty dining room on the second floor of Kresge, the campus dining hall. We chose a big round table in the far corner overlooking the Charles River, a sparkling blue ribbon on that sunny summer day.

I liked Regi immediately. She was the type of woman I would want to emulate. She had been determined to have a career, she told me, just determined, as far back as her undergraduate days at the Massachusetts Institute of Technology. She had run her own consulting firm for years until she found that what she really liked to do was business research. So she went back for her doctorate, then joined the faculty of the Business School, then worked her way up the academic ladder until she received tenure. The award hadn't come at the price of her personal life either, and that impressed me. She was married and had two children. Their pictures had been placed on the windowsill in her office, and she spoke of them fondly.

We talked about women at the Business School, and she told me that there has been a big change since the early 1970's. In those days, there were only a handful of women in each section of about ninety students, whereas now there were twenty to twenty-five women in each group. "It's like day and night," she said.

Then we talked about women in business. Regi said her perspective on women's progress in business came from a look at the mid-career management programs the Business School sponsors throughout the year for corporate executives. In the advanced management program for senior managers, those individuals who generally have reached the level of vice-president, only 1 woman had been enrolled in the group of 160 the previous year. "And she was a nun running a large hospital," Regi said with a smile. But in a similar program for middle managers, people who were five to ten years into their careers, women comprised 10 percent of the enrollment. "So it's getting there; the number of women companies send to the middle-management program is following the curve [of those who graduated from the business schools a half dozen years earlier]," she said.

"But what concerns me"—Regi's voice grew more serious—"is what's happening at the middle-management level. It is there that the percentages will stop following the curve."

I nodded, knowing precisely what she was starting to get at.

She began to elaborate. "It is possible, perhaps, to do it all in a professional career—as a doctor, a lawyer, an academic"—she looked at me—"a journalist. But . . ." She was forming her thoughts carefully now. "It is not possible in management." She paused, then continued. "Management involves a process, not techniques or skills. If you are not *there*, so that people can see you, you cannot be an effective manager."

She was pinpointing the conflict for women between career and family. The reason why they wouldn't be "there," as the career development officer had pointed out, was because they tended to drop out to raise children. "The real question is, can a woman reenter on a full-time basis three or six years after having dropped out?" Regi asked.

Then she continued in a different direction. "Of course, some women decide not to have children, not to get married. But those are fantastically difficult choices. Women who make those choices, what happens when they become more senior? Where will their [emotional] support come from? What will their existence be like as a single . . ." And then she mentioned the name of a noted businesswoman who had never married. "The isolation is enormous."

I didn't disagree that the isolation could be "enormous." But I thought fleetingly of Suzanne Sheehan, and I wondered if the choice was necessarily "fantastically difficult." Could it be that for some women—women like Suzanne, women like the businesswoman Regi mentioned—there was no other choice? Could there be something in their makeup that makes them different from most women? Could it be that they don't *care* about marriage, about children?

Regi talked about the alternatives that have been suggested as solutions by academics studying the issue: shared jobs, flexible work hours, corporate day-care centers. A smile crept slowly across her face, and she shook her head. "That's a lot of crapola," she said. "Those solutions are not solutions [for managers]."

I steered the conversation back to her major point. "Why do women cop out at that level, at middle management?" I asked.

Regi had a ready answer. It was a simple one. "Childbearing pressures," she said, and I was disappointed. Her answer was too simplistic, too rote.

She picked up her own ball and began talking about how women tend to scale down because of those childbearing pressures. They make less than the kind of commitment it takes to make it into senior management. Not that scaling down is all that bad, she added. "People can still have satisfying jobs in middle management." But to make it further up the ladder in corporations, one simply can't do that. "Corporations that permit scaling down at no detriment to one's career—you can count them on one hand!" she exclaimed.

As she talked, I wondered if she hadn't gone off on the wrong course. She was serving up the popular explanation. I thought about Tess Beckett, her pregnancy the spur that had propelled her full speed ahead to accomplish what she couldn't accomplish just one year earlier: graduation from the Harvard Business School. I thought about Martha Davis, her future bleak and cloudy, to be sure. But motherhood certainly wasn't what made it bleak and cloudy. Rather it seemed as if she had decided to adopt a child because she couldn't solve a deeper, more complex problem.

I looked at Regi, and I decided to risk her criticism. "I don't think that's it," I said, starting slowly in an effort to muster the courage to make my point. "I don't think it has anything to do with childbearing pressures."

She looked at me quizzically, a touch disturbed, and I continued. "I don't know that childbearing is the real problem," I said, thinking about the women I had interviewed and knowing that Regi didn't have that perspective. "I sometimes think that that is the excuse for a lack of commitment on the part of a lot of women."

To my surprise, Regi didn't disagree. "You are suggesting," she said slowly, "that the problem is psychological. I don't know. I haven't looked into the hearts and souls of these women. But if the problem is psychological, the solutions are more complex."

I thought back once again to my year of interviews with the women of the class of 1975. Certainly, I had opened the door only a mere crack to their innermost thoughts and feelings. But I had been permitted even that small glimpse, and no one else had. From what I saw there, I was convinced that women struggled not with childbearing pressures per se. Those were just the surface problems. What they struggled with was deeper and infinitely more complex—psychological, if you will. So I was gratified that Regi, the first woman to have received tenure at the Business School—a person who, I thought, would know the Business

School women far better than most people in a position to judge them—wasn't disagreeing with what I had pointed out to her.

The third person I talked with at the Business School was a beady-eyed professor whose name had been given to me by a friend in publishing who knew I was writing this book. My friend suggested I call this professor, who he felt could be helpful to me. The professor agreed to talk to me, with the understanding that I not quote him by name.

In his office, late in the afternoon, the professor began by telling me that there was a difference between older women who came to the Business School to change careers and younger women who knew from the beginning that they wanted to be managers. The older women were more "uncertain" of themselves, he said. They didn't take easily to the back and forth banter in the classroom. "You can watch them watching the younger women, because the younger women don't have those uncertainties," he said.

The younger women were "like young female athletes," he said, with obvious pleasure in his voice. "When they got clipped in the classroom, as invariably happens to everyone, they'd laugh in a way that said, 'That's okay. I'll get you next time!' "

"So all of the problems for women in business will be solved once this younger, more knowing group of women gets into the mainstream?" I suggested.

Well, no, not exactly, the professor said, slowing the pace of his voice and becoming more hesitant. There were other issues, which he would be happy to discuss, but only because I had agreed not to quote him by name.

"Like what?" I asked.

He looked at me, his beady eyes glowing. He broke into an embarrassed smile, and he faltered a bit as he tried to explain. "Like, well, you know, sex," he said. "I mean, men just don't have to deal with the issue of getting into bed with some executive they are trying to impress. It uses up energy unnecessarily."

He began to elaborate by citing an example, the case history of Mary Cunningham who had, the previous fall, made national headlines in the business press. She was a recent graduate of the Harvard Business School who had been promoted to vice-president for strategic planning at The Bendix Corporation by its chairman, William Agee, because of, it was alleged, their "personal relationship."

"Look what happened to Mary Cunningham," the professor said. "We don't know that they slept together. But what we do know is that they behaved in such a way that gave people ammunition for gossip. She was the hostess in his suite at conventions; he stated publicly that he regarded her as a friend. The whole thing was naive on both of their parts. I mean, in corporations, this is just one more element that women have to deal with that men don't."

Then the professor veered slightly, going into a different, but more interesting territory. "Did you read the recent column by Ellen Goodman?" he asked, referring to the columnist for *The Boston Globe* who writes about women's issues.

I shook my head no, and the professor continued. "Ellen Goodman talked about two women in gray-flannel suits and button-down shirts. She said she couldn't tell them apart from men in gray-flannel suits and button-down shirts. 'Is this what liberation is all about?' she wrote in her article, suggesting that it shouldn't be." The professor took a deep breath. "My reaction was, from the point of view of the corporation, yes, this is what liberation is all about. We are striving for a sex-blind corporation. Those women who are succeeding, that's what they're becoming— men."

I could see the professor's point, and I felt uneasy about it.

The professor sighed. There were some things I should keep in mind about the Harvard Business School, he said. Contrary to the prevailing wisdom, not all of the people who graduate from the Business School are aiming for the top. "There are a lot of men who graduate from here who would be happy simply to have a good job for the rest of their lives," he said.

"Like what type of job?" I asked.

"Like vice-president in charge of a division—running something big," he said.

I did a double take. Of the eighty-two women I'd interviewed, only a handful were striving for such a goal. Certainly not Phoebe Holstrom, for all she knew about playing the game, or Martha Davis, for all of her brilliance. Certainly not Mary Pat

Horner, even though she had a fine analytical mind of which people would speak with respect. Not even Tess Beckett, for all of her determination. Only a few women were aiming that high. A Holly Lane, perhaps. Only one was aiming for the top, Suzanne Sheehan.

Yet the professor spoke of jobs such as vice-president in charge of a division as if they were suitable for the type of man who wasn't particularly ambitious, who certainly wasn't among the cream of the crop of Business School graduates. His comment made me think again about the women I had interviewed, who they were and what they wanted and why they seemed so different.

In the fall of 1981, when I was conducting the second interviews with the six women I had chosen to be the major figures in this book, I also researched and wrote a few articles about the Business School for *The Wall Street Journal.* One of the reasons I did was to get a better feel for the Harvard Business School, a better sense of what it is all about.

So that fall, I wandered about the campus as if I belonged there. I talked with many professors. I sat in on their private sessions with students and research assistants as they discussed class assignments or research for the cases they were developing. I observed a number of classes, delighting in my chance to see the windowless, self-contained room I had been shown in the summer come alive with a group of students.

I marveled at how the case method could be used to teach a business concept. In one instance, I watched Regi teach her students a business concept that had been popular in the 1970's, a strategy that was supposed to help stagnant companies start growing again. The strategy held that companies should be in a mix of businesses: some mature businesses that generated a lot of cash, some brand-new businesses that offered hope for growth. That way they could use the profits from the mature businesses to get the new businesses started.

Regi began by summarizing the case history of a company that wanted to diversify. Then she asked question after question regarding what that company should do. Students picked up the ball. Hands went up all over the room. There was a lot of shouting: Students argued with each other's theses. Until finally, by the end of the eighty-minute class session, they had begun to understand the concept Regi was teaching.

In the evenings, I would wander over to the Pub, order a beer, and take a seat in the far corner of the room, waiting for a group of students to invite me to join them at a round table, as they invariably did. I would confess, after a while, that I wasn't a student at all, but rather a reporter working on a number of projects about the Business School. And that would be the trigger that would make them start talking about their schoolwork and their professors, the reasons they had come to the Business School, and the plans they had for the future.

One Friday evening late in September, as I wandered through the campus, I spotted a group of students in the far corner of one of the broad lawns that, like a courtyard, separates the dormitories from the main street of the campus. They had gathered in a polite little circle, and they were drinking beer and talking, their hands slung jauntily in their pants pockets, their heads thrown back in casual laughter.

I passed the group and walked along the main street of the campus, then turned right toward the Charles River. Crossing the bridge, I glanced back and thought to myself: How beautiful the campus looks, shaded as it is in the twilight of early fall, in hues of lavender and rose, the river shimmering like a ribbon of diamonds in front of it.

I wondered to myself, irrationally perhaps, whether I had made a terrible mistake about my own career. Where was I, what was I doing, a decade ago, when I could have come to Harvard and been the beneficiary of what the school has to offer—the chance for money and power, the allure of limitless opportunity? I felt twinges of envy toward the group of students I had spotted, talking casually in the polite little circle, and I felt profoundly sad that I could not turn back the clock ten years and be in my early twenties and be a student at the Harvard Business School.

Yet, deep in my reverie, I knew from talking to the women of the class of 1975 for the previous year and to the people who worked and taught at the Business School that it would not have been the same for me, as it had not been for the women of that class. "I'll be happy to talk to you, but I'm not typical . . . ," so many of the women had said to me when I first approached them.

One woman made the point best of all: "I've always considered myself very different in terms of why I went to Harvard, what I've done since Harvard, what my life represents. I mean, all of those things. I don't consider myself the least bit typical of the Harvard stereotype male. Perhaps your research or somebody else's research will figure out what the Harvard stereotype female is, and maybe someday they'll decide whether or not I fit into that. But I'm sure I don't fit into the Harvard male image."

I hadn't brushed aside comments such as those. I had heard them too often to dismiss them. But it wasn't until I had completed all of my interviews with the women, and talked to the professors and administrators at the Business School, that I began to realize how sharp those differences were and how they worked to keep women from becoming full participants in business.

There was no question in my mind that part of the reason for the difference was the system, of which the Harvard Business School was representative. I remember talking once to a woman who counsels women about how to advance in corporations. At one point in our conversation, in her dimly lit New York apartment, she was explaining why women shouldn't, mustn't, ask for special treatment because they are women if they expect to be taken seriously in companies. "Hey, Liz, nothing's changed," she said stridently. Then louder, *"Nothing's changed!"*

But I was convinced that part of the reason had to do with the women themselves. I was beginning to have a new respect for what the young career development officer had told me: "The probability that a woman will drop out for several years is much higher than for a man. . . ." The professor with the beady eyes had suggested the same thing in a more sophisticated way, and even Regi, the first woman to have received tenure at the Business School, hadn't disagreed with me when I suggested that women seemed to be less committed.

So when I went back to talk to the women of the class of 1975, I knew that most of all I wanted to explore this issue: What holds women back? Why do they seem to be less committed to their careers?

3.

SUZANNE:
The Making of a
Female Chief
Executive Officer

As a staff reporter for *The Wall Street Journal,* I was in the unique position of being able to observe, at close range, the chief executive officers of the biggest and most powerful companies in the country. As *Journal* reporters, we dealt mainly with senior executives. Often they stumbled over themselves to return our telephone calls in an effort to get their names in the newspaper, and heaven help the underling who talked to us rather than refer our calls to his superior, who expected to be the spokesperson for the company in the premier business newspaper in the country.

As a woman in her twenties and early thirties, I had only to pick up the telephone to engage a chief executive in a private meeting, in the business interviews I would do from time to time to talk about a company's financial prospects, or in the quick telephone conversations for their comments for stories we were doing about the national economy or business trends in general. Sometimes, these chieftains would parade dutifully into my office in downtown Boston, where they would be ushered into a back conference room, sparsely furnished and windowless, to proclaim that this or that quarter had been the best in the company's history or to cry on my shoulder: Things were so bad that it had been the worst quarter ever.

Other times, for interviews I considered especially important, I would hail a taxicab or rent a car and head for their offices, sequestered as they were on the top floors of shimmering downtown steel-and-glass office buildings or in secluded settings in the suburbs or in the country. Going to interview them on their turf, I would take note of their handsomely appointed corporate domains, retreats almost, furnished with antiques or prized possessions, the family photographs adorning their desks and bookshelves, it seemed, as obligatory as their leather briefcases and smiling secretaries.

I had a chance to view these chieftains in public settings, as spokespersons for their companies at forums such as annual stockholders' meetings or security analysts' meetings held from time to time by the company or at the invitation of an analysts' society. And while I wouldn't ever presume to undercut the individuality of the chief executives I had interviewed and observed, hundreds and hundreds of them over some dozen years, I always felt a jolt when I had to admit to myself that I found them to be largely very placid and ordinary individuals.

The more obvious flamboyant exceptions notwithstanding, most appeared to be one dimensional, simple in a way that President Ronald Reagan can be said to be simple—not unintelligent, of course, but subscribers to a cut-and-dried way of looking at the world. They were ambitious, to be sure, always eyeing the next opportunity, ready for the next step on the ladder. While that was a trait they tried hard to conceal from me beneath a calmly professional if not polished demeanor, I couldn't help but see it come out, here and there, when posing some of my questions about their companies or industries.

Few seemed to have interests beyond the narrow sphere of their businesses. And indeed, it hardly ever occurred to me to presume they would have insightful opinions when I explored topics other than business for articles—the social sciences or the arts, for example—or when I would write about the human aspects of business stories that were making headlines: the effect of inflation on ordinary people, the progress of women on the job. I wouldn't have expected them to have cared much about such things.

Rather, they seemed to blend homogeneously into an archetype who, in my mind, became the chairman of one of our biggest Fortune 500 companies. I would interview this man every year after his company's annual meeting in suburban Boston. I always knew precisely what questions I planned to ask him, about earnings for the recent quarter and his company's new products, and I usually knew what his answers would be. No comment on earnings. No comment on new products beyond the press release. This individual's tight-lipped and expressionless countenance, just a few shades lighter than the obligatory gray of his business suits, was to become forever frozen in my mind. If I had ever harbored fantasies when I was a young reporter that the leaders of American business had to be among the most personable and creative individuals in our society, I had only to turn to thoughts of this individual to remember why I had long abandoned that notion. The sobering reality was that chief executives were no more than ordinary individuals, albeit a touch less colorful.

So what must have struck me, when I first met Suzanne Sheehan at Il Monello on that May evening in 1981, was that she appeared to be so ordinary. She was, after all, nothing but a small-town girl from Alvin, Texas, a tiny hamlet a few dozen miles from the port city of Galveston. She was the oldest of four children, the daughter of an owner of a small manufacturer of drilling bits, who had made decent money after World War II only to continue to live as if he were still middle class.

"My father and mother would go out to dinner and stuff like that, but there really isn't much in Galveston," Suzanne said, somewhat reluctantly toward the end of our interview that evening, revealing the details of her family background only because I specifically asked. "Now the city is starting a decent symphony, but there still isn't much to do. It's a very outdoor life, and on weekends when we were little, we had a summer house on the coast. We would go there and go out fishing, go on the boat, deep-sea fishing. We would do outdoor things like that, which my father and brother liked and I hated."

She wrinkled her nose when she said that, sitting kitty-corner from me in the restaurant, and I immediately recalled how she had made such a point of telling me that she was different in that respect from the executives she worked with at the Fortune 100 company. They were all athletic and she was not. Recently, one of the executives had told her she was eligible for the company's executive health club. She really wasn't; as director of planning for the $2 billion North American Group, one of the three big operating arms of the $6 billion company, she wasn't quite that senior. But she had accepted his invitation to join, if only because she wanted to lose ten pounds. The alternative was to diet, which she had been doing religiously for the past several weeks, to the dismay and amusement of her colleagues.

At a recent luncheon, one of her best friends in the company, her first boss, in fact, had offered to sneak out and buy her an orange at a fruit stand downstairs. She wanted fresh fruit, and there was nothing on the menu but raspberries, which she didn't particularly like. "I really will get an orange for you, Suzanne," he had said. "Don't go off your diet just for that. You know you're going to hate these managers, you're going to be mad at yourself, and I'm going to pay. I really want you to have an orange." So she had met him in the lobby, and when they couldn't find an orange at any of the fruit stands, they had gone back to the restaurant. "And I had raspberries for my main course and raspberries for dessert."

Suzanne wasn't any stranger to diets. She had dieted like crazy the spring of her senior year at the University of Texas at Austin, in 1967, when she wanted to look great in a bikini for her honeymoon to Honolulu. She was going to get married in June, to Butch, the guy she had been dating for years. "I wanted to go to Honolulu and swim, and then I got sick—I really had never been thinner in my life, I was so thin." She laughed shortly as she recalled this aspect of her past. Not too long before our meeting, she had been in Honolulu with a group of people from the company. "It was really funny," she said. "I was in this little van taking eight or ten people from our company to the site of my first honeymoon that I never had, and they were all embarrassed when I told them that."

As she spoke about the honeymoon she never had, I thought

about that point in her story when her life had taken a twist that wasn't ordinary. She hadn't married Butch. She hadn't taken that honeymoon to Honolulu. Instead, she had climbed on a plane and gone to Boston. And once in Boston, she had the great good fortune to have been twenty-two years old at a time that likewise wasn't ordinary, at least not for young women with dreams for the future.

For a while in Boston, Suzanne played the role she had been playing all of her life, and she seemed to delight in telling me about that: how she had landed a job as a pediatric nurse at the Boston Lying-In Hospital, which she thought she'd do until something better came along; how she had found a beautiful apartment in the Fenway with two stewardesses and a dental hygienist; how she had had what she called "a reasonably active social life," which meant that she went out all of the time.

But then she met Jonathan Price, and her life took yet another twist. Jonathan was a young engineer for Polaroid who roomed with three coworkers in a big old house in Arlington, a working-class community just north of Cambridge. For the two years she was with him, Suzanne would listen in amazement to the way he and his roommates would talk about their careers.

"These guys really raised my expectations about what twenty-two- or twenty-three- or twenty-four-year-olds could expect to do with their lives," she began. "They were all working at Polaroid and they expected to go straight up. They had high, high expectations. They were very critical of management, and they felt they were capable of criticizing and analyzing a lot of things I didn't feel I was capable of criticizing and analyzing. But when I was with them, I really began to enjoy what they were doing. I identified with it immediately. I began to understand that it was okay to think you were going to go to the top. It never occurred to me that I could go to the top of some big thing."

It was Jonathan in particular who used to tell her how important it was for his career that he be accepted at a first-rank business school, the best among them being the Harvard Business School. She hadn't understood at first, because where she had come from business school was "the lowest of the low"; people who were smart and going into business would become engineers. But Jonathan explained that Harvard was different. "That it was so special!

So critical!" she said, her eyes aglow as she recalled how he had built it up. "That was the ticket. That was critical to his success in life."

So the following year, when Jonathan applied and was accepted at both Harvard and the University of Chicago and decided to go to Chicago and Suzanne was named head nurse at the hospital, which "scared [her] to death"—she really was a nurse, she wasn't just doing it as a temporary job anymore—she took a step that she probably otherwise would not have taken.

She took the step by means of a circuitous route, which she delighted in describing, for this was one of her favorite stories. The year that Jonathan left and she began looking but couldn't find even a typing job, she took a night course in business administration at Boston State College. She did so well that year that she won the only scholarship the school offered to a special M.B.A. program for students whose undergraduate degrees weren't in business-related subjects.

"And as soon as I got that, I took a taxicab, which was a big deal. Took a cab, and I was just this little pediatric nurse. From my apartment in the Fenway over to Harvard. Picked up the application. Stayed in the apartment the entire weekend. My roommate took the day off on Monday to type it. She was the dental hygienist. She typed up my application. And I had already written one application because Jonathan had applied the year before. I pulled out the application and really went through it and restructured some of the essay questions since I was a little bit exposed to the way you're supposed to fill out those things. And you sort of can tell. 'What are your two greatest weaknesses?' 'I'm impatient with myself for not being perfect.' Of course! So it's pretty easy to figure out what they want to hear. And I, I got in! And as soon as I got in, I dropped any consideration of going to the M.B.A. program at Boston State.

"Since I got that scholarship, you know, I figured, 'Whoa! If I'm the best they've got, why should I go there?' So then I went to Harvard, which was really the right thing to do."

When Suzanne spoke about her career later that evening at Il Monello, I began to see that she was ordinary in yet another way.

She was ordinary in the way the chief executives I had come to know over the years were ordinary. She appeared to be one of them. Close my eyes and I could almost feel myself at that annual meeting in suburban Boston, listening to my archetype say, "No comment on earnings."

She was, at that point in the interview, talking about her job at the Fortune 100 company, as director of planning for the North American Group, which she had gotten a year and a half earlier. It was considered a huge promotion for her, a chance to go down into an operating unit, where decisions are made, from corporate headquarters, which is really just a consolidating entity and where she had had the title she loathed, assistant to the director of planning for the corporation. "Notice that the phrase 'for the North American Group' has been added," she said of her current title. "I began working on that the day I took the job."

Not only had I not noticed, but I couldn't conceive of why it would be important to have the phrase "for the North American Group" added to her title. But Suzanne explained that her superiors had deliberately kept it from her because they wanted to soften the blow for a man who had wanted the job and didn't get it. "So they abbreviated the title and called it director of planning. And they graded it at a lower level, which, of course, caused me to get less money. The day I walked in I let them know that I knew that. And I said I really needed the full title because I really thought I should have it. So finally, a year later, I got it."

I was astonished that it had taken a year for something so simple. I raised an eyebrow, but Suzanne already had begun to explain. "He was one of the good old boys and the company really owed him something," she said of the man they were trying to appease. "Just that nobody wanted to have him back. Nobody particularly gave a damn about him."

Suzanne herself hadn't been wanted by her new boss, the vice-president for planning for the North American Group, when she was named director. He was forced to take her because his boss, the chief administrative officer for the group, had gotten to know Suzanne at informal company gatherings and had heard of her work from her superiors at headquarters. He thought she could be a solution to a problem he was having: He needed someone who could do a better job of analyzing new businesses for the group because his boss, the president of the group, wasn't pleased with what was being done up to that point.

"So my boss didn't want me. He wanted someone else. And he hated the guy who was working for him before me in that job. He saw me as another person that he didn't want. And it took me four months to win him over. Four months! I worked on it. Once I came back from a vacation three days early just to be a hero. So he'd think I was the type of person who chewed bullets because he was that type of guy. It was stupid and inconvenient and I could have stayed away. It was just sort of a silly thing to do. But I did it in order to show him, 'I'll chew bullets because I know that's what you want to see.' And I let him know that. 'You want to see me chew bullets? I'll chew bullets! Want to see? Watch it!' I just did it. It wasn't a big deal to me. And he really began to respect that, and we really developed a fairly reasonable relationship."

She laughed when she told me this story, a short thoughtful snicker. She had his number. He was just under forty and an "accountant's accountant," a workaholic who expected his subordinates to be that way too. People were petrified of him. He drove them like slaves and treated them badly, because that was his way of making them work.

"But"—Suzanne set her jaw and continued—"if anyone screamed at me, guaranteed he's not going to get me to move my little bottom from one chair to the next. Our relationship has worked because before he ever put pressure on me, I showed him more than he ever would have wanted. That forced him not to ask me. I mean I knew what he was going to do so I tried hard to trump him. Before he asked me, I already had given it to him. So our relationship was established on . . . on a different level."

At that point in the interview, having had a feel for Suzanne's style on the job, I felt as if I had to put it into perspective. I asked her for a precis of her progress at the company. She immediately began rattling off the titles she had held, and the titles of the people who had hired and promoted her. She had started as an analyst in the department of planning at corporate headquarters. Then she had been named assistant to the director of planning, the title she had held for years and loathed.

She had been hired by three people at headquarters, the assistant planner, the director of planning, and the vice-president for planning. Two of the three left or were otherwise removed a few short months after she took the job, and she was left with no one but the junior person from the group that had hired her. So she had had to get a feel for the new people in her department at headquarters, the new director of planning and the new vice-president for planning. It was during that time that she had begun branching out to meet other people in the company, such as the chief administrative officer of the North American Group, who eventually brought her into his unit.

"So it was the vice-president for planning at headquarters who suggested you for the job in the North American Group," I asked, repeating what she had told me about her effort to shed the horrid title of "assistant to," because I wanted to make sure I had the story right. I felt as if I were suddenly swimming in a sea of titles, and I was too embarrassed to ask Suzanne to set me straight. "As opposed to the chief administration officer of the group?"

"Yeah, he didn't even know my name at that point."

"Okay," I said, scrambling to buy a few minutes to sort through my confusion. "You say your title at headquarters was assistant to the assistant planner . . ."

I had obviously made a mistake. Her title at the time had been assistant to the director of planning. A look of exasperation crossed her face, as if she were wondering why she was bothering to explain all of this to me. Then she said, "We should go back a bit." And very methodically, she ran through the titles of all of the people again. But she was speaking so rapidly and I was so rattled that I had to keep asking her to stop.

"Hold on! Hold on!" I said at one point. "You talked about the three guys who hired you. I'm clear about what happened to them. Now for that vice-president for planning at headquarters who you said was just named president. . . ."

So it went until finally, much later in the evening, when the restaurant was clearing out and I was so mentally weary that I could barely think, I shook my head and let out a little chuckle. "I've got to hand it to you, Suzanne," I said. "You talk about women in corporations. Anyone who can play this type of game, figure out all of these little moves, belongs there, for heaven's sake. I mean I can't even keep these guys straight!''

The following November, when Suzanne and I spoke for a second time and discussed her role as a boss, I was to come to precisely the same conclusion about her ability to maneuver in a large company.

That Saturday afternoon, we met in the lobby of her apartment building, which was located, as she so often made a point of telling me, just three short blocks south of the United Nations, and the first thing that struck me was that she appeared every bit as disheveled as she had the previous spring. She sauntered into the lobby well past four o'clock, the time we had set for our meeting, side by side with a female friend with whom she had spent the afternoon. She seemed oblivious to the fact that she had kept me waiting.

As before, her ensemble appeared to be wrong in so many little ways that the sum was somehow off. She was wearing a heavy woolen dirndl that was two inches too long, and as such, made her look heavier than she really was. (Her diet notwithstanding, she was still about ten pounds overweight.) The sleeves of her fisherman's knit sweater needed to be rolled up, her hair needed a trim, and she would have looked far better had she bothered to put on some makeup. Her face was pale, her expression wan, and she didn't smile as she approached me where I was seated on a couch in the otherwise barren lobby. She introduced me to her friend, whose name was Betsyanne, and when they had said their good-byes, she motioned for me to follow her up a cramped elevator, down a dark corridor, and into her apartment.

When she opened the door to her apartment, I was more shocked by what I saw than I suppose I should have been. Like Suzanne herself, the apartment appeared to be a collection of elements that were each a little bit off, and as a result, the whole setting seemed awry. It reminded me of a stage setting from a Tennessee Williams play about the decadent South. The living room was painted a musty shade of lavender and furnished with an ornate Victorian couch that needed a shampoo. Antique-satin drapes wrinkled and curled their way to the bottom of the two tall

French windows, as if they mightn't quite make it. In the bedroom, a lace coverlet was thrown haphazardly across her bed, and in the kitchen, the counters were lined with empty wine glasses, tall glasses with graceful stems.

That afternoon, Suzanne and I sat together on her sofa, sipping red wine and listening to hard rock. She had turned on her stereo so loud that finally I had to ask her to shut it down. We eased our way from topic to topic, from her career to her personal life, then back again to her career. But it wasn't until much later that evening, when we had retired for a late-night supper at a little quiche-and-salad restaurant a few blocks from her apartment, that we talked about her subordinates. Although she was exhausted by then—the interview in her apartment had lasted more than six hours—she seemed more eager than usual to discuss what she considered to be one of her most important functions, that of developing people.

The point that seemed to be coming through strongest of all was that she made her decisions about whom to promote strictly on the basis of what was best for the company. Recently, for example, she had forced a bright young female M.B.A., whom she had hired to work directly for her, to work under a man she just had brought into the department as manager of planning. "I forced her to go under him because it was the right thing to do," she said insistently. "If I had kept her separate, he never would have gained any experience managing people, an area he was going to be working in."

Suzanne's decision had been particularly difficult for the young woman, because she had wanted the job that Suzanne gave to the man. What made it even worse for her was that even Suzanne had admitted that she was qualified for the job, whereas he was not.

I raised an eyebrow when Suzanne came to that point in her story. But she didn't seem to share my sympathy for her young subordinate. "I think she could have done the job, but she was just too junior," she said brusquely. "She really was. I didn't think it was the right job for her right now."

There were other considerations, Suzanne explained. The man had come from a department that was beginning to suffer from low morale, because people in that group didn't think they were being given as many opportunities as people in other areas. The problem was a particularly difficult one for Suzanne's boss, who had been trying to make some opportunities available to them. "So I took it very seriously that there was a morale problem there. I have two guys working for me now that came out of that group."

Then, too, the man she brought in was perceived by his superiors as someone who would be promoted into the field. He had been with the company for about six years and had done very well in a narrow specialty. Therefore, it would be better for the company if he first did a stint under Suzanne in the planning department before going to a branch office.

As Suzanne spoke, I tried to get a handle on all of the dynamics that had played a part in her decision: the need to boost morale in a department that had been presenting a problem for her boss; the need to give a candidate who was due for a promotion the type of experience he didn't have and could use; the need to prevent a younger individual from being promoted too soon and perhaps forever typecast as someone familiar with only one area. The interplay of all of these factors was reason enough for rejecting the pleas of a young woman who had expected (and certainly deserved) to be promoted into a bigger job at that time.

Still, telling her had been tough, Suzanne said, and when she told me the story of how she had done it, I got the feeling that she saw herself in the young subordinate she had rejected. "She's not a bad person, but she's an aggressive person and she has her requirements, thank you," Suzanne explained. "And I understand that. I think I'm very willing and cooperative, and I kill myself, but frost me and you're dead. That's the way it is with her. So I really had a hard conversation with her about that guy I named to be her boss."

The interplay of these many factors whenever Suzanne had to decide whom to promote also suggested her thinking on a related issue, I reasoned. That was that she probably couldn't afford to be biased against anyone because of factors such as sex or marital status.

And in many ways, I was right. A little bit later in our discussion of this topic, Suzanne made a point of telling me that she just promoted a thirty-seven-year-old woman to be the other manager in her department. The woman was married, had three children, and had to be transferred from the Midwest, which meant that Suzanne had to spend department funds to put her up in a hotel until she could settle her family into the area. "And it was very hard on me because she would go home to see them and she would be at the office and not really be there," she said.

Suzanne's decision was particularly heartening for me. For one of the theses that was emerging from new research on the topic of women in management and the professions was that bosses tended to be less likely to promote married women because they perceived them to be less committed to their careers. This was thought by the researchers to be one of the major stumbling blocks for women when it came to upward mobility in organizations.

I mentioned the theory to Suzanne, then said it apparently hadn't been an issue for her when selecting the thirty-seven-year-old woman. She looked at me curiously, a touch bewildered that I had even made the point. "For me? No," she said, quickly dismissing it. "The fact that she needed to go home as much as she did for a while was all part of the deal I made going in."

As we discussed the issue of whether an individual's personal situation makes a difference when it comes to getting ahead, Suzanne tried hard to direct the discussion away from a focus on women. "Nor do I care that this guy who works for me needs to go home because it is eight o'clock at night and he won't get there until ten," she said. "That's not my business, that he lives two hours away. He made a choice. He wants a bigger yard. What can I say?"

I studied Suzanne for a moment, her lips drawn into a taut little line now that she had had her say. I felt as if I had put my finger on yet another characteristic about her that made her appear so much like the chief executives I knew.

"You're very impersonal about the whole process," I said.

"You absolutely have to be," she replied, a firm little edge in her voice. "Once I've made a commitment to them, I'm very interested in their careers. I'm not interested in their personal lives. I can't do anything about the fact that somebody who works for me doesn't see his kids a lot because it's been a tough week. What can I do? I don't see anybody I want to see either."

95

"You're very impersonal," I repeated.

"But I'm not any more impersonal than my employer or the men that I deal with," she replied.

"Exactly," I said.

The more I came to know Suzanne Sheehan over the course of our two interviews, the more I came to believe something about her that I wouldn't have otherwise believed about any human being, let alone a woman. And that was that her inclination to be impersonal seemed to go beyond just the way she behaved on the job. Rather, it appeared to be a characteristic of her personality, every bit as much as a good sense of humor or a facility with numbers.

The concept of Suzanne as the impersonal woman was to emerge from our discussions about her personal life as well. For the woman who had left Butch so many years before at the University of Texas and who had seen Jonathan off to the University of Chicago seemed to be even more willing to let go as the years went on. There appeared to be no reason for pretense anymore; that she didn't particularly care became more and more obvious.

Her feelings for another were perhaps at their peak when she spoke about the man she had dated at the Business School, a Pakistani named Revi Bengas. But even when she spoke about him, she seemed to emphasize what he had done for her. He had given her support and encouragement at a time when she had been "scared, very scared"—she had, after all, gone to Harvard after a six-year stint as a pediatric nurse at the Boston Lying-In Hospital.

"But then I met Revi, and he was really supportive and he taught me a lot," she said, explaining, for example, that she couldn't bring herself to speak in class at the beginning. That fear subsided once she got her grades back and they were mostly Satisfactories—not great grades by any means, but good enough to convince her that she was home free. But at the beginning, "It was Revi who kept saying, 'Don't just speak about it in our study group. Speak in class!' He kept pushing me."

The fondness she felt for Revi, at least when measured against the fondness she had felt for the others, was to continue even after graduation. Revi went back to his country to run the family business, and she to New York to join the Fortune 100 company. But they continued to see each other every six months or so. "I remember that as a wonderful period," she said, and then she told me about a vacation she took with Revi to the Middle East. "There was waterskiing. I water-skied among the tankers in the Gulf of Oman."

Her enthusiasm was to pale, however, when he told her a few years later that she had changed. "It was true," she said, and this time there was a sharp little edge in her voice. "I remember his saying, 'You used to need me a lot and now you don't.' And I said, 'That's right. Number one, you're not here, and number two, I'm not sure you're as smart as you used to be.'"

Perhaps no one was, to her way of thinking, as she herself became more confident of her own abilities, and her own ambition. The next man she spoke about was someone she could barely remember, even though she had lived with him for practically a year when she first went to New York. He was a Frenchman who was an administrator for a company hers did business with. She just about moved in with him—something she hadn't ever done with anyone because, she explained, "It's too difficult to move out again." But she had taken an apartment on Sixty-second Street with Claire Jacobsen and Holly Lane at the time, her two friends from the Business School. And Holly had left shortly thereafter to go to Dallas and marry Chuck Pfeiffer, while Claire had begun dating the man she would marry and someone Suzanne couldn't put up with. "The last thing I wanted was to see this little turkey walking around the apartment, the two of them cooing and oohing," she said.

Perhaps because she thought it was what I wanted to hear, she began telling me stories about her days with the Frenchman. But even her best stories began coming across as flat and dull, and we both wearied of them. We both also wearied of the charade. When I asked her who came next, she replied without hesitation that there hadn't been anyone, no one serious since the Frenchman.

Toward the end of our evening at Il Monello, I remember asking Suzanne, mostly in an effort to satisfy my own curiosity, why she hadn't ever felt the need to marry and have children. She had reached way back for her explanation. "Well, it might have been from my first relationship with Butch," she said. "I mean, I could have had that. If I were really worried about waking up in the morning and being alone, that was a way to fix it. And I almost took that solution many years ago. But I figured out, in some way that I don't quite understand, that that wouldn't have been a good idea. And I deeply believe that was the right thing to do. I mean, I would just be divorced with three kids right now."

Her thinking on the subject was hard for most women to understand, she had continued. She and Claire Jacobsen, for example, couldn't discuss it, because Claire had felt the need for someone who was "warm and supportive and kind and understanding" from the time she first went to New York. "But I'm almost like a divorcée who got divorced at the age of twenty-two and who doesn't feel that marriage is the solution anymore to feeling lonely or unhappy or incomplete," Suzanne had said, turning away from me, reluctant to continue the discussion.

So the next time we spoke about her social life, the following November in her apartment, the topic had become a rote and necessary one for me to cover, a perfunctory one for her to talk about. There wasn't much to discuss, in fact, at least not in terms of the men in her life. She was dating about five or six different men, she said when I asked, and she made a less-than-enthusiastic effort to describe them.

There was a painter who was about her age and who wanted to settle down, an attorney who was about forty and still single. "Absolutely never wants children," she said of the attorney, and when I asked her why, she replied that he was just as selfish as she was. There was another attorney, who was divorced and had a small son, and about whom she could care, if only a little. And this time when I asked her why, she threw back her head and laughed. "Who knows? Chemicals!" she said.

The more she talked about her social life, the more I began to see how fundamental were the differences between Suzanne and myself. Whereas I had approached the subject from that most universal of human themes, the forming of relationships about which one could care deeply, Suzanne felt far more comfortable discussing the topic from another perspective. When I stopped pushing her for information about the men she was dating, she eased instinctively into a discussion of her circles of friends in the city, whom she said she made every effort to see.

There was the group of academics at New York University, with whom she felt "comfortable sitting around in a T-shirt and jeans in bare feet all day Saturday and Sunday just talking philosophically." There was a group of young professionals, of which Betsyanne, the woman I had met that afternoon, was a part. Those people didn't mind spending their weekends talking about one person's problem on the job, "in enormous, excruciating detail, just one problem, to help the person really work it out."

Then there was an eclectic group, with whom she had a standing date every Thursday night at the Delegates' Lounge in the United Nations, and when she told me about the organizer of that group, she spoke with a softness that was uncharacteristic of her. The organizer was a bizarre individual, a "poet who was more of a sketcher," she explained. He often behaved outrageously and when she told me about some of the things he had done—he had once set off lighted paper napkins in a restaurant and had been thrown out—I became exasperated. But Suzanne shook her head, adding hastily that she enjoys that streak in people if there is "real brains and fun and interest there."

"They all meet at five-thirty, and about once a month I trickle in at about seven-thirty just before the bar closes," she said of her eclectic crowd, "and we start drinking. And we keep on drinking until one in the morning and we have a wonderful time!"

Many of the men she was dating came from these circles, Suzanne continued, comfortable now as she discussed her dates from this perspective. But from my own perspective, that of a long-married woman with a young child, I remember feeling as if I had to cut her off at that point, my curiosity piqued. "These dating situations, do they just go on and on or . . . . I'm just trying to think back to junior high."

And when I said that, she became indignant for the first time during our discussion of her personal life, perhaps because what I said might have been interpreted as a put-down. "That is the thing you cannot do," she snapped, "because in these groups, a number of people have lived together and have split up and are still part of the group."

A man she had dated from the academic circle, for example, just began living with another woman from the group. Everyone had assumed they were just casual acquaintances. Now Suzanne, the man she had dated, and his new girlfriend went places as a threesome, Suzanne said, adding, "She's darling! Sure, no big problem. Now if I had fallen in love with him, that wouldn't be a good idea. It would be awkward, and I'd be hurt, and you know, whatever. But it was really quite casual."

She giggled a little at that point and so did I, if only in relief. "Apparently you haven't fallen in love with any of these guys," I said, and Suzanne laughed again. "My little circle of casual dates? Oh no!"

My only other observation was that women such as she, women whose social lives consisted of a continual round of casual dates, or women who had no social lives at all (the flip side of the same coin, perhaps?) seemed to be those who, for whatever reason, didn't want to form a deep and lasting relationship with another human being.

"I don't think that's wrong," Suzanne said. "I think that's definitely there in my case. I know how not to be around when it's going to be serious. I look for situations that are manageable. Controllable."

The concept of Suzanne as an individual who was inherently impersonal would have been neither here nor there had it not been for the fact that organizations and, most particularly, large corporations are also impersonal entities. From that perspective, I could see that the characteristic served her well when it came to advancing as far as she had in management at a major company. But the quality also had its sinister side, as I was to discover, quite by accident, at two points in our interview that Saturday in November when she talked about her relationship with two women who weren't as impersonal.

The first was the woman who had been her roommate at the Business School, Holly Lane Pfeiffer, whose name came up midway through our conversation. The point Suzanne was making was that she was planning to get in touch with Holly, of whom she had always been fond, as soon as Holly was settled in New York. She was being transferred from Dallas to New York just that month for a big promotion.

Her feeling for her friend took a sharply acerbic turn, however, when I told Suzanne that I, too, had been impressed with Holly. I told her that I had been particularly impressed that she was able to have both a family and a career without having compromised either. The transfer was proof positive that she hadn't compromised her career, I continued. She had been apprehensive about that step in her career the previous December when I had interviewed her. She had been worried that she wouldn't be asked because all of her bosses knew Chuck and might have suspected that she couldn't relocate. So she had taken it upon herself to tell them that she was able to move in spite of Chuck—something she didn't like to do. She had always thought it unprofessional to bring up the issue of her family when discussing her career with her superiors.

"Well, Chuck doesn't have a job," Suzanne said. Those were the first words out of her mouth when I stated my case for Holly, and from that oblique perspective, she began to explain that Holly wasn't transferring as much to advance her career as to save her marriage. She explained that Chuck had set up his own consulting firm and was spending so much time with clients in New York that the marriage had begun to suffer. The last time she had seen her friend the previous fall, in fact, Holly had admitted as much. "As Holly explained it, 'It will be better for me living in New York because at least some of the time Chuck will be there,' " Suzanne said. "Since last January he has not been home Monday through Friday. She has three tiny babies!"

Suzanne's distaste for Chuck Pfeiffer was to become more obvious the more we talked about Holly. She started slowly at first, reluctant, I presumed, to say much against the person who was her friend's husband. She hadn't ever liked his pranks, which she found childish, she began, and when I mentioned that she had made a point earlier that evening of being so fond of the bizarre individual from her eclectic circle who set off lighted paper napkins in restaurants, she retorted that he was different. Her friend was witty and insightful about people, whereas Chuck was just "a big overgrown teddy-bear type who thinks he's adorable but isn't."

About Holly, Suzanne had opinions that were equally firm, and she began to argue from a perspective that annoyed me, a theoretical perspective. Her major point was that Holly wouldn't have moved if Chuck had had a job in Dallas, because she was more committed to her family than her career. "But that's theoretical," I protested, forgetting for an instant that we were interviewer and subject, and that I had come merely to elicit her opinions. "Let's see what she actually does. The fact is that she is moving to New York to accept this transfer." And then, Suzanne shot back angrily, "She isn't leaving her family behind either."

The other point at which I was to get the same feeling about Suzanne came much later that evening, at our late-night supper. She mentioned casually that she had attended a meeting at the company hosted by the chairman of "some women's committee." He wanted to get ideas from the company's female managers for a speech he was writing. A woman at the meeting who just had had a baby suggested that the company could improve its benefits for working parents, and her comment had annoyed Suzanne. Turning belligerent, Suzanne told me she had said to the woman, " 'Don't you know? They don't even want you here. Why do they care about the fact that you have a kid at home, that you're paying a nursemaid to take care of her? Until you're wanted by yourself, don't try to sell them on the fact that you have a child at home. The first issue is that they want you here, that you can play the game.' "

Suzanne's attitude horrified me, even though I knew she was right—women err in thinking they can bring personal concerns to the work place. Employers don't, in fact, care. But my horror stemmed from a feeling I had about Suzanne. Considering what she had said, both about her colleague and about Holly, I couldn't help but spot an ever-so-slight touch of envy—or of longing. She appeared to be devastated, subliminally at least, by the thought that women who were successful in business could also be succeeding in that other arena—women's own—as wives and mothers.

The thought wasn't one that I posed to Suzanne, of course. But by the time we had finished our supper and were walking back to her apartment, I had found myself recoiling from her. She wasn't the type of woman I'd want to be up against on the job, the type of woman for whom I'd want to work.

At the doorway to her apartment, she turned to face me. She asked me casually about my baby, and I remember drawing back from even that simple question. The fact that I had a baby, had a husband, diminished me in her eyes, I sensed. I also remember wanting to grab her and straighten out all of the little things about her appearance that had always disturbed me. Trim her hair, put some makeup on her face, and in the case of her outfit that night, shorten her skirt, and roll up the sleeves of her sweater.

But then, just as casually, she began telling me about a store I should try for shoes if I were planning to shop in New York. And because I was so grateful that we were now discussing a topic that didn't cut close to the emotions, I allowed her to write down the name of the store on a scrap of paper as if I were interested, which I was not.

At the beginning of our second interview in Suzanne's apartment, I saw another side of the woman who I had determined was the most likely to make it to the top of a major American corporation. She was talking about her future at the company, and the point she wanted to make was that she already might have gone as far as she could go. The thought was devastating, of course, not only because she felt she had done all that she could as director of planning for the North American Group but also because she felt she could handle bigger jobs. The problem was even more formidable because there wasn't anything more she could do to improve her chances, she added. The promotions at her level in a big company started going to people senior executives felt most comfortable with, and those people were most likely to be white men.

"I'm increasingly aware of . . . of a ceiling," Suzanne began, faltering a bit as she tried to explain and looking curiously demure, her hands folded in her lap as she sat poised and proper on her Victorian couch. "I'm at a ceiling right now and I know it. I knew it in May. I've gotten my department in order, so it's like,

'Now what? Okay, I've chewed bullets for you. Thank you. What's next for me? What's in this for me?' "

The thought that there wouldn't be anything else in it for Suzanne struck me first of all as ironic, even as I surveyed her from the perspective of her status as a single woman, seated as she was like a lady on an overbearing couch in her musty apartment, somehow out of synch with the neatly put together pin-striped men for whom she worked, they with their wives and children and conventional suburban homes. It was ironic that she who lived so differently from them was, in fact, their temperamental counterpart; ironic that she who thought like them was perceived as different—and was being penalized for that.

As Suzanne related anecdote after anecdote that made her believe she was being held back because she was a woman, I paid particular attention. For she was describing a problem that scholars and writers have theorized to be at the crux of the barrier for women advancing into senior positions in management and the professions. The theory professes that women are held back at that level, not for lack of skills or desire, but because their mostly male superiors perceive that they somehow don't "fit."

"Well, at any moment, I never see the next job for myself," Suzanne began, explaining that the men who were her colleagues assumed they would be able to jump from job to job, whereas she did not. They saw themselves, for example, going from a mid-level job to senior management in charge of an area of the world or a major product line. "But I don't see myself being accepted in those senior roles," she said.

She told me, for example, that her first boss at the company, and one of her big boosters, had given her name to executives at other companies who called from time to time looking for planners at the level of vice-president. But the moment he would mention that the person he was recommending was a woman, they would lose interest. Never had she gotten even one call from those firms.

Then there was her recent dinner with a colleague who had been named a director in her department after she had been named to her directorship. A remark he made at dinner had set her off. "You know, I am able to accept you as my peer, but I wouldn't want to work for you," he had said, and she had replied,

"I am able to accept you as my peer, but I wouldn't want to work for you." Angrily, she explained: The point was that he had had "the audacity to make that remark to the person who was established in the department, when the real issue was, was I able to accept *him* as my peer?"

An even more frightening point about the incident was that senior managers took remarks like that as evidence that men were beginning to accept women in management whereas precisely the opposite was true, Suzanne continued. The remark showed that they weren't willing to work for a woman, the ultimate test of acceptance, she said. "It's like my saying, 'I don't want to work for a gray-haired man.' It's like, who cares? But no one says to him, 'Who cares?'"

Suzanne and I talked for a while about whether it would be best if she just left the company, which a friend of hers had been recommending for years. This friend was an extremely powerful individual who led "sort of an idealized quasi-consulting, quasi-academic life in circles I couldn't operate in for years," she said. He had been telling her to go to work for a small company and actually run it or get herself on some boards so that her name would become known to people who could help. But whenever she thought about what he had said, she would decide once again to stay with the Fortune 100 company.

She hadn't ever been a risk taker, she explained, and as such was best suited for the relatively riskless confines of the large corporation. The risks she appeared to have taken—putting herself on that plane to Boston so many years before, leaving a secure nursing job for the Business School—weren't really risks at all. "I mean, how can you lose by leaving someone you don't really want to marry? You can't really lose that way," she said. "How can you lose by going to Harvard, when all of those people you really respect tell you it's the answer to everything?"

So recently she had identified the job she wanted next at the company and, very methodically, she had begun the process that she would have to go through to get it. She had sat down with her boss and expressed her interest, and when he hadn't responded, she had made a mental note to try him again in six months. "You mean he didn't get it the first time?" I asked, and Suzanne, a touch surprised by my obvious naïveté, said, "Oh no, they don't hear."

The job she wanted carried the title of vice-president and involved responsibility for the production of one of the products made by the North American Group. She would have to go down into one tiny division of the group rather than be involved on a group level as she was now. But the advantage was that she would have what companies call a line job, actual profit-and-loss responsibility for making or selling a product. As director of planning for the group and in all of her previous positions, she had what companies call a staff job, which meant that she could merely advise line managers about a course of action. The reason it was so important for her to have a line job was because only managers who have had such experience can be considered for senior positions at most companies.

I remember asking Suzanne at that point what she saw for herself in the future should she get the line job she wanted. Her response was that she'd like to come back to the planning department as vice-president, her current boss's position and a job clearly within the ranks of senior management.

And when I asked her what appealed to her about that job, she gave me an answer that made me realize what had really been propelling her for all those many years, ever since she put herself on that plane to Boston after college. She had looked away from me when I had asked the question. Then, with a passion I was to recall from the way she had spoken from time to time about her future, she replied, "Power."

Throughout the course of both of my interviews with Suzanne, the theme of power had run like a thread through all of the topics we had discussed. Most especially, it was running oddly parallel to the subject we were discussing then, the reticence she felt as a woman at her level in the corporation.

As I thought about this, I found myself recalling the way she had spoken at our first interview about a psychological test the company had administered a few years back for women they expected to promote. Her results had baffled the executive who reviewed them with her: She had scored equally high on two values that were supposed to be contradictory. Specifically, the results had shown that she put a premium on both power and her social life, which had immediately caused the executive to jump to the conclusion that she would leave to get married. "The guy took one look at the results and said, 'Well, you are not married now, but you are going to get married.' And I said, 'No, I'm not.' And he said, 'Well, you have a very high social score, and I would have assumed that meant you were interested in a family.'

"So what we figured out was that I resented being a pediatric nurse," she continued, digging deep into her past for the explanation. "I didn't want to be a nurse, so I chose against everything on the test that looked like nursing. But I still chose a lot of social things such as helping a blind person across the street as long as it didn't appear that I had to say I was a nurse when doing it."

There was another contradiction. She had scored equally low on two values that similarly were supposed to be at opposite poles, specifically charity and physical prowess. "There was this grid and I had this really bizarre peak that went down when it shouldn't have gone down, the physical prowess value. Because I am extremely nonathletic. I don't like to go out in the sun; I don't like to get dirty; I don't like to get sweaty; and most people who are very interested in power like that a little bit."

By this point in our conversation in Suzanne's apartment in New York, the shadows of late afternoon had turned into night, and the rose-tinted glow of lamplight from her Tiffany fixtures fell across her face, softening her coarse features. As she talked about her future, I found that I was no longer surprised to hear her speak with reticence and humility about the power she said she wanted. The contradictions in her personality were ultimately what set her apart from the men for whom she worked; they were what would make it so difficult for her to advance any further in the still-so-wholly-male milieu of senior management.

Later that night, I told Suzanne about my meeting with the beady-eyed professor at the Business School. Despite our obvious lack of rapport, I suspected this might be one story of mine with which she would empathize. I told her how shocked I had been when the professor had talked about people who aspired only to the level of vice-president in charge of a division—well within the ranks of senior management—as those who weren't especially ambitious. "And I did a double take and said, 'Wait a minute!' " I said to Suzanne. "He's looking at them as sort of the nonachievers. The grunts of the crowd. And they're the best of the women in your class. Why is it so skewered?"

Suzanne didn't dismiss what I had said as she so often did whenever I made a comment. Instead, she asked, very thoughtfully, "Why is it, I wonder? What do you think? What's your thesis?"

I told Suzanne I had seen a tremendous lack of self-confidence among the women in the class, and she shot back, annoyed, "I also think there's a tremendous lack of identification."

Then I told Suzanne that I wasn't referring to her own situation. I said I found her to be among the most self-confident of the group, and I asked her whether she agreed.

"Let's think about that for a minute," she said in her studied and cautious way. "Yeah, I think I'm self-confident. But the manager of planning whom I just brought into the department and who works for me now . . . he's been working for me for a few months. And one of the things he said to me is that he'd like to be in the job for about a year and then move on to another job out in the field. And then be promoted back from the field. Every time he says that to me, I am shocked. Because he has not done a thing for me yet. I'm his boss, right? He has to perform here first.

"And I began to realize that he expects to have continued promotions. And that is what I mean. He is so self-confident and so unhumble that it surprises me. I am self-confident, but I truly feel I am more humble. I don't dare ask for something more until I feel sure they can't say no. And that in a way worries me about getting into senior management. Because I don't believe it's my birthright."

The only other time I saw that touch of caution in Suzanne was midway through our discussion in her apartment, when we were talking about her friends from the Business School and she made a point of telling me she had tried to keep up with Elizabeth Conner, the woman who had tried to stand me up for our interview in Philadelphia. I was to recall how Suzanne had made a point of talking about Elizabeth that night at Il Monello; how she said she considered Elizabeth a friend; and how that made me feel sorry for her, as I considered Elizabeth's opinion of Suzanne. " 'Suzanne what's-her-face?' " Elizabeth had said at our brunch, with a little smile and a shrug of her patrician shoulders.

"We probably never had very much in common," Suzanne was saying now, a bit sadly, almost admitting as much to herself. "We don't have career things in common for sure. I don't know exactly what she does for starters. I mean, I have a concept. She's one of those people who goes out and tries to keep northwestern Brazil from being quite so poor. But I don't know how she does that. She puts up cement-brick factories. I'm guessing."

The only explanation I could think of for Suzanne's curious fascination with Elizabeth could be found in the way the two of them differed. Whereas Suzanne was striving for advancement in the male milieu of corporate management, Elizabeth, her Business School degree notwithstanding, was doing a job that could be said to be "feminine" in orientation, her job at the international foundation of helping people less fortunate than herself.

Suzanne's admiration for Elizabeth struck me as a longing, however subliminal, for a side of herself that she had lost a long time ago, or perhaps never had in the first place. In a deeper sense, it made me realize how frustrating would be the task ahead for Suzanne, a woman who had chosen to live as a man. The conflict to which she herself had alluded would continue to plague her, I assumed, and, perhaps most sadly, keep her from making that final push up to the apex of American business.

Suzanne's story nonetheless revealed a lot about what it would take for a woman to come near to that apex. Most of all, it made me realize how much harder it would be for most of the rest of them. As Suzanne and I walked back to her apartment on that brisk and beautiful evening in New York, I thought back to my interview two weeks before with such a woman who shared many of Suzanne's characteristics but who was nowhere near as ordinary —Phoebe Holstrom.

4.

PHOEBE: The Antithesis of the Corporate Woman

During my years with *The Wall Street Journal,* the type of story I liked to do best was what is called a corporate profile. This is a long article, usually for the front page, that puts a single company and its people under what we hope will be a very perceptive microscope. The story generally has to have a purpose. I couldn't just write about a company at random. There had to be something happening at the company, some new development that was important above and beyond the scope of its business, before I could proceed.

My fascination with close-up looks at the country's corporations was perhaps ironic considering my belief that corporate leaders were for the most part very ordinary individuals. For, as any writer knows, the people make a story. And what could be worse than doing an article about an organization whose movers and shakers turn out to be, as did the Wizard of Oz, not quite what the reporter had in mind.

The explanation is, of course, that we writers generally will not do such profiles unless we find the individuals who are running the show to be a cut above those that we ordinarily deal with, no matter what the importance of the development. In my case at least, I paid particular attention to what is generally referred to as an executive's "style," the sum and substance of all of a person's characteristics. Should the executive's style appear to equal more than the sum of its parts, I would have found a person, and perhaps therefore a company, worth writing about.

The chief executives with style will always remain in my mind, set apart from the pack by a set of mannerisms or an aura that enabled me to remember them fondly as individuals as well as corporate leaders. There was the mild-mannered, pear-shaped man with spectacles whom I had interviewed in the mid-1970's and whose quiet style somehow stood apart from the merely ordinary. He had been brought into a company that had been in turmoil for years, plagued not only by an extraordinary set of business problems but also by the ramifications surrounding the suicide of his predecessor. So it was the way this man stood in contrast to the chaos around him that made him memorable in my mind. I will always remember my interview with him in his office, as he sat like a contented peacock behind his desk and told me when I asked that his favorite hobby was reading. He would sweep through a certain bookstore at periodic intervals and emerge with his arms full, he said.

Then there was the chief executive of yet another company who stood apart for what he had done, which was to put together a multibillion-dollar company from bits and pieces, scraps of everyone else's throwaways. He also had a sharply individual and somewhat grandiose personal style. A man who appeared to have had experiences that cut like a broad brush across all that life has to offer, he had done everything from sail his yacht to raise prizewinning horses on his country estate. Yet the characteristic I found most interesting about this executive was that his style was no predictor of who he really was. The more I came to know him, the more I began to see that the person beneath the unique and appealing exterior was no less ordinary than most of the others I had come to know. He had been able to build his business because he, in fact, shared many of their mundane qualities.

The demystification of this executive brings to mind another thing that had struck me about the leaders of American companies. And that was that even those with charisma and personal magnetism were more often than not likely to be ordinary when one peered beneath their surface. What lay beneath was usually nothing but the gray-haired, dull-spoken chief executive who had become, in my mind, the archetype for all of them.

This observation is all the more meaningful, I believe, because much is made in the business and general press about an executive's style. It seems as if a lot of writers, myself included, would like to believe that the nation's corporate leaders are more akin to the maverick, as epitomized in American culture by the cowboy. They are thought to be individuals who strike out on their own to build a future in a place or from a situation in which there was nothing before they saw the opportunities therein.

It was perhaps only because I had the privilege of having been able to observe them up close for so many years, when I was young and still idealistic enough to believe that I had to call the shots as I saw them, that I was able to see this for the myth that it is. There are far fewer cowboys among the leaders of American business than one might suppose, no matter how much their personal style might be conveying precisely the opposite point. The fact is that American business hasn't ever found a way to deal with its mavericks, and thus has been more likely to disregard or dismiss them.

The thought that there may be no place in American business for individuals who are truly mavericks was to persist as I came to know Phoebe Holstrom. The very first thing I noticed about her, in fact, when she whirled into the lobby of the Berkshire Place on that warm May afternoon, afloat in a sea of black voile and dark hair, was that she was anything but ordinary. The sense that she had a finely honed and highly individual personal style was apparent, not only from her appearance but also from the story she told that evening and from the way she chose to tell it.

I was to come back time after time to the way she had taken her place in the high-back chair across from me and, like some bountiful snow queen about to dispense her favors upon one of her subjects, had begun her story in a way that would elevate her somewhat ordinary background into that which was extraordinary. The young woman who had grown up in the upper-middle-class suburb of Greenwich, Connecticut, in the mid-1960's and who had dated the football heroes and been named Miss Greenwich her junior year really wasn't that person at all, she appeared to be saying. The real Phoebe Holstrom was the young woman who had spent her summers and her holidays on the Caribbean island of Jamaica and who was old beyond her years, considering all that she had been exposed to.

"That's where I first learned to dance to reggae music, calypso music," she began, her eyes aglow as she told me about how her father would take the whole family out to the bars on the island —his wife and three children, Phoebe the oldest and her brother and sister just babies—for where was there to leave them? There were no baby-sitters on the island in those days. "I mean, in those days Jamaica had no electricity. There was one little native bar, and the women didn't go out, only the men did. And there were a lot of men from other islands who were out working so that they could send the money back to support their kids on Tortola or wherever. So we'd all go out together, and there'd be like scratch bands, steel bands. Makeshift instruments. And I'm sitting there right with my father, and he'd let me dance. That was an astounding thing because there were very big differences between the races in those days, and it was always considered really special that Mr. Holstrom would let his wife and daughters dance with the local people, because white people who came to the islands didn't do that."

It wasn't that her father was all that extraordinary, Phoebe said, except for the fact that he had emigrated from St. John, Newfoundland, and put together his restaurant business from scratch. He had been entirely on his own, because his parents had died when he was in his early twenties. He had married young, and the babies had come quickly, which may have accounted for the rigidity that Phoebe had always hated about him. He had been able to dominate her mother, refusing to allow the woman to work even though she was gifted, in a way that he would never be able to dominate her. She would run away as soon as practicable, fleeing to the only college he would let her attend if she wanted to live away from home—Connecticut College, ninety miles east of Greenwich.

He was also insecure in a way that she was not, Phoebe continued, always needing other people's approval, never able to be comfortable by himself. "And I, I don't compete with people directly," she said. "I compete against my own standards."

Yet the life that she was to come to know as a young adolescent on Jamaica was something that met with his approval, and so was the way she chose to take advantage of it. Much later, in my second interview with her, she was to pull out a photograph of her former husband, Johnny Carellas, the Venezuelan of mixed racial heritage, that showed him at a Holstrom family gathering, his big black arm slung affectionately around her father's neck. In the same way, her father must have known and silently approved of what she had done way back when she was but a child in Jamaica. Her father must have known about Carney, the black man who was older than even he was and a friend of the family's, the first man she ever slept with.

Phoebe chuckled softly to herself as she came to this point in her story, secure in the knowledge that she had captured my attention by then and that I was enraptured by her. "Well, you know, it's funny, sometimes I've laughed about it," she said. "I think I never wanted to sleep with him. First of all, this is a man who was interested in me. I was this sort of very cute, sexy little fifteen-year-old kid, I'm sure. I know what I looked like. I had long hair and I'm sure that I was actively enticing. I was not a flirt, but sort of, at a distance, very enticing.

"I'm also sure that deep down inside somewhere I wasn't going to have some fifteen-year-old guy messing around with me. I didn't know what this was all about, but if I was going to do it, I was going to make sure it was done right and I was going to have a good time. Well, I had a great time! And one of the net effects of that— It's fascinating, God knows, I've slept with hoards of men, but I've never slept with anyone I didn't like. Anyone who wasn't a friend. They're all people I care about, who care about me. The same with this guy. He's now seen me grow up. This guy has watched me for fifteen years. He really knows me well."

The sense of caring for others on the broadest of scales, from the impersonal perspective of a leader for his people, was to cut like a knife through the rest of the topics we discussed that afternoon in New York. For her father's legacy had done nothing if not make its way into the philosophy by which she had chosen to live her life. She wanted "the widest array of options" for her career, for example, which was why she finally had chosen to go to business school rather than law school, the latter having been the way she had been leaning in college. "I wanted to be able to work in any number of different institutions at different times in my life," she said. "I wanted to be able to go into government, to go into business, to be in the U.S., to be out of the U.S. If I were a lawyer, I was gonna learn U.S. law, gonna get stuck in the U.S. I'm too action-oriented to be writing briefs and all that stuff. Deadly!"

The conviction that she wasn't ever going to be stuck, in the broadest sense of the word, was matched by an equally strong conviction that she had to help those who were. "This was sort of a radical leftist lady here," she said with a touch of swagger in her voice, when she explained that it had been Johnny who had convinced her that she should go to the Business School and that she had scoffed at first. She wanted to "fix the problems." The summer after her freshman year in college, when social activism was very new, she worked for an antipoverty program in the Lindsay administration in New York. In the summers that followed, she did the same type of work in Boston and Chicago.

She hadn't ever been apprehensive about mingling with the people she was helping—although whenever she spoke of doing that I was to get the impression once again that she thought of herself as stooping down from on high to mingle. The time she met Johnny, for example, at a party for her community workers when she was eighteen and working in the Lindsay administration, she was to recall that he had noticed her because she stood apart. She had been the only white woman at the party. "He said he noticed me right away," she said. "He said that my hair was very long. He said I was wearing a yellow dress." And when he asked, she agreed to go out with him because he, too, stood apart. She explained that he had led a "duplicate" life, having been reared in a family of Venezuelan intellectuals, then sent to boarding school in the United States and to Brown University. "By the same token, he had friends who were drug addicts," she said approvingly, for that split appealed to her.

The most extraordinary aspect of Phoebe's story was to occur, however, at that point in our interview when people had begun to fill the lobby of the Berkshire Place, and in the midst of swirling cigarette smoke and loud chatter, she had shut her eyes and issued me an order: *"Shut that thing off."* She wanted to tell me what had gone wrong with her ten-year love affair and marriage to Johnny and why she had chosen to leave him, and she didn't want this side of her story to be imprinted permanently on the uncompromisingly honest record of my tape recorder.

This aspect of her story was the most extraordinary because it seemed to be a complete contradiction of who she had made me believe she was, a young woman self-confident enough to be considered a leader. What Phoebe told me was that she had left Johnny because he had been beating her, repeatedly and ever more viciously as the years went on. The beatings had started shortly after their marriage in the spring of 1975, just before she graduated from the Business School and went to New York to marry him and to start her job at the consulting company. And the attacks had been nothing if not a surprise, she said, a brief little look of horror and amazement crossing her face. "Johnny was an incredibly fair player. He never hit anyone after the whistle," she exclaimed.

But the summer after she married him, she made a decision that I would have thought bizarre had anyone but she made it. She decided to leave for six weeks on a trip through northern Africa with Karen Muller, the older divorcée who had been her best friend at the Business School. Her explanation was that she felt the need to "shake the Business School out of [her] system" before she could buckle down to her work. But the point was that when she returned, Johnny wasn't the same person and never would be again.

The details about the beatings came in fits and starts. But there were more of them than I suspected she would have revealed, and I remember making a special effort to record as many of them as I could in my mind. I didn't dare flick on the recorder, and I was even afraid to start jotting down notes in my notebook. So the details remain a hazy jumble of images: the way she would return home late at night from work and the lights would be out in the apartment and he'd be sitting there—she could see the whites of his eyes in the darkness—and he'd go after her; the time he beat her when she had a presentation to make before the board of one of her client companies at nine the next morning—he pulverized her in all the right places so that it hurt but didn't show—and she was able to get to her meeting, albeit a half hour late; how finally, the following spring, when a woman friend—she didn't want to say who—was due to be a houseguest for a weekend, she provoked him so that he would beat her in front of a witness. And beat her he did. "You know how it is, the eyes literally changed," she said, opening hers wide in a gesture of amazement. He dragged her naked and screaming into the bathroom, and while her horrified friend rushed to a neighbor for help, he swung her back and forth by the hair.

They were apart for a year and a half, and then, in the fall of 1977, at Johnny's suggestion, they went together for counseling. He wanted to go back with her. And that lasted until the following summer, when she came home from work one day to find the apartment in shambles. The furniture was tossed about and broken, the pictures torn from the walls. She knew he had been at it again. So she turned the key and left, and when she was able to reach him, she told him it was over. "And I never saw him again after that," she said with an air of finality reminiscent of the way one closes a book.

She said she had heard that Johnny had joined an order of priests that was affiliated with Mother Teresa, the third-world religious who won a Nobel prize for devoting her life to the cause of India's poor. The branch that Johnny had joined was in New York, but its mission was the same. He'd be helping the poor throughout the ghetto neighborhoods of Harlem and the South Bronx.

The story of her marriage completed, Phoebe turned to other topics. I flicked on the tape recorder again and listened to her, as I had throughout the afternoon, with rapture. But though these aspects of her story were fascinating too—we talked for a while about the men in her life: the Jewish businessman, the Italian duke, and the rancher from Nevada—they paled by comparison to the story of her marriage and of why it had failed. So as we walked out of the lobby that evening and said our good-byes on the busy corner of Fifty-second and Madison, my watching her intently as she made her way up to the roller rink, I could think of nothing but the beatings, those brutal beatings.

The contradiction in Phoebe's story was what sent me, the following October, back to interview Karen Muller for a second time. I had been shocked, and then puzzled, the more I thought about how the beatings were at odds with a woman who portrayed herself as Phoebe did. Not only did she have such a distinctive personal style, unlike most of the others, but she was able through her style to portray herself as a winner. And she seemed always to have been able to do that, I was to recall, thinking back to the way she had made the Century Club her second year at the Business School and how she had turned the tables on her professor with her handling of the J. M. Smucker & Co. case involving the wide-brimmed ketchup jars.

The contradiction was too sharp, too blatant. And for a while I didn't worry about it, because I didn't decide for a long time to include Phoebe in this book. The facts of her story were so startling that I suspected they would have no broader significance for other women in business. But one of the surprises of the project, as I tried to decide whom to include, was that everyone I consulted had been taken by her story. They always singled out the sketch of her that I had written on a three-by-five-inch index card from the stack of sketches on all eighty-two cards. And because they kept coming back to her story, I realized that I wanted to find out why. I wanted to find out what there was about her that so appealed to them—and me. The first step in the process became coming to terms with that contradiction, and because it was so sharp and blatant, I felt it best to get the perspective of someone who had known Phoebe so well when she was a student at the Business School.

The Karen Muller I interviewed on an unseasonably warm October evening in 1981 didn't strike me as all that much different from the woman I had interviewed at Casa Mexico the previous January. She lived where I would have expected her to live, in a ramshackled second-floor apartment in the student section of Cambridge. As I made my way over to her apartment that eve-

ning, through the streets of a neighborhood where I had lived so
long ago when I was young and could be expected to appreciate
its bohemian cache, I wondered for a slight moment why a sophisticated businesswoman a half dozen years out of the best business
school in the country would still be living there. But I didn't
wonder too long, certainly not after thinking once again about the
woman I was about to see again.

I found Karen reclining on a high-posted bed stuck in the bay
window of her darkened living room. There she would remain for
the entire interview. She had been hurt, she explained; over the
summer, she had been hit from the rear by a car when she was
riding her bicycle on Storrow Drive in Boston. She had been
thrown from her bicycle and had sprained her back. She would be
out of work for months, she said.

Then she mentioned that she had been three weeks pregnant
when the accident occurred. The grand plan for her future that she
had outlined to me the previous January, to be artificially inseminated and to have a child, had begun to come to pass. But she
had miscarried in the accident, she said, in the same monotone I
recalled from our previous interview. The loss of her child-to-be
seemed to have affected her as had the loss of her infant daughter
many years before. If she were torn or saddened, she wasn't about
to express those emotions to me. And because she was such a
curious woman, I didn't think I was capable of making a judgment.
Whatever clue there might have been to her real feelings continued to elude me.

Karen's feelings about Phoebe were less the victim of her unwillingness or inability to share. When I asked her about Phoebe,
ever so casually as we slid into the rhythm of the interview, it was
apparent that she did have a point of view. She and Phoebe had
parted company after one especially horrible incident in Phoebe's
apartment in New York about a year out of the Business School,
Karen began. It was a beating to which she had been a witness,
for Karen had been the houseguest in front of whom Phoebe had
provoked Johnny. Karen had been appalled by what she already
knew, of course, by the late-night phone calls she had been getting
from Phoebe, who would intimate in a plaintive little voice that
there were problems. "I knew that there were some awful things

going on in her life," Karen said with a swift shake of her head that told me she really cared. She was the type of person who would do anything for her friends. But she had been even more appalled by what Phoebe had done to her, setting her up to be a witness to such an occurrence without telling her what was going on or why she was doing what she did. That offended the very tenets of friendship, according to Karen's way of seeing things.

The friendship between Phoebe and Karen at the Business School had always prompted a raised eyebrow on my part, because Phoebe appeared to have an eclectic attitude when it came to the women in her life. On one hand, I saw nothing but the most callous contempt, the kind women stereotypically are said to have toward others of their own sex. There was the way the very first words out of her mouth to me had been a put-down of two women who had been in her section at the Business School, for example, Pauline Adams and Alexis Drake. Prim, conservative Pauline was to be put down in Phoebe's view, it seemed, for being afraid that she would lose her husband to Phoebe. And Alexis, sadder still —for at least Pauline had a career that she was building brick by brick, having just been named vice-president for the insurance company. But Alexis! Phoebe had shaken her head when talking about her, even though she knew better than to wonder why even a Baker Scholar could be unemployed.

The concept that she was a woman that other women feared was definitely one that Phoebe wanted to get across to me. The thought ran like a subtheme throughout the entire course of our conversation at the Berkshire Place. For example, she said, just recently, a client she had been doing work for in Latin America had had her to Thanksgiving dinner with his family. "And he said, 'I know why I am attracted to you, but I can understand why other women don't like you.' He said, 'You're like a black hole. A person gets too close to you and he's not sure whether or not he's just going to get sucked in. And I think that's what the women feel like, that you're like a black hole, and if their men get too close to you they'll get sucked in.'"

Yet the funny thing was that she had always cared about at least some of the women in her life in that impersonal style so characteristic of her. There had been the way, in high school, she had so abhorred the manner with which some of the big men on campus treated their women that she had conceded to go out with them and then had given them what she called "the old dump," just so they would feel what it was like when they did it to women. That was one of her methods of helping women. Then there was the intense, almost passionate way she had felt about a friend who had died the summer after their graduation from high school. "Listen," she had said, almost angrily at one point that night, gritting her teeth so that she wouldn't cry. "I saw my best friend die, and there was nothing I could do. I had absolutely no control over that situation."

Finally, there was her friendship with Karen which, even to Karen's shock and amazement, Phoebe had pursued with all the zeal of an evangelist converting a heathen. She had asked Karen to join her discussion group in one course the fall of their first year, and when Karen had agreed, she had stepped up her campaign for Karen's friendship. She would call every night and talk for hours. Karen's roommate had given up in disgust, and the new man in Karen's life had chided her about her lesbian relationship with Phoebe. "Were you?" I asked, raising an eyebrow and picking up the cue from Karen. Karen shook her head firmly. No, they were not, she said. "But if you've ever seen a process of seduction, that was what Phoebe was doing to me," she continued, in her discussion of Phoebe that night in her Cambridge apartment. "It's an amazing process, and it works on men and women."

The process of what Karen called seduction was clearly Phoebe's strong suit, both at the Business School and in business. And that could be said to be a good thing, because the ability to seduce, in the sense of making others perceive you as an individual whose judgment should be valued, was central to the process of getting ahead. In addition, it was respected, indeed revered, by people in positions of power. "The ability to gain credibility with the decision maker"—that is what it is all about, Karen said, and Phoebe had that ability in spades.

For a good portion of our evening together, Karen and I talked about this characteristic of Phoebe's, the one I had come to realize was present in its most polished form the night we talked at the Berkshire Place. Back at the Business School, the trait may not have been as refined, but it was there nonetheless. Karen opened her eyes wide with amazement as she related example after example of how Phoebe would seduce whomever she felt would be important to her. She mentioned the time Phoebe had taken all of her crib notes for the final in finance and managed to pull off an Excellent after having done no work all semester. Karen had busted her behind and had gone into the exam and frozen. "Which I didn't even resent," she said, referring to Phoebe's Excellent grade. "That is a good example of how she can pull anything out of the fire to bring about the results she wants."

Then there was the matter of the Century Club, which I had brought up. I wanted to get a feel from Karen for what the club was and how important it was. Was it as important as Phoebe had made it out to be? "It wasn't important to me," Karen said, and for the first time that evening I noticed a touch of hurt in her eye. She knew I had come to talk about Phoebe and not really about her own situation. "But that is an excellent example of how she operates," Karen continued, back to the point now. She told me that Phoebe had been truly shocked to have gotten in; she hadn't even known that such a club existed. But she was "the first to go to her professors and protest that she didn't have good enough grades to get in, thereby getting feedback that 'even though your grades aren't superior, you, Phoebe, can be chosen in spite of everything!' "

But there was a dark side to Phoebe's ability to seduce, Karen continued. And it was when I brought up the subject of Johnny Carellas and the beatings that this point was to emerge. Karen had been reluctant to discuss the beatings. She agreed only because I pointed out that Phoebe herself had told me about them, and Karen was shocked that she had. "Why did she tell you?" she asked, and I replied honestly that I did not know. The major issue I wanted Karen to address was the contradiction. Why had someone with Phoebe's ability to project herself as she had, as confident and self-assured, allowed herself to be beaten by her husband? And when I asked that, Karen suddenly bolted upright in her bed, as if she were about to lunge at me, she was so angry. "Listen, if you don't like it, you lock the door and call the police, right?" she cried. "You don't consistently forget to lock the door, forget to change the lock, leave your complete itinerary with Johnny. And if you do, you do that once or twice. You don't do it for several years straight."

Karen's thesis was, of course, that for some reason Phoebe wanted to be beaten. She had come to that conclusion the day she had been a witness. That was why she had decided never again to associate with Phoebe. She didn't want to be a part of something like that. And it was then that Karen came back to what she meant by the dark side of Phoebe's ability to seduce. "Phoebe wants to be in control of the images she projects," Karen said, explaining, for example, that Phoebe didn't project just one image. Rather she projected different images at different times and to different people. "And if you've happened to have been around at a time when she was projecting an image she's since discarded, you're out of the picture until the need for it arises again," she said.

Karen herself, who had been the object of Phoebe's ability to seduce the fall of their first year, had seen more than just one image. When she met Phoebe the first day at the Business School, for example, she had dismissed her as a "totally inexperienced little girl." Phoebe had been standing ahead of her in the registration line, wearing a skimpy sundress and flirting with the man ahead of her. By the fall of their second year, she had begun to believe that Phoebe used people without realizing it. That fall, for example, Phoebe had so monopolized and mesmerized a group of executives from a trucking firm at a campus cocktail party that she had prevented twenty-five other students from the chance to talk to them. The worst part about it was that she hadn't had any interest whatsoever in the firm or in trucking.

When Karen told her she was wrong for having prevented the others from talking to the executives, Phoebe had told her she was talking to her like a mother and simply stopped speaking to Karen for the rest of the year. Then the following spring, when she was planning to travel through northern Africa and had heard that Karen was planning to make the same trip, she approached Karen as if nothing had happened and suggested that they be traveling companions. That had suggested to Karen that Phoebe used people ruthlessly. Then the next year, when she saw Johnny beat Phoebe, she had switched to believing that Phoebe was the victim of a horrible situation. "But I can't keep up! I don't know!" Karen cried. She had come to the conclusion that she would never fully understand Phoebe.

But there was one thing that Karen did understand about Phoebe. The fact that Phoebe projected not just one image but several could only mean that she wasn't as self-assured as she would have liked to have believed, that she would have liked others to have believed about her. She probably hadn't ever been that person, even as far back as the Business School. "See, I originally thought that Phoebe wasn't intimidated by the Business School," Karen said. "But that's something I've changed my mind about. Because it takes a person who is very easily intimidated to have a need to systematically cut off anyone who knows a great deal about you. A great lack of faith in people. A great lack of faith in emotions." By tailoring her images, each for a particular reason in a particular situation, Karen explained, Phoebe had arranged it so that different people knew different things about her. But no one could put the pieces together. No one could get a grip on who she really was.

The issue of who precisely Phoebe was, was one that had eluded me too. For throughout the course of my interviews with Phoebe at the Berkshire Place and with Karen that night in her apartment, I still didn't feel as if I knew what Phoebe wanted out of life—from her work, from her relationships. The irony was that someone who could project the image of being successful hadn't really expressed a desire for success in any concrete terms. She didn't appear to be striving, as was, say, Suzanne Sheehan, for the next rung on the ladder in her career. Indeed, she had made a point of telling me that she didn't want to be a partner at the consulting firm, no matter how much the partners wanted that for her. "I'm pausing because what I am about to say is a little unbelievable," Karen said, when I asked her about this. "But I don't think Phoebe has any goals at all. And that does seem strange considering her charisma. But I feel that with Phoebe it's more the *process* of being on top, of being in control, rather than anything she really wants, that dominates her."

Which brought Karen back to Johnny Carellas and those terrible beatings. Looked at from this perspective, she said, there could be only one reason why Phoebe had tolerated them. That was because with Johnny she had been the self-confident one. She had controlled him, not the other way around. As unbelievable as Karen's thesis was considering that it had been Phoebe who had been beaten, I began to understand her reasoning. The reason was rooted in competitiveness. Karen felt Phoebe had chosen Johnny precisely because with him there would be no way in which anyone could judge how well she was doing when it came to that aspect of her life. "Johnny's black, Johnny's Venezuelan," Karen said. "He comes from a completely different place. At eighteen, she loses with him because he's the more powerful and interesting person. But later in life, she wins because one can measure how well she's doing there."

Karen explained that with other men Phoebe could have been judged. "If she married a presidential candidate, there was always the president. But with Johnny there's no way to understand. He's out of the running! He's out of the game! He's absolutely not measurable. So she could define for herself how well she was doing in that aspect of her life. She could say, 'This is the most unique person, the most unique relationship.' And there's no way in the world that anyone could second-guess her."

I had but one last question for Karen. "The only thing we have to figure out is why Phoebe wants to be in control merely for the sake of being in control," I asked.

And Karen had an answer for that too. "She wants to take care of herself," Karen said.

The most extraordinary thing about my second meeting with Phoebe was that she appeared at first glance to be a touch more ordinary than I remembered from the previous spring. I had flown to New York to interview her on a blustery cold Saturday morning in November. We had set the date the week before, when I had called, as I suppose I always knew I would. She had answered as if she always knew that I would call again. The first weekend in November would be fine, she had said. It was her birthday weekend and friends were coming to help her celebrate. But she would work around that. As she spoke, I remember fondling a warm image of her in my mind. I envisioned her standing in her kitchen with a wire wisk in her hand, preparing a meal for the friends who had come from around the world to help her celebrate.

As I made my way out of the taxi that Saturday morning, the wind tore through my thin navy-blue blazer and corduroy slacks. It whipped about so fiercely that I could barely open the door to her apartment building. Once I was inside the lobby, the doorman rang her bell, and I made my way up the elevator and down the corridor to her apartment. There was no answer when I knocked on the door, but it was ajar, so I walked in. "Hello?" I called, and again there was no answer. I glanced around me: There were floor-to-ceiling bookshelves in her foyer, replete with cookbooks from around the world, and, in the far corner, a pair of roller skates.

From the other room, Phoebe finally called out and told me to make myself at home. I took my place on the off-white sofa in her living room, which was buried amid a forest of potted plants, and waited. "Nurse Phoebe," she said with a little smile when she came out to greet me. Then she explained that a friend of hers who was visiting for the weekend had come down with the flu and she was nursing him.

That she appeared to be more ordinary than I had remembered may have been the case because I was now a bit more familiar with her than I had been in the past. From my conversations with her the previous spring and with Karen Muller in October, I may have come to a point where my perception was skewed. She was beginning to appear to be the norm; the rest of the women in the class were those whose lives were awry.

Then, too, there was the way she was dressed on this Saturday morning. She was wearing a red sweatshirt and baggy corduroy jeans; her long hair was swept back from her face and tied at the crown, Alice in Wonderland-style. She appeared more young than old this time around, and I was reminded once again of the waif.

The main thing we talked about that day was her career at the prestigious national consulting firm, and the chief point she wanted to make was that she didn't want to be a partner. That she didn't was something we had discussed the previous spring, and it had surprised me at first. Once again, I felt as if I were up against an inexplicable contradiction in Phoebe's life: that the woman who sat like a leader on the high-back chair in the lobby of the Berkshire Place wouldn't be striving for the goal of partnership, the ultimate goal in a consulting career.

The point that Phoebe had made back then was that her reasons were difficult for almost everyone to understand. No one understood that she "didn't give two hoots" about all of that—about, to be precise, her career at the consulting firm—except for Will. A little smile had crossed her face when she mentioned Will, the rancher from Nevada whom she had been dating. It wasn't a playful smile, the type of smile she'd reserve for the Italian duke when she'd call from the airport on a Friday night and say, "Come on and get your skates!" because she wanted to go to the rink. Rather, her smile was one that told me that she and Will understood each other, which was precisely the point she was trying to make. He understood when she'd say that she was going to pack it all in and go run a ranch. "It will be that he's said he's going to buy another ranch and I've been laughing, saying, 'You know, I've got to turn it all in now. I've got this working life and I've done it enough. I know I can do it, and now it doesn't interest me anymore. I need to do something else. Maybe I'll move to the ranch and become a cowgirl.' And it's a standing joke, but it's not completely out of the realm of possibility."

The people for whom it was a joke were the partners at her firm, who never believed her when she'd say she didn't want to be one of them. The previous December, for example, when the senior partner and her dear, dear friend had called her into his office to ask her once again if she wanted to go for it, he also had some news for her. He told her that she had just been promoted to managing director, the step before partner. And when he told her that, she had bristled and said, "Look, let's be clear about what you can expect from me." Then she had told him that she wasn't going to change, not ever; she wasn't going to write reports for the firm or associate mostly with people from the firm. She was going to continue to do what she liked to do, which was to work with her clients, and if she could do that and still be made a partner, that would be fine.

Then she told me that, in March, she had had dinner with the wife of the senior partner. They were friends, Phoebe explained, because they had discovered a common interest in music and had friends in musical circles. Whenever she and the senior partner and his wife got together socially, they would talk about music, no matter how many people at the firm thought she was using her friendship with the couple to promote her career. "So I knew when she asked me what she did that something was going on," Phoebe said. "She asked me, as the wife of the head of the firm, 'You know, from what I understand, all you have to do is want it and you'll be a partner.' Then she said, 'Do you care?' And I said, 'No, I don't care, it's not going to make any difference to me.' Now it was interesting to me to see how comfortable I was saying that. Because what was clearly happening in March was that the senior partner and some of the other very senior people were organizing to put me up for partnership. All I had to say was that it made a difference to me. And maybe I was crazy. But that's part of my personality. Once I know I can get something, I just don't care."

The reason she didn't care was to emerge from our conversation in her apartment that Saturday in November. We were seated at the big oak table in her dining room, finishing the mushroom omelets she had prepared for lunch. (I had watched as she had wisked the eggs in her galley kitchen, looking very much as she had in my imagination a few weeks earlier when I had called to set the date.) As the bright noon sunlight turned into the muted hues of late afternoon, I remember thinking that she seemed a bit more apprehensive than she had when we had discussed the topic the previous spring.

She told me that she hadn't, as it turned out, been put up for partnership that year. The fact that the firm wanted her wasn't enough to make them do it. She had to indicate that she wanted to be one of them, and she just couldn't do that. "It's mutually understood that when I told them I didn't want to be a partner, they weren't going to take the risk and put me up for partnership. I mean, that's sick. That's really stupid. Why would my office put me up for partnership if I didn't want it? I mean, that's foolish. They'd have to secure my complete and total commitment."

That Phoebe wouldn't ever forfeit complete and total commit-

ment to an entity apart from herself was something that the partners probably sensed from the day she joined the firm, she said.
At his meeting with her the previous December, for example, the
senior partner who knew her so well had alluded to just that
characteristic about her. He had called her a maverick. "He said,
'It's very hard for us to deal with maverick people. We need them
in our environment, for sure. But we usually lose them before too
long because we don't know how to handle them,' " Phoebe said.

The concept of Phoebe as the maverick was the one that struck
me as the missing link. It appeared to be what had been eluding
me, partly because she had seemed more ordinary the more I
became familiar with her. Then, too, I suppose, I hadn't ever
really been up against a real maverick—a cowboy, if you will. The
executives with style that I had come to know over the years were
more likely than not to be ordinary within.

Yet as I thought about Phoebe, I thought back to the summer
of 1981, when I was deciding whom to include as the central
characters in this book. I remember placing each of the women I
interviewed into categories that appeared most typically to define
their lives. There were women who were clearly ambitious for
their careers, others who were not. There were many who were
ambivalent, and another large group who had decided firmly that
they wanted both careers and families. Yet Phoebe had defied all
of these categories. I remember making up a new one, which I
called In a Class by Herself, and placing her name under that
heading.

Then there was the way she herself told me she acted as a
professional in the consulting firm. She wasn't afraid to be critical,
even though that wasn't the most diplomatic way to behave. "It's
a standing joke; they call me 'the troublemaker,' " she said. "Monday morning, I'm in there early. The senior partner is at the spiral
stairwell, and he's with another senior partner from Germany, and
he says, 'We better get moving. Phoebe's gonna get after me
about all of the stuff that's not right in here.' And we all laughed.
But it's right. I'll go through and I'll figure out all of the things
that are wrong. And if he asks me, I'll tell him exactly what I think
is right and wrong. And that's the way I am."

The reason why she was inclined to be the maverick was to

perplex me until much later that afternoon, when she was talking about the reasons the partners had given for not putting her up for partnership that year. They told her she was "too controversial" and that they weren't sure of her commitment to the firm. "One day I show up on the cover of a major national magazine out of nowhere with some guy and . . . I seem to be too many personae and have too many options. It's like they don't know me. They don't know enough about me. What I am, what makes me tick, what I want to do"—and then Phoebe made another comment.

This comment seemed to suggest that she knew, down deep, that as a partner in a major national consulting firm—as would be the case for a principal of any partnership, a senior manager of any corporation—she wouldn't be in control of the firm. No matter how badly she may have wanted to believe precisely the opposite, the firm would control her—just as her father had once done so long before on that Caribbean island of Jamaica.

"They don't have any control over me—that's actually the most important reason," Phoebe said. "Here I am, I'm going to buy their shares, they're going to make me a part of their organization, and they don't have any *control* over me?" She raised her voice just a little when she said that, as if to indicate that the firm simply wouldn't tolerate such a situation. Then she said, "There's no hot button. There's no particular thing I seem to need them for."

It was late by the time we finished talking about her career, and Phoebe had switched on the track lighting in her living room. The lighting cast dramatic shadows across the leaves of her many potted plants and gave her face a surreal appearance.

She was talking about her life in a way that excited me, just as she had so many months before. She was "like a sparkler," even for someone such as Will, she was saying, because hers was a life of many facets. "My friend Pandy comes and stays for a week, and we're off with big Hollywood producers. My friend Selma is here from Kuwait, and we have a bunch of Arabs around." Then there were her friends from the roller rink. "I'm known at the rink as sort of a roller-disco queen," she said with a smile. "I'm the only one who's ever fully clothed in the place."

At one point, when she was talking about the special rapport that she had with her girl friend Pandy, who had just sold her first movie script to a big Hollywood producer, she did something that she hadn't done throughout the entire course of our first interview or up until that moment during our second. She asked me a question about myself. The question had arisen when she was trying to explain that rapport with a friend was different from that with an interviewer. "It's one thing to sit here talking to you," she said, and then she turned to face me. "How old are you?" she asked.

The question did more than take me by surprise. It excited me. I remember feeling flattered that she had noticed me. And I remember hoping that my answer would be one that would satisfy her, for I wanted her to think of me as a friend. I wanted to be a friend of hers, plain as a peanut though I was compared with her.

My own reaction to Phoebe was to remind me of something Karen Muller had said the night we talked in her apartment. The point Karen had been making was that Phoebe's inclination to project several different images would be the factor that would prevent her from going as far as she otherwise could have gone in business. The truth was that for all of its glamour, business is nothing but a trade (and as a microcosm of business, the Business School nothing but a trade school), Karen had said. "So people who do well are basically very simple people. They have the ability. They have the capacity. They have no doubts about what they are doing. And they can just barrel ahead."

Then Karen had brought up the name of Pauline Adams, whom Phoebe had scorned for fearing she'd lose her husband to Phoebe. The fact that Pauline was doing exceptionally well in her career at the insurance company and would continue to do well in the years ahead was a case in point, Karen had said. "She's just, you know, stable, dependable, do-a-good-job."

But then Karen had said that it was precisely that facade that made Phoebe the far more interesting person. And at that point, she had turned on her side to face me as she spoke from her high-posted bed. "So if you ask me who I care about, whether it's Pauline Adams or Phoebe, for all of her weak points, I'd choose to be friends with Phoebe."

Phoebe and I parted as we had before, on a street corner in

New York. We left her apartment late and walked up First Avenue to New York University Hospital on the corner of Thirty-third Street. Phoebe wanted to visit a friend before calling hours were over. We stood on the corner for a moment, saying our good-byes. She was dressed in a long, flowing black coat, and she looked like a beggar or a character in a Russian novel. She told me not to hesitate to call if I needed to talk again, and I remember hoping that I would have a reason to do so.

I also remember thinking that I agreed with Karen about Phoebe's being such an interesting person. And I remember thinking it a shame that there wasn't more of a place for someone like her in American business. For hers was the story of a maverick, and even in organizations such as consulting firms, supposedly the loosest of business structures, there hadn't been a place. While hers was an extreme example, the thought crossed my mind that all women were in some respects mavericks in American business. The issue of fit was such a critical problem because, like the maverick, women didn't naturally fit. As I watched Phoebe swirl through the revolving doors into the lobby of the hospital, I decided I wanted to explore the issue of fit from the perspective of a woman whose story would point up the problem more starkly —Mary Pat Horner.

5.

MARY PAT:
Femininity
and Fit

Throughout the course of my research for this book, one question nagged me as I put together the pieces for the women of the class of 1975. The question predated my work on the project. As a reporter for *The Wall Street Journal* in the late 1970's and early 1980's, when I had begun to research and write articles about women in business for the news and editorial pages, I had come across the same issue. The question could best be posed in the form of a riddle: Take one fairly ordinary young woman—Suzanne Sheehan, for example—who had come of age in the late 1960's and early 1970's at a time when doors were first opening to women. Give her a reasonable intellect, a decidedly above-average degree of ambition—enough at least so that she would somehow find her way into the finest graduate business school in the country. See to it that she stayed single so that husband and children couldn't be said to be getting in the way of her ambition. Put her in one of the biggest Fortune 100 companies in the country and watch her climb the ladder.

Not that she wouldn't have disappointments and setbacks, of course. A job that she wanted in the Far East would go to another because the company had political debts to pay; a full title with-held from her so that a man who had wanted the job she had gotten would be appeased. Nor would she be free of apprehension about her future at the company, for she was the first to admit, haltingly and not really wanting to believe it, that she may have hit what she called a ceiling and not because of an inability or a lack of desire to advance into senior positions, but only because she didn't "fit" as a woman in a man's world.

Disappointments, setbacks, apprehension about the future, all of that notwithstanding, she had made it into upper middle management at one of the country's biggest corporations in the short span of six years after graduation from the Business School, and in the even shorter span—psychologically speaking—of a dozen years after she had first gone to work as a pediatric nurse at a major Boston-based maternity hospital. At age thirty-five, she could look around her with satisfaction. She was earning $78,000 a year, including bonus, and even more important, at least to her way of looking at things, she was beginning to have a little taste of what she really wanted—power, the feeling of being in control of her destiny at, as she would put it, "some big thing."

Then take another young woman who appeared on the surface to be just as ordinary. Like Suzanne, she had graduated from a big state university—Penn State, in her case. She had come of age when women for the first time were getting opportunities in the country's companies and professional associations. She, too, was ambitious enough to have found her way into the best business school in the country; she was single; and as an extra filip, she was far brighter than Suzanne. She was bright enough to have graduated, without undue effort on her part, in the top 10 percent of her class at Harvard, the cut just below that for Baker Scholar.

Take that young woman, put her into three Fortune 100 companies, and watch her pull rabbits out of hats: kick off a successful marketing campaign for a product no consumer in his right mind would want to buy—a sugar substitute called Sparkle that was half cane sugar and half artificial sweetener; bring her department in on budget as a group product manager for a line of processed meats at the second company for which she worked, during one of the worst years of the decade for the processed-meats business;

start up a brand-new credit-card business for yet another company and shepherd its growth from zero to revenue of $50 million in one year. Watch her do all of that and fail—so miserably that she left the first company for the second after an especially bitter falling out with her boss, the second for the third after realizing for some reason that the same thing was happening all over again; so miserably that even now, at her third company, a time in her career when presumably she should have learned from past mistakes, she was in the same predicament. She had failed to be promoted to vice-president, which she would have expected by this point, and she was already thinking about leaving.

In terms of money, her salary was at the lower end of the spectrum for the women of her class, even though she wouldn't have thought in those terms. At $45,000 a year plus bonus, which kicked her total compensation up to $50,000, she would consider herself affluent. For that sum, in fact, she would have once thought that there wasn't anything anybody could do to her that could be all that bad. Only now she knew better. Even for 45K plus five, there were things people could do that were "that bad." The bad things, in fact, were showering down on her with such a vengeance that toward the end of our second interview, on a beautiful Saturday in October 1981, she admitted in an emphatic but decidedly defeated tone of voice, "I do not have control over the environment in which I am functioning."

The theme of a lack of control over her environment at work, the male milieu of business, was what I myself kept coming back to whenever I considered the riddle, the riddle that had predated my talks with the women of Harvard. For one of the clearest points to be made from my conversations with all of the women I talked to, both the Harvard group and their counterparts, professional and managerial women who hadn't gone to the Business School but who were similarly in the process of forming such careers, was that the difference between those who were succeeding and those who weren't couldn't be traced to the factors that at that time dominated the thinking on this subject. There was no correlation between success on the job and choice of life-style, for example: Successful women in business were just as likely to be married and have children as they were to be single, divorced, or married and childless. Nor was there a correlation between success in a career and one's background, be it socioeconomic or religious. Successful women in business were just as likely to have come from poor, middle-class, or wealthy families; Protestant, Roman Catholic, or Jewish homes.

So what set successful women apart from their less successful counterparts had to be traced to something else, and it was only when I met Mary Pat Horner at Zapata's, awash in the reddish-gold hues of late afternoon as she approached my table, that I began to get a hint of the reason. For it had become very obvious by the end of the evening that here was a woman who was failing in an environment that someone who was nearly her exact counterpart, Suzanne Sheehan, was succeeding in, at least to a certain extent.

That theme of a lack of control that I was to believe underscored Mary Pat's problem in business could be traced way back, to her childhood days in the moribund industrial city of Allentown, Pennsylvania, on the New Jersey border. Even though she had done the unthinkable back then—break away from an environment that would have stifled all but the hardiest souls—it was almost as if she had done it without willing it for herself, as if it were predestined that she do it. This was the world of the lower-middle-class Roman Catholic ethnic—Irish, in Mary Pat's case—the world of row houses, triple deckers, or cramped bungalows; a limiting world where "having enough to eat," as Mary Pat so proudly said her family always had before she caught herself and smiled sardonically, was an accomplishment in itself. This was a world in which vacations to the shore and a home of one's own, as her family was able to have only because they were extraordinarily frugal with the $6,000 her father earned as a state trooper, were considered luxuries of which to be proud.

"I mean all I ever knew was that there wasn't enough money to do additional things," Mary Pat said at one point during our interview. "You got one new dress for the summer—that was your Easter dress and you wore it every Sunday to church. In the winter, you got one new good outfit and that was for Christmas, and you wore that all winter to church. That made perfect sense to me. I mean, if that were lower middle class, and I guess it could have been . . . isn't that funny? I never asked that question. All I ever knew was that I got the feeling everybody would have been more comfortable if there had been more money. My father wouldn't have had to work as hard, my mother wouldn't have had to worry as much, and I would have gotten the one thing I always wanted in life and that I have never gotten—which is one of the great ironies of my life—a horse."

Nor was her family one to offer her much encouragement, for its members were hardly stereotypes of the upwardly mobile turn-of-the-century ethnics. Hers was a father who had ordered her down to the better restaurants, where the tips were good, when she graduated from high school, because he couldn't afford to send her to college. It made no sense to spend the ten dollars to apply if he couldn't afford to send her, he had said. Hers was a mother who had turned to Mary Pat when she had escaped to the extent that she was awarded her fellowship to the Harvard Business School and, because she feared for her daughter, had said: "But, Mary Pat, I don't think our kind of people would fit in there."

The escape that Mary Pat hadn't willed for herself began at the telephone company, where she got a job as a statistical clerk shortly after waitressing for a year, just as her father also had suggested. There she took a look around her and found, as she put it, that "lo and behold, there wasn't anything cooking for women in that world." The young men who went into the telephone company after high school were marked for bigger and better things, for the managerial track. But women who had been there ten years—"ten whole years," Mary Pat exclaimed with shock and dismay, even now, so many years later—were just the senior grade of what she was starting out as. They were senior statistical clerks. The ones who had really, really made it were supervisors of statistical clerks. "So I took a look around and said, 'Whoa! A person can die hungry doing this. Never make any money, never get any advancement. The answer must be a college degree, because it certainly isn't struggling along at this pace.'"

So she applied and was awarded a full scholarship to Penn State, where she majored in applied mathematics for computers, because she told her father that when she graduated she wanted a job that paid $10,000 a year. At that time, her father wasn't making such a sum. So she needed to study something that would prepare her for a field in which qualified people were in such short supply that no company could discriminate against her because she was a woman. That field was computers. When she graduated, she got her job—it paid $11,000 a year—as a systems analyst for a steel company in Pittsburgh. And there she happened upon the second event that propelled her forward, almost in spite of herself. The company she joined had been the one that had sponsored her college scholarship. The personnel office asked for a copy of her transcript, and when the vice-president for personnel noticed that she had received the highest grade point average in the history of Penn State, he immediately recommended that the company continue to fund her education.

He called her into his office, told her even before she started to work that the company would sponsor her at any graduate school in the country, and she remembers backing off. She wanted to work; she wanted to make $11,000 a year. What did she know of the value of a graduate degree? What did she know of a graduate degree, period? So it wasn't until a year later, when she saw herself slipping into the same rut at the steel company as she had at the telephone company, that she went back to see the vice-president. "About that fellowship," she told me she said to him, a knowing little half smile on her face. The vice-president told her to apply to Harvard, that she'd be a shoo-in, and she remembers asking, in what she called honest naïveté, "Do they accept women?" The vice-president said yes, and so she applied. "And that was the first time I even knew, not so much that the Harvard Business School existed but whoever dreamed they took women and whoever believed I would go there."

Mary Pat's naïveté was to run parallel with that other sense I had about her, that she was being carried along in the world of the corporation almost against her will. For throughout the course of both our interviews, at Zapata's in May and at the Marriott Hotel near her home in Larchmont, New York, the following October, she would come back again and again to this quality about herself. It would be an understatement to say she was embarrassed by it; she was embarrassed and humiliated and too ashamed even to try to cover it up. She dealt with it by talking about it, incessantly, as if to a priest in a confessional. The most obvious area of her innocence was her clothes, she began. Her classmates at the Business School all wore chinos, LaCoste shirts, and loafers with little tassels, whereas she came to class in her bell bottoms or one of her little dresses, the navy blue one with the red cherry on the boob, for example. She was so hopelessly out of it that she didn't even know she was. "I remember sitting in class in wonderment, saying, 'I wonder why all these people look alike. How did they all happen to choose the same outfit? Isn't that incredible! They all have those shirts with alligators on them.' " She understood now, of course. It was a uniform; it was her classmates' way of showing each other that they belonged. "But back then, I was so out of it that I just thought it was very coincidental that they all wore the same outfit."

She was naïve in the classroom, too, and it was only because she was so bright that she was able ultimately to catch on and graduate with honors. The standard for success in the classroom at the Business School was like nothing she had ever seen before, she began. First of all, her classmates weren't even as intellectually curious as she had been way back at a place such as Penn State, where she had loved to learn a little bit about many things. She loved those big introductory courses that everyone else hated: Geology 101, in which she learned why a river ran or meandered through a channel, why volcanoes came into existence, Economics 101, in which she sat in the front row and asked so many questions that the professor even knew her by name.

She would have expected people who went to Harvard to be like that, but they were not. "They were all, generally speaking, very conformist," she said. "All wearing the same clothes, all thinking the same way, getting their ticket punched, either because they were expected to or because they really believed that getting a Harvard degree would single them out for success."

She would have expected something else in the classroom, too, but the professors seemed to pay no heed to people who studied hard; they seemed, in fact, to put a negative value on hard work, to scorn the students who showed up with nineteen pages of notes for every case. "What they loved was that detached cynicism,"

Mary Pat began, "that attitude of, 'It really would be beneath my dignity to try terribly hard, but if I must make a comment, this is what I observe, my keen insightful observations . . .' I think the profs enjoyed students who showed them almost . . . scorn."

For some women, the process was a difficult one, Mary Pat said, and toward the end of our second interview, she lashed out at what had happened to a woman who had lived on the same floor as she in McCulloch Hall and whom she had particularly liked. The woman was Esther Micholov Boron, the lovely blonde I had interviewed in the coffeehouse in Berkeley, California. "The profs could get away with humiliating someone like Esther," Mary Pat said with a mixture of anger and sorrow that told me she would have liked to have protected her.

She saw Esther as someone who had such a love of learning that she should have been a scholar, and from that perspective, she wasn't surprised that Esther dropped out at the end of first year. "She was like a piece of crystal in a diner, like an orchid in a desert" in that environment, Mary Pat exclaimed.

But as for herself, she was so bright in that analytical sort of way that no professor could victimize her, Mary Pat continued. Her second year, figuring that the process was a game, she didn't read one single case from October through April and still managed to graduate in the top 10 percent of her class. She made it through using what she called her Exhibit Thirteen strategy. She knew that none of the professors would call on her to state the facts of a case at the beginning of class, because she always talked so much in class anyway. So while someone else laid out the facts for everyone to hear and others chimed in based on what they knew from having pored over the first twenty pages and the first twelve exhibits—they were usually too exhausted to have gotten much beyond that—she would turn to the thirteenth exhibit and the ones beyond that.

She would analyze those exhibits based upon what the others already had said and based upon what she thought to be the central issue in the case from having skimmed it as they spoke. "So they're talking, and I'm reading and listening and deciding on the key question, and then I'd go to exhibit . . . the last five exhibits which all the guys who read the whole case never had time to look at, and I'd draw some conclusions from the last five exhibits, and . . . and my comments were always coherent, because after all, I was only talking about data in the exhibits and how it related to the problem.''

That she could do so well in spite of herself was part and parcel of what I had supposed about her: that she had been propelled almost against her will into the environment of a place such as the Business School. This was to become even more apparent as she discussed her social life. She told me that during both of her years at the Business School, she had done something that was fast becoming a taboo. She had had affairs with men who were her classmates. The first had been a sectionmate; this was especially frowned upon and had caused Esther to let her know, in the nicest way possible, that she didn't want to be friends with her. The thought of Mary Pat having opened herself up to ridicule for the sake of such a man had disgusted Esther.

"You don't sleep where you shit," Mary Pat told me flatly, in an even tone of voice that was uncharacteristic of her. The phrase, which repulsed her, was a favorite of the professors when defending the taboo, she said. Her tone of voice seemed to be her way of emphasizing the seriousness with which the taboo was taken, for professors and students alike knew that such behavior could cause problems once an affair had run its course.

The affair Mary Pat had her first year had run its course by the end of the second semester; even she had to admit that the man wasn't right for her. He hated the Business School and wasn't doing well and seemed to be leaning on her throughout the year for help with his studies.

But she had done it because she was lonely, so lonely when she arrived on campus, she said. She had just broken up with the man she had dated throughout college, a military man who wouldn't make a commitment to her, and she had been dismayed to discover that practically none of the men at the Business School seemed to consider her a potential date. She would have thought that there would have been at least some who would have from that group of so many men.

Her second year, she didn't strictly have an affair. The man she had been referring to was someone she had noticed for a long time but figured would never notice her. "You could see him as one of those fraternity brothers who had been elected an officer," she began. "He was very good-looking, real easygoing. He always seemed half-bombed, but he had a charming way about him."

Then she explained that the day before she was about to leave for Christmas vacation, he did notice her. He spotted her in the hallway and asked if she would like to go with him to the airport where he was planning to drop off a friend. She agreed, and on the way back, basking in the glow of his attention, she said, "You know, this is one of those nights when you wish you could sit in front of a fireplace, play Nat King Cole records, and drink wine. Just relax." To her surprise, he replied, "I have a fireplace. Why don't you come over? We'll just sit down and relax."

The night she spent with that man was one of the most wonderful in her life, Mary Pat said, her voice warm and soft even as she remembered it years later and in spite of what was to happen thereafter.

"I remember that it was like a fantasy to me, like a dream come true," she said. "To think that a guy like that would really like me. There we were talking and laughing and having a good time. We spent a wonderful night together, and then he literally got up the next morning"—at this point her voice metamorphosed into tense hurt—"dusted off his hands, and said, 'Well, see you around, kid.' "

The shock was too much for her, and she wouldn't accept it. Over Christmas vacation, she nurtured a fantasy that he would call when she got back to school. When he didn't, she called him. "Why didn't you call or something?" she said on the phone. So he came over to her room that night, and as before, they had a couple of drinks, went to bed, and then he said to her, "I hope you don't think this is anything serious." She replied, "I kind of hoped, you know, that there was something . . ." And he said, "Oh, no, no, no . . ." He was interested in someone else who had just begun to show an interest in him. So he left quickly, refusing even her offer to drive him back to his apartment. "He didn't even want to be seen with me," she cried. "He was just so brutal! What a shock!"

Whenever I thought of this particular incident, in the weeks and months after I had heard Mary Pat's whole story, I began to believe that it could have been the event that might have caused her to do then what she finally would do only years later, after her graduation from the Business School and her three jobs in three different corporations. It could have been the event that might have caused her to leave the environment for which she was so ill-suited.

But as it turned out, something else happened on the heels of that jilting by her Business School classmate. The night that he dusted off his hands in her room was the very night the whole second year class had a very important paper due in one of their most important courses. The paper was one that would be graded on a curve, and as such, it was a very competitive assignment. Students certainly wouldn't be likely to swap ideas, because they could add someone else's ideas to their own and come out with the better grade.

"So that night I was sitting there, and I was really crushed, and I couldn't write the paper," Mary Pat began. "And I sat there that night and my girl friend Sheila Brummel, who lived down the hall and knew what had happened, brought me her typed paper at eleven o'clock at night. She handed it to me, and said, 'Maybe this will give you some ideas,' and then she walked out of the door.

"And I really was in no condition to think of anything more than what Sheila had written in her paper. So I subtracted one idea, one idea out of Sheila's paper, because I couldn't think of anything to add to it. I didn't have the heart for it. And she got a Satisfactory Plus and I got a Satisfactory. I ended up with an Excellent for the course, but the point is, I don't think I ever would have turned in that paper otherwise. In fact, what she did struck me as a turning point, that out of this disastrous thing with a man had come a bond of real friendship."

That Sheila Brummel in no way considered herself a friend of Mary Pat's, as she had indicated when we had spoken the previous February, wasn't the point. The point was that she had been generous to Mary Pat at a time when Mary Pat had all but given up on generosity at a place such as the Business School, at a time when she had begun to believe that competitiveness all but excluded an emotion as human as generosity.

"Fascinating woman—so closed!" Mary Pat exclaimed as she told me about Sheila Brummel during our interview at Zapata's. And as she continued, Sheila's face flashed before me. I had flown clear across the continent to interview her in a godforsaken town in the Pacific Northwest and, indeed, Sheila had been closed. She was working as a line manager for a timber company, she said, and dating a man in another city, which she refused to identify. Beyond that, she would say nothing. But that same woman had taken pains to make my hotel reservations, and to plan an outing for me at a famous resort in her area. That evening, she had treated me to dinner at a fine French restaurant, with a view of the majestic Cascades and had toasted my project with a bottle of wine she selected especially for the occasion.

Now at Zapata's, referring to what Sheila had done for her years earlier at the Business School, Mary Pat said, "It was one of those turning points, because I really couldn't say what my attitude would have been if I hadn't gotten that paper in."

Perhaps because she had behaved as she had at the Business School for such a fundamental reason, Mary Pat was to repeat the error years later in business. At the second company she worked for, she had an affair with a colleague, a senior executive who was married and had three children. This man was Lloyd Whitmore, with whom she had been living when we first spoke in May 1981.

The subject of Mary Pat's affair with Lloyd was to dominate the better part of our second interview the following October. The topic had come up from the moment I placed my call to her in September to ask her if she would talk with me again. "Oh, it's *you,*" she had said when I identified myself, as if she had stumbled upon a long-lost friend and couldn't decide whether to be pleased or apprehensive.

Then she had said in a resigned tone of voice that she had finally found the strength to leave Lloyd. There was something about him that she hadn't told me the previous spring, and the minute she said that, I knew. I could feel myself stiffening as I accepted the explanation. "Yeah," she had said, "he's an alcoholic. I couldn't bring myself to admit that back then. I just couldn't."

The matter had come to a head at their home the previous

weekend, she continued. For the first time ever in their relationship—and God knew, there had been plenty of bad times before
—he had abused her physically. In the midst of a fight, he had
thrown her against the wall, so violently that she thought for sure
he had broken something. And she knew that she couldn't live
with that. So she had called the police. They came and asked him
to leave, which he did, meekly almost, failing even to gather his
clothes. He had told her he would come back for them later.

The second time we spoke, Mary Pat put together the pieces
that had led up to that parting. I flew from Boston to LaGuardia
early that morning, then took a limousine from the airport
through the rolling New York countryside to New Rochelle, and
the first thing I noticed about Mary Pat, when I walked through
the revolving doors of the hotel and saw her sitting in the lobby,
was that she had cut and curled her auburn hair. As she waved to
me, it seemed to bounce along with the rhythm of her undulating
wrist. Rays of sunlight streaming through the windows made it
appear more reddish-gold than brown. Perhaps this detail struck
me first because I remembered how plain she had looked the
previous spring, with her straight hair parted severely in the middle. Or perhaps it was because my own hair was stringy and dirty;
I hadn't washed it because I had been so busy that week.

Whatever the reason, Mary Pat herself picked up on that detail.
The first words out of her mouth, as we walked toward our table
in the dining room for a late breakfast, was that she had cut and
curled her hair for a purpose. That is what a woman does, she
explained, when she leaves the man in her life and wants to make
a fresh start. She gets a new hairdo, tries a new perfume. And as
she spoke about what had led up to her need for a new hairdo,
the story of her relationship with Lloyd winding its way in huge
bursts of monologue in and out of the other topics we talked about
that day—breakfast sliding into afternoon coffee, which slid into
dinner, so that ten hours later we were still sitting at the same
table, still talking—I was to note that she had done the same thing
three years earlier, in the fall of 1978, just before she met him.

She had been working for her first employer, the consumer-
products company at the time, and when she decided to leave for
the processed-meats concern, she had decided to make a new

beginning. She hadn't much liked the woman she was back then, a single woman who hadn't ever shed the twenty or so extra pounds that she had carried around since adolescence. The excess weight marred even her stately five-feet eleven-inch frame. She had been living in a singles complex just outside of Manhattan and she wasn't happy there either. She had no friends, except for an acquaintance with whom she played tennis on Saturday mornings. Nor did she date. From time to time, there'd be a casual encounter with someone she'd meet at a dating bar, someone she'd hope would be interested but who never was. So that three years after graduating from the Business School, she was lonely in a way that she didn't think anyone could be—desperately lonely.

When she joined the processed-meats firm, therefore, she bought a new wardrobe, changed her hairstyle—anything to give herself a boost. And that fall, when she met Lloyd, she was ready for him. One afternoon, he passed by her desk and gave her a copy of a book by an Indian mystic. The book was a treatise on the misery and loneliness of human existence, and from the moment Lloyd put it on her desk, she knew that he wasn't the confident, devil-be-damned executive that everyone assumed he was. There was another Lloyd Whitmore beneath that facade, and he was reaching out to her.

The following January, in 1979, there was a shake-up in the managerial ranks, and Lloyd was demoted. She had been there when it happened. But even more frightening than the fact that it had occurred, at least from her perspective, was the way Lloyd had reacted. He had stayed at the office to commiserate with his colleagues, which was the last thing Mary Pat would have done if something like that had happened to her. Assuming she had had a family, as he had, she would have wanted to be home with them, the people who loved her.

That night, she and Lloyd left the building together. It was about 7:00 P.M., already dark out and snowing hard. She had taken her car to work for the first time that day and wasn't sure of her exit off of the turnpike. So Lloyd suggested that she follow him. At the proper exit, he signaled, and she turned off. She arrived home at 8:00 P.M. Much later that evening, when she was in the shower, he called. "Mary Pat?" he said. And she replied,

"Lloyd?" He just wanted to know whether she had arrived home safely, he said. And that was the extent of the conversation. But Mary Pat knew better. His call would have been reasonable at 9:00 P.M., but not at 11:00. There was another reason for his call, she deduced. He wanted someone to talk to, and he couldn't talk to his wife.

For the next several weeks, she became convinced that Lloyd was reaching out to her. That, coupled with her own growing loneliness, made her so distraught that for weeks she couldn't eat. The pounds began to melt off, which would have frightened her had she not had to lose weight anyway. By the end of February, she was slender—the same slim young woman I would meet two years later at Zapata's, for the pounds just never returned.

Finally in March, she devised a reason for taking a business trip to Miami and convinced Lloyd that he should come along. She bought a new dress for the occasion, because it had been her fantasy to walk into the Fontainebleau Hilton wearing a new dress. The night before the business meeting, she met him at the airport. They shared a taxi to the hotel, and he suggested dinner. At the restaurant, they had to sit side by side, "which delighted me to no end," she said with a soft smile. She ordered a standing rib roast which she hardly touched—he was to remind her of that much later. After dinner, they had a few stingers at the bar, then retired to his room for a few more. "And he began talking about my career ad nauseam," she said. "And I just never liked that conversation that much. So I said, 'Look, I've had enough. See you.' "

She went back to her room and tried to sleep. But she could not. She knew that he hadn't wanted her to leave. "He'd been telling me that all night long!" she exclaimed. "You see, I wore the fancy dress to dinner, and he didn't like it. I met him at the airport in a pair of pants and a sweater, which he liked much better."

So she put the pants and sweater back on, walked down the hall, and knocked on his door. He opened the door, looked at her, and said, "You've changed your clothes." She walked into the room. "And he put his arm around my waist. I'm holding my key in my hand. That's all I brought. And he said, 'What's that?' And I said, 'It's my key.' And he took it out of my hand and said, 'Well, I guess you won't be needing that anymore.' "

They saw each other for a year and a half surreptitiously, because Lloyd was still living with his wife. Mary Pat remembers that as an especially happy time in her life. "I was so happy," she said, and I remember being happy for her as she spoke. That was the first time in either of our two interviews that she had mentioned happiness. "People who knew me said I looked wonderful. I sounded happy. They said, 'We don't know who this guy is, but whoever he is, hang on to him. He's done wonderful things for you.'"

The happiness lasted until mid-1980, when Lloyd separated from his wife, and Mary Pat agreed to live with him. She had just left her job at the processed-meats firm to join the big bank, and the first problem was that the move to Larchmont was yet another disruption in her life. The house they rented was much more expensive than her apartment. They had agreed to split the expenses, but he could never seem to meet his half, because he had huge support payments. So they began to fight. "Suddenly, it was like we were having arguments over things I couldn't explain," she said, a touch bewildered.

As the arguments became more frequent, the signs that Lloyd was an alcoholic began to appear. Mary Pat hadn't noticed them before, or perhaps she hadn't wanted to. Whatever the case, she began to notice, for example, that he'd be slurring his words after dinner. "No, I'm tired," he would say. Which she would accept as a reasonable explanation. After all, how was she, a thirty-two-year-old woman, to know how a fifty-year-old man behaves? "You really do believe that," she said plaintively, as if to convince me. "You never see the bottle. Never, ever. Now you can say to yourself, 'How could a person not know this?' But it's very possible."

The events that Mary Pat described next were so startling that I hardly had time to digest one before she hit me with the next. There were four of them; they occurred in rapid succession in December and led finally the following April—just a few weeks before our meeting at Zapata's—to what Mary Pat called yet another turning point in her life.

The first of the four events was that she and Lloyd were robbed. When the police came to write the report, Lloyd had been drinking. As she tried to tell the police what had been taken—all of her jewelry was gone, and she was there sobbing—Lloyd stood over her, calling her a liar. She didn't have any jewelry, he kept shouting to the policemen, while she sobbed even louder and tried to convince them that she had. "I mean, I couldn't justify his behavior that night," she said to me with a firm little shake of her auburn curls. "It was just so brutal."

Then there were the dogs that Lloyd insisted they buy to protect the house. They were two big German shepherds that chewed the rugs, scratched the furniture, and clawed at each other so incessantly that Mary Pat thought she was going to go mad. The same week they got the dogs, Lloyd's wife attempted suicide, and Lloyd took that out on Mary Pat. Their fights became more intense. Whatever she did was wrong in his eyes. If she cooked him dinner, he would tell her that he wasn't hungry. If she didn't, he would tell her that he was going to drink because she hadn't made dinner for him. Within weeks after his wife's attempted suicide, Lloyd quit his job. He told Mary Pat that he was planning to start his own company, but he never did.

By the middle of April, saddled with a man who was disintegrating before her eyes and struggling to pay all of the household expenses herself, Mary Pat knew she had reached the breaking point. "Finally, what you do is . . . I mean all of this time, you never tell anybody because you are so ashamed. You're smart, you have an M.B.A., you're five feet eleven inches tall and not that bad looking. So why would you be living with a fifty-year-old man who's drinking himself to death and brutalizing you? I mean, no one who hasn't been exposed to an alcoholic can understand how the alcoholic can get you to the point where you think you are going to lose your mind. You literally stop sleeping. You stop eating. You have no peace. A person who is key in your life is driving you crazy. And the person who lives with the alcoholic becomes sick, but you don't believe you're sick. So you don't seek help for yourself, you're constantly trying to help the alcoholic. You do everything. You pour out bottles. You argue. You fight. You plead. But your life becomes a war against itself.

"Finally, you reach a crisis point in your own survival, which I reached in April. You must do something to survive or you know you will die. You literally feel like you can't go on. And when I did that I guess there was only one person. . . . I remember sitting there on Easter Sunday, and I said to myself, 'Make the key admission. You must be doing something wrong.' For the first time you say, 'Not him, me.' "

And it was then that Mary Pat told me about the discovery that, quite literally, had changed her whole life. In the few short months since April, she was able to stop smoking. All of a sudden, she just stopped, she said, her eyes wide with amazement. "Liz, you are a witness," she said, referring to the fact that she had been a chain-smoker. And I smiled, remembering how she had been desperate for a cigarette that night at Zapata's. She had stopped seeing the psychiatrist she had been seeing ever since she had met Lloyd. And finally, she had been able to leave Lloyd himself.

But as Mary Pat spoke, I remember envisioning her, not as the person she said she had become but as the desperate figure, all alone in the house in Larchmont on that beautiful Easter Sunday, making her admission. "So I prayed that day, not to God, because I had given up on the God of my childhood," Mary Pat said. "I prayed to my Uncle John, who had died two years before and whom I had loved dearly. I said, 'Uncle John, wherever you are, you've got to hear me, you've got to see what a terrible mess I'm in. I must be doing something wrong. I don't know whom else to ask. If there's a way of letting me know, let me know, because I'm going out of my mind. Send me a sign.' "

A week after she prayed to the memory of her uncle, Mary Pat had a casual conversation with her landlady, who was a member of a charismatic church. The woman referred Mary Pat to the minister of the church. Mary Pat dialed the minister's number that very day. And, over the telephone, she said, "I turned my life over to God, to Jesus."

The single most important thing about Mary Pat's admission was that it bore direct relevance to another decision she recently made, that she could no longer work for a large corporation. The subject of her career had come up from the moment we had met in the lobby of the Marriott that morning. Again, her new hairdo was our jumping-off point. The only thing she had asked of her hairdresser was that her new coif be trouble-free and very femi-nine, she began. But though it was becoming, it was hardly trou-ble-free. Shaking her head in dismay, she said the first thing she had to do was to buy a blow dryer to keep it up.

Things like that were always happening to her, she continued. "When I look at my business career, I was always believing some-one. I have looked three bosses in the eyes who have made pro-mises to me. They said, 'Don't worry, it won't be a problem.' And it ends up being a problem. My gut told me it would be a problem, but I believed them anyway. Because I'm a believer!"

With that, she began to tell me about a career that wound its convoluted way in and out of three jobs at three different compa-nies in the six short years since her graduation from the Business School. And in the course of doing that, she told me she was up against a world she couldn't have imagined existed, let alone understand. The world that she had expected to find was rooted in the fantasies of her adolescence: that if she went to college, then to graduate school, and then to work at a job that paid good money, the rest would follow—a life of happiness and prosperity. Yet, just as she had at the Business School, she found that the milieu in which she would have to operate in business didn't reward hard work per se. It rewarded something else that to her was far more esoteric and, as she was to say again and again, "confusing."

The confusion began from the moment she joined the consum-er-products company after the Business School. As product man-ager for "Sparkle," the sugar cut with artificial sweetener, she was responsible for launching the product to the public, a task she felt possible only if the company agreed to spend a reasonable amount of money to advertise it. For who would want to buy sugar cut with artificial sweetener unless convinced it was tastier than the real thing? And how could anyone be convinced unless the com-pany advertised? The confusion arose when a new man took over as vice-president for marketing and told her to cut down on the advertising for the product. The man had a financial background and felt she was spending too much money.

The order enraged Mary Pat and sent her back to a headhunter who had been contacting her at that time. The headhunter had a job opening at a large processed-meats company for a group product manager to handle bulk sales to institutions such as restaurants, hospitals, and schools. When that company came through with an offer of $36,000, a full $12,000 more than she was making, she quickly changed jobs.

The job that Mary Pat took at the processed-meats firm was to disappoint her as well, and what was most disconcerting, it was to disappoint her for precisely the same reason. There she was, trying to cut the best possible deal for meats sold in bulk to large customers, and her boss ("good ol' Andy," she said with a slick little smile. "I mean, Andy really was a little whippersnapper") ordered her to charge the same price to all customers. Which just didn't make sense to her, especially that year, 1979, one of the worst for the processed-meats business. Didn't it make more sense to give a bigger customer a better price, especially during a year when the loss of a large customer could mean the difference between a profit and a loss for the business?

"I hate to sound like I'm telling the same story, but this man was brought into a very troubled division and he did nothing," she said, shaking her head in disbelief. "He was convinced that I was running my business totally wrong. I was the only group product manager who brought a business in on budget that year, but he was convinced I was wrong. I tried to explain to him why a customer that orders three million pounds of hot dogs a year should pay less per pound than a customer that orders a hundred thousand. But he thought I was being recalcitrant. I mean, if all I were doing was playing for a position, if I hadn't cared about the business, I would have done exactly what he told me to do. Which is what the next guy did and which is exactly why the company sold thirty percent fewer hot dogs the year I left."

As Mary Pat talked about her career, I began comparing her attitude with, say, Suzanne Sheehan's. The point Mary Pat kept emphasizing was that she cared about making a go of her businesses. Yet Suzanne hadn't even raised that issue. Suzanne's whole orientation had been to try to determine what would most please her bosses and to act accordingly. Her strategy had been to make her bosses think highly of her so that they, in turn, would see to it that she was promoted.

"Did I ever tell you the story about my baby bunny?" Mary Pat was saying at this point during our interview at the Marriott, and the story she related illustrated the way she felt about her businesses. She told me that, recently, a friend had given her a baby bunny that would have died if she hadn't taken it home. A dog had mauled it, and if her friend had brought it to his house, his children would have killed it.

"So I said, 'Give me the bunny, and I'll take care of it.' I took it home. It was so small. It was so scared that it wouldn't eat. I tried for a whole day to feed it with an eyedropper and finally I had it wrapped up in a towel so it couldn't move. I'm practically drowning it in milk, and finally it starts to swallow. Every day when I came home, I fed this bunny. The first night, it got out of the milk carton I had put it in, and it was sitting on the basement floor. I came down and looked for it, and there it was, sitting on the newspaper on the floor. And I looked at it and said, 'You little turkey, where are you going to go? You know you can't survive out there. You can't eat grass. You have to drink milk, and I'm your source of milk. Get back into that box!' You wouldn't believe the look! This rabbit hated me! But I got it to the point where it could eat broccoli tops and junk like that. After eight weeks, it grew into a big strong bunny, and finally I had to let it go. It hopped off, and I've never seen it since.

"But, anyway, that's the kind of person I am. That rabbit hated me, and I loved it. It wanted to die, it wanted to escape. But I was determined to feed it and take care of it and make it live. I mean, I adjusted my whole schedule so that I could get home to feed and take care of my baby rabbit. I mean, here I am ruled by a rabbit! But I loved the thing! I took care of it and it got better and I felt good . . . and you see, I'm that way with my businesses. I love them. They're terrible. They're cantankerous. They're going all the wrong way—people don't like sugar mixed with artificial sweetener. But I love them. I'm trying to make them work. I'll force-feed them. I'll work for them. I'll do anything. I want to make them live!"

Six years out of the Business School, Mary Pat understood that making a business go wasn't always an executive's top priority. "There's a word in the corporate vocabulary called 'good soldier,' " she began, and then she explained that she knew what was happening at the processed-meats concern. The company had hired her to improve the bulk-sales business. Yet besides refusing to allow her to give special prices to big customers, her boss wouldn't let her hire the assistant she desperately needed. Nor would he see to it that the business was played up in the company's annual report to stockholders. Any other manager would have read that as a subtle signal from senior management to "bleed" the business. "But you see, I'm the kind of turkey that says, 'Hey, look, you guys are pushing down on me. If you'd just get off the top of this rock, we wouldn't have such a hard time pushing it up.'

"The point is, if you can imagine the analogy of the ship. . . ." she continued. "The ship is sinking. The processed-meats company is sinking. It's sinking very slowly. In fact, it's sinking imperceptibly. But the most important thing that management wants is a report showing the rate of sinking. The key thing for every officer up the line is that his boss asks him, 'What's going on?' So that he can now tell his boss when he asks, 'What's going on?' You have five or six or ten levels of management whose only job is to ask, 'What's going on?' Therefore, the job of all the levels of management is to produce information for the next layer so they can answer the question. The job of management becomes to produce reports showing which way the ship is going, and if it's sinking, how fast it's sinking and, most importantly, when it's projected to hit bottom. But don't tell me you didn't produce the report today because you were fixing the leak. Because the most important thing is not for me to know you were fixing the leak. The most important thing is for me to be able to answer my boss when he says, 'What's going on?'

"And you see, for people like me . . . I'm just not the kind of person who is interested in producing reports on how fast the ship is sinking. I mean, I see sink, and I think, 'Let's fix the leak!' Even if I can't fix the leak, I'd rather go down trying to fix the leak than producing a report saying when we're going to hit bottom." She looked at me, deadpan. "But that's just me."

What she had discovered from the admission she had made to herself about her personal life was that she would have to make precisely the same admission about her career. It wasn't the corporation that was wrong. It was she who was at odds with the ethos of the corporation. Nor was the reason for this what she had thought it to be, her naïveté about a world so far removed from the one in which she had grown up. No, the reason for her inability to fit was far more fundamental.

The point Mary Pat was making became graphically clear to me when she explained that she wasn't promoted to vice-president at the bank for which she was now working, even though she had successfully launched the new credit card business. Her problems had begun when a new vice-president, Keith Foster, was brought in to be her boss's boss. The first thing he did was march over to her office and tell her where she was going wrong. She wouldn't have minded if he had taken the trouble to read her business plan and study the results, but he had not. "Just from a superficial analysis," he had said to her—he was a little pipsqueak, she said, and he had kicked off his shoes and was padding around her office in his stocking feet, which annoyed her—"I think you could be a little tighter here and a little more strategic there."

"And I looked at him and thought, Get your ass out of here," Mary Pat said to me. "Take those claws and dig them into something that has problems. This is your idea of management? This is nonproductive! You think the rocks out of your mouth are words of wisdom, but you are stupid. You couldn't mend your way out of a paper bag. You could no more have brought this business from a standing start to where it is now than the man in the moon."

Mary Pat's attitude toward the new boss's boss was so harsh that I found myself pointing out that he hadn't specifically asked her to do anything. He obviously had to justify his job, so he merely made a few suggestions to show her that he was on top of things. Why not play along? Why not tell him his suggestions were good and just continue to do what she had been doing?

"Liz, if I could just do that, my life would be easier," Mary Pat said, ever so slightly conceding a point.

But when I added that she had taken the man's comments personally, she stiffened and said, "Because I identify very personally with my businesses."

The next thing Mary Pat mentioned was that her business was doing so well that Keith had upgraded it to a full-fledged department and brought in a new man, Garry Levin, to oversee it. And when she said that, I was incredulous. She had been passed over, and the reason why was just as I had suspected. She hadn't paid due respect to Keith Foster, and it was he who would make the recommendation about whom to name to head the department. Without Keith to go to bat for her, how were the senior executives at the bank to know that it was she who had done the grunt work to get the business off the ground? From their perspective, it was Keith (and his predecessor) who had gotten the job done.

"But I guess the problem I have with this whole thing . . ." Mary Pat was saying, wearily now, as if she were vacillating between hoping she'd still be promoted and acknowledging that she wouldn't be and didn't particularly care. "I guess it's not the title I wanted. It wasn't even more money. What I wanted was recognition. New titles and money happen to be the way they recognize things in the standard language of business. But I didn't want these things just to have them. I wanted them because I wanted to be recognized for doing a good job. I'm the sort of person who . . . when I spend a whole year to put them into a new business, I want to hear something about it. I would like to be made to feel as if I were part of the management team. It doesn't have anything to do with titles or salary per se. It's what they symbolize. It's my way of keeping score that they care.

"But you see, the game is played by people who can throw their hearts away," she continued. The man Keith brought in to be her new boss, Garry Levin, for example, came into work at eight every morning and worked until eight every night. He even came in on Rosh Hashanah, and when Mary Pat told me that, she gave her auburn curls a swift shake. "I mean, I don't know much about the Jewish religion. But coming in on one of the highest holy days seems . . . creepy."

The fact that she wanted business to care about her in a way that it could not suggested the answer to my riddle. She had been pursuing the wrong dream for the wrong reason, which became even more obvious when she mentioned another thing that had happened the previous summer, just after she had become a charismatic.

That summer, she had seen a movie that she first saw when she was thirteen years old. The movie was *Yellow Sky* with Gregory Peck and Ann Baxter, which she described as a "great old western, a black-and-white gem from 1948, the year before I was born." She had always identified with the heroine. "The heroine was a tomboy—packs a gun," she explained. "But when she falls in love, she realizes it isn't such a bad thing to be a girl after all."

Seeing the movie again, Mary Pat suddenly realized that that had always been her fantasy. "That I, rough-and-tumble Mary Pat, would meet a guy who would see beyond what I was into the depths of my soul," she began. "He would see the gentleness and affection that were really there and draw out what I always wanted to give. The most important thing was that at the heart of finding out who I was I would be loving a man. And so I was always waiting to be discovered by a man who would love me and teach me what I was. The way Gregory Peck taught Ann Baxter." She laughed shortly, but it was a sincere laugh. "It worked great in the movies," she said.

The path she had chosen instead couldn't have been more at odds with her fantasy, she continued. For it was a competitive world for jobs like hers, jobs that paid $50,000 a year. "You are not an unnoticed individual in jobs like that," she explained. "You are a target in a competitive, difficult, and stressful environment. Now, I'm sure there are people who enjoy it, but for me it's been taxing . . ." She stopped herself, because she wanted to be precise. "Not taxing in terms of performance, because I always knew I could do the work, but taxing in terms of emotional . . . I mean, psychologically, it's been very taxing. Which was a shock to me because what I wanted was security. I didn't want a sense of disruption and nonacceptance. I didn't want to find another place where I didn't fit. I wanted to belong."

The irony implicit in what she said was so obvious that she smiled in spite of herself. "I recognize—not that I regret my education or anything," she said, "but I recognize that there were probably better places for me to be in terms of an emotional and psychological fit than the place I'm in now."

It was nearly midnight when we left the dining room of the Marriott Hotel, and as I had been after our first conversation, I was expended. So when Mary Pat invited me to stay at her house, I accepted gratefully. I didn't even feel as if I had the energy to check into a hotel.

As we drove back to her house, a cold and uninviting split-level wedged into a sunken piece of land by the side of a winding country road, Mary Pat continued to talk. The monologue continued even as we made our way into her converted basement, where the guest quarters were located, and as she made up my bed with garish orange sheets.

The following morning, I accompanied Mary Pat to the charismatic church she had been attending for the past several months. The previous month, when I had called for the second interview, she had made a point of telling me that she could not do it on Sunday, because she had to go to church. Because she had sounded so intense when she said that, I had asked her if I could accompany her. She had seemed pleased that I asked, and told me she would be happy to let me come.

That morning, as we drove through the beautiful New York countryside, only a few clouds in the sky foreshadowed the rainstorm that would come with a vengeance in the afternoon. Turning to face me for a moment, Mary Pat said she wanted to warn me. Her congregation was a spirited one. People hooted and hollered and sometimes fell to their knees in a frenzy of exaltation and love for Jesus.

At the service, which began at 10:30 A.M., I sat beside Mary Pat in a pew toward the center of the church. The minister approached the pulpit, and I flicked on my tape recorder. He opened his Bible to a Psalm and began to read: "In the day of my trouble, I sought the Lord. I am so troubled I cannot speak. . . ."

Then he asked the congregation to bow their heads in prayer. Mary Pat turned to me and noticed that the spools were spinning in my tape recorder. Flushed with embarrassment, she whispered, plaintively, "Please turn that off. People will wonder what this is all about."

I flicked off the machine immediately. I felt ashamed for having embarrassed her among people who apparently meant so much to her, in a place where, finally, she belonged.

Then the minister asked the choir to sing a hymn, and leaping out of her pew, Mary Pat rushed down the long aisle and stepped up to the altar. There she joined fifteen men and women in tattered coats that smelled of winter. The choir burst into song. "Now He wants me beside Him every day! He means everything to me!" they caroled. And as I watched Mary Pat, towering above most of the other people in the group, I wondered once again how she had come to this: a shattered career, a personal life in shambles.

The thought I kept coming back to could be symbolized by one of the first things I had learned about her, when her classmates spoke of her with ridicule: that she had dressed up as a Playboy Bunny and danced on the tables of the Pub. We finally had talked about the incident the night before at the Marriott, and Mary Pat had been embarrassed when I had asked. "Oh, I never told you that story," she said with that same sad expression I remembered from our evening at Zapata's when she realized I was pregnant.

The real story, as it turned out, wasn't as her classmates had remembered. What they remembered was a composite of three incidents. The first happened early in the first year, when she ran for social chairman of her section. As a campaign gimmick, she reached back for a stunt she had pulled years earlier at the steel company. One day back then—who knew why? Perhaps because she was so unhappy—she marched into work dressed in gold lamé boots, purple-velvet hot pants, a little purple top with a choker, and a blond wig she saw Raquel Welch wear in a movie about prehistoric dinosaurs.

"Well, I was a very popular girl that day," she said, as we both started to laugh. "Men who had never spoken to me were coming into my office and leaning on my desk. I remember those guys, those starchy old married men, those drippy engineers, those have-a-sandwich-for-lunch-that-they-pack-from-home-everyday guys, coming into my office. I mean, it was just terrific!"

161

The gimmick worked just as well in a classroom at the Business School, the morning that candidates for social chairman had to give their campaign speeches. The first two candidates gave tame little discourses about how they had contacts at all of the women's colleges in the area. Then, when it was Mary Pat's turn, she stood up in the back of the room and peeled off her raincoat. In her little outfit—the blond wig, the gold-lamé boots, the purple-velvet hot pants, and the little purple top with the choker—she marched down the aisle. She turned to her classmates, and in a breathy Marilyn Monroe tone of voice, she said, "Well, I just like to throw parties where everybody has a good time!" And she was elected by an overwhelming majority.

The other two incidents were at a Halloween party where everyone had to come in costume, and she dressed up as a Playboy Bunny, and at a Friday-night gathering at the Pub the night after the deadline for a big paper. That night, somebody—"some delightful human being," she recalled—dared her to dance on the tables. "I mean, I should have said no, but I said yes, you know," she said sadly. She told me she was wearing jeans that night.

The story must have rung true about Mary Pat, however, or else why would so many of her classmates have recalled an incident that hadn't even happened? And I knew that it did for me. For Mary Pat seemed to symbolize what some women have to deny for the sake of access to the alien world of business—alien because it isn't a woman's world but a man's. In Mary Pat's case, the lie was something she ultimately could not live with: The asexual female executive was crying out to be recognized for the sexual woman she really was.

After the church service that Sunday morning, Mary Pat invited me to have breakfast with her Christian friends. We drove to a nearby diner and joined two middle-aged women from Mary Pat's church. They were both overweight, wore their hair sculpted in beauty-parlor coifs, and kept giving each other knowing glances. They asked me at one point, for example, if I were a Christian. When I replied, politely, that I wasn't religious, they turned to each other, shook their heads, and said, "Praise God! She'll find

Jesus." Mary Pat smiled and echoed their words. "Praise God," she caroled.

That afternoon, when her friends left and she once again had to confront the reality of her life, we sat facing each other in two easy chairs at her house in Larchmont. And it was then that she brought up the name of Esther Micholov Boron, whom professors at the Business School had intimidated to such an extent that she finally dropped out.

Mary Pat's affection and affinity for Esther no longer seemed as unusual as it once had, for the more I got to know Mary Pat, the more I began to see how much they had in common. Her awkwardness notwithstanding, Mary Pat was every bit as personal a woman as the charming, soft-spoken blonde I had interviewed in Berkeley.

If there were any differences between the two, in fact, they were that Mary Pat had chosen to work in management, Esther a profession. As Mary Pat had thought she should do, Esther had enrolled in a doctoral program after she dropped out of the Business School. Her field was Egyptian studies, and she spoke about it with interest and ease. She was just completing the research for her dissertation, she said, and she was planning to spend the following year abroad writing it.

The ease with which Esther had spoken about her career, in sharp contrast to Mary Pat's desperation, was to make its way into her conversation about her personal life. On her trip abroad the following year, she was planning to rendezvous with her lover on the same uninhabited Mediterranean island they had visited the year before, when she had met him.

I remember having raised a skeptical eyebrow as Esther had talked about her lover, as calmly as one would discuss the events of the day, pulling a snapshot out of her wallet, and saying to me, "Would you like to see a picture of him?" For she was married to a man she purported to love. But she had shaken her beautiful blond hair to make me understand that it was not only possible, but desirable, to love two men. "Being seduced!" she had exclaimed. "That is one of the great things in life!"

"Is Esther married?" Mary Pat asked as she drove me to the

airport later that afternoon, the expression on her face tense and anxious. She was battling with the blinding rainstorm that was obstructing her vision. And when I told her that Esther was, she seemed satisfied. "Good," she said.

As we neared LaGuardia, I asked Mary Pat what she planned to do next in her career. And her answer was one that I suppose I suspected, even though I found myself buckling ever so slightly as she spoke. It seemed a shame that such a bright woman would come to this, I thought.

She responded obliquely. She wanted a different type of work, she began. She wanted to work for a much smaller organization, in a place that would be close to wherever she chose to live. Ideally, she wanted to work for "the Great Commission."

She caught my blank stare. "What is 'the Great Commission'?" she said. "I'm glad you asked. The Great Commission is the preaching of the gospel of the kingdom of God to a world that is dying."

As I thought about Mary Pat, the woman whose story so graphically illustrated the reason why women such as she have such a difficult time fitting into the structure of business, I knew that it nonetheless begged an important question. There had to be some women who cared as much as Mary Pat did—about husbands, about children, and indeed, about people—who were able to survive and prosper in management. My next area of exploration was to talk to a woman who had won the fight for control in that alien environment—Tess Beckett.

6.

TESS:
The Fight
for Control

Of all of the reasons I decided to write this book, the issue of whether a woman could have both a career and a family was the most important. It became even more crucial in the wake of completing my research. For the findings that had become obvious when putting together my assessment of Mary Pat Horner—that there wasn't any correlation whatsoever between a woman's success in business and the way she had chosen to live her personal life—seemed to suggest that the problems we writers had been pointing up as the central concerns for career-minded women were overemphasized at best, and at worst not really the issues at all. Those were the logistical concerns associated with combining careers with marriage and children—the difficulty working long hours and, should the job require it, traveling frequently, to say nothing of the potential for a major dislocation should husband or wife have to transfer or risk stagnating on the job. The undeniable fact remained that at least some women in the class had managed to circumvent such concerns.

Then, too, the very essence of Mary Pat's story seemed to suggest that the issue couldn't be primarily those logistical concerns. For here was a woman who wasn't married, didn't have any children, and hadn't even been in a serious relationship for most of her years since Harvard, and still was plagued by a conflict that, when dissected, appeared to come perilously close to that classic conflict between family and career.

The essence of this conflict—that the major issue for women in business wasn't whether a woman *could* combine these two facets of life but rather, to be brutally honest, whether she *wanted* to and had arranged her life so that she could—was to come directly to the fore on that hot summer night when I interviewed Tess Beckett in the continental restaurant in the basement of the Boston townhouse. For here was a woman who, like Mary Pat, had come from a background of near poverty in a moribund factory town. Only hers had been far worse than Mary Pat's. Her father drank when she was a child growing up in Pawtucket, Rhode Island. She still remembers hiding beneath the covers with a flashlight so that she could continue to read when he'd come in in a drunken stupor. Her home wasn't the neat little bungalow Mary Pat's family had scrimped and saved to buy, but rather a tenement, a second-floor flat in the first of four brick buildings, each with a storefront on the ground floor: a bowling alley and a bad restaurant, a grocer and a barber shop.

Yet here was a woman who, so very much unlike Mary Pat, could sit across the table from me in one of Boston's poshest restaurants, and with a persistence that I would come to believe was the major quality setting her apart from most of the others in the class, speak with enthusiasm about all that she had in her life today: her upwardly mobile job with the fledgling personal computer company, her beautiful home in the fine Boston suburb of Belmont, and most of all, her husband, Kevin, and their five-year-old son, Chris.

The dichotomy was even more startling given the disparity between the two women when it came to natural ability. Whereas Mary Pat had been among the brightest members of her class, Tess had just about scraped through in the bottom third, and then only after having first dropped out and having had to make a virtual round-the-clock effort in her studies when she returned. And it was even more startling considering perhaps the most important factor they had in common: that the conflict that had so plagued Mary Pat had also been a part of Tess's life, and in a far more direct and tangible way, ever since the beginning.

As a child in Pawtucket, Tess had always known that she wanted to escape the plight that had been her father's: that of a life spent as a laborer in a place with no future. And like generations of young women who had grown up poor in dying factory towns, she knew of only one way to do that: She would marry the rich kid on the block. She had chosen him very specifically, in fact, during their junior year in high school, where he sat unsuspectingly across the room from her in English class. His name was Curt Rodgers, and his family owned the biggest furniture store in town, which she envisioned running with him someday.

She and Curt dated throughout her junior and senior years. Six months later, when she had gone to work as a clerk in his family's furniture store and he to a third-rate junior college in Worcester, Massachusetts, he returned one memorable weekend to dump her. But even then, she didn't think to forgo that philosophy. Indeed, in the years ahead, she continued to date the boys from Pawtucket who had gone away to the good colleges in Rhode Island and Massachusetts or to the jobs behind the desks in all of the little companies that dot southern New England. Finally, when she had joined the fast-growing minicomputer maker in Westboro, Massachusetts, she met and married Kevin Beckett, a rising star in the ranks of financial management.

Yet the jilting years earlier at the hands of Curt Rodgers, whom Tess wouldn't easily forget, threw a huge damper on her perception of the only way she knew to make it out of Pawtucket. It planted the seed that perhaps she wouldn't be able to do it through a man, that perhaps she would have to do it on her own. In the years after Curt left, therefore, she simultaneously threw herself into a haphazard, almost desperate, scramble to find a way out on her own. She thought about becoming an airline stewardess until five carriers turned her down. She dreamed of being named an administrative assistant, which she thought was the ultimate job for a woman. Throughout it all, she read voraciously, everything from trashy novels to the self-help books that were beginning to become popular in the mid-1960's until finally she discovered

Helen Gurley Brown's *Sex and the Single Girl.* She read that book five times because it said so much to her. "For me, liberation was *Sex and the Single Girl,*" she was to repeat time and time again throughout the course of both our interviews.

That it was helped me see Tess from another perspective. Whereas she had awed me when we first met at the continental restaurant, she with her larger-than-life story that I felt had the makings of a novel or a screenplay, from this other angle I could see how very far behind most of her Harvard classmates she had been, and in many respects, still was when she arrived on campus. She had come not from the entry-level jobs in management and the professions, as had most of the other women in her class, but rather from the route common to successful women of the past generations: from having been discovered in the clerical ranks by some powerful male figure and carefully massaged into something more.

After clerking at the furniture store, Tess had gone to work as a secretary to the general manager of a sweater mill. There she ingratiated herself to her boss to such an extent that it was she he thought to send to a computer seminar for employees. The company was just beginning to computerize, and he figured she'd be interested enough to learn about the new machines. At that seminar, the spark was lit: She could see that computers were the future, perhaps even her future. So that three years later in 1968, when she spotted an advertisement for secretaries placed by the fast-growing minicomputer maker, she knew enough to apply. And it was there that she began her dizzying ascent in life, nurtured primarily by her second boss at the company. One of the founders, he saw in her the makings of a woman who could be more than a secretary. It was he who guided her career into the marketing ranks and cheered her on when she went for her associate degree at night at the local junior college. A few years later, after she had left the company to marry Kevin Beckett and go to college full time in the Springfield, Massachusetts, area, where Kevin had been transferred to run a branch office, it was that executive who wrote her recommendation to the Harvard Business School.

Tess's decision to apply to Harvard during the spring of her second semester of senior year, the semester she spent at Smith, was perhaps the first time in her life that the two courses she had been following openly collided. After having made it to Smith for that brief semester from, going backward in time, a semester at a good but not great private school, a year at the University of Massachusetts at Amherst, and the two years at the local junior college, Tess knew that she wanted even more. She wanted a professional degree. Although the thought of applying to Harvard had always been with her, lingering there in the back of her mind even as far back as her days at the junior college, she felt uncomfortable with the idea in a way she couldn't fully explain. She only knew that an alternative course, that of getting a doctorate in economics, which was her major, and teaching on the college level, seemed more comfortable, or as she would put it, "more socially acceptable for a woman." After all, she had seen her professors at Smith drop off their children—and the thought of someday having children had also occurred to Tess from time to time—with the secretaries in their departments who were only too willing to babysit while the professors taught or did research in the library.

"Kevin and I spent long hours that spring talking about how, as a tenured professor with a [hypothetical] three point two children, we could work it into our lives," she explained. "Not inconvenience us, right?"

So that semester, she applied to doctoral programs in economics throughout the Boston area and was accepted at two good but not great universities. Then she sat back and considered her options. Of all of the things she understood about herself, she knew that she wasn't brilliant in that academic, top-of-the-class sort of way. "I am not a genius," she explained, underlining the word "not" with a little smile and a shake of her head. "I've known that for a long time. I've always known that. I have reasonably good abilities. But my strength is a street sense. It's a sense of humor and perserverance and an ability to deal with people."

She also knew that as a professor of economics, she would want to be "advising presidents!" She certainly didn't want to be, as she put it, "some lowly person who taught in night school!" And with top scholars from the best schools being denied teaching positions that year, what hope would there be for someone whose most likely fate would be just-passing grades from a less than top-notch school?

So finally, on the day of the deadline for applying to the Harvard Business School, Tess picked up an application at the Smith College placement office. She filled it out that very night "under the influence of a considerable amount of wine," and carried it by hand to the post office. "And when I was accepted, I said, 'That's it! I'm going to do it!' "—and then with a firm little slap of her hands—"Did it!"

"I'm really one of the lucky ones," she continued triumphantly. "I'm doing what I want to do. When I first had the confidence to say 'I'm going to be happier doing what I want to do than conforming to what all the signals say I should do,' it's been like the world cut me free and I've been soaring!"

If the semester at Smith had been the first time that the two conflicting forces in Tess Beckett's life came into open collision, the years at the Business School were when she resolved the conflict. For it was during those years that she fought and won the battle to put her career first in her life, a subject that was to weave its way in and out of both our interviews and to become the dominant theme of her story.

The battle wasn't won until it first decimated her to such a degree that she had to drop out for a year before marshaling her resources to return on a far different, and perhaps more mature, basis. And it wasn't won until, as I was to note curiously from the moment of her outburst in the Prudential Center parking garage, she incorporated into her life what is commonly thought to be an obstacle for women in business: her pregnancy.

Nor was the battle something she would easily forget. Even years later, as she spoke about her life with me, she was to approach the subject first from an oblique perspective. She told me when we first spoke at the continental restaurant, how different she felt from the women who had been her best friends at the Business School, Maureen Graham and Polly Drascovitch, even though they were ostensibly very much like her. They were both married and not really a part of the Business School community, commuting as they did from off-campus apartments.

Yet it was the way in which they viewed the Business School that confused Tess, she explained, and even more so because, unlike she, they had had all of the advantages. They had come from the upper middle class and had gone to fine women's colleges as a matter of course.

The problem was, she explained, that she would have suspected that women who went to the Business School would have been just as ambitious as she, and Maureen and Polly were not ambitious at all. They seemed to regard the Business School as little more than a finishing school, in fact, as "something one does after college or after being a medical technician or whatever one does," she said scornfully. And that made Tess feel even more like an oddity. Not only was she a lower-middle-class person among people who were well-to-do, but she was an ambitious woman among women who for the most part were not. The feeling that had first struck her the previous semester at Smith, that perhaps a woman shouldn't be going to the Business School in the first place, grew stronger.

"If being one of the crowd means you go to Wheaton or Bryn Mawr," she explained, referring, respectively, to the schools that had been Maureen's and Polly's alma maters, "and then you marry the guy who is a classmate at the Business School and proceed to settle in the suburbs and raise your three point two children, whatever the stresses and problems in that role, they're relatively minor to what they might be if you step out into another role."

The particulars of stepping out into "that other role" were what Tess was to describe, graphically and in her methodical point-by-point way, during the course of our second interview, which took place leisurely over the course of six evenings the following September at her beautiful contemporary home in Belmont. This approach was a luxury for me. On those evenings, I would drive out to her home with anticipation, the windows of my car rolled down and the soft late-summer breezes pouring in. I would consider what we had already talked about and think about what I still wanted to ask her.

Tess would greet me at the door in a chic business suit or, if she had had the time to change, a flowing kimono that hid the problem spots in her lumpy figure. There would be a glass of wine in her hand, and with it she would usher me into a little study that was every bit as sleek as the clean lines of the house itself. She would offer wine, which she would pour from a bottle she had just decanted—a visible symbol, I thought, of how far she had come. No jug wines for Tess Beckett; she lived in Belmont now! Then we would settle kitty-corner from each other in the study, Tess on the black leather couch and me stretched out on the matching easy chair, and after a few pleasantries that grew warmer as our nights together continued, she would begin.

The fact was that even before she set foot on the campus of the Harvard Business School, she "knew there was going to be a crisis," she said. That summer she had gone back to the minicomputer maker to see the boss who had supported her during all of those years and who had written such a beautiful recommendation for her. He was just thrilled that she was going to attend. But his enthusiasm only frightened her. What if she should fail when people such as he thought so highly of her?

The prospect of failure hovered on Orientation Day, when the urbane associate dean spoke to the incoming students with nary a hint of speaking down to them—that was how suave he was, Tess thought—and it continued into her first month of classes, although, to be fair, she explained, the classroom was intimidating. "They threw you into this little mini-circus of a section of eighty people, all of them brilliant! Walk into accounting class and there would be C.P.A.'s! Walk into finance and there would be people who had worked for banks!"

Then there was the teaching method, which confused her to such an extent that by the end of the month she had already stopped reading her cases through. "The professors would say, 'Analyze the case,'" she explained. "But what does it mean to 'analyze' a case? So I thought, since I can't figure out what I'm supposed to be doing anyway, why not just skim and wait?"

The first sign that she was in trouble came as early as mid semester, when she got an Unsatisfactory in a mandatory writing course that wasn't even considered up to the standards of a "real" Business School course. At the end of the semester, she received Low Passes in two of her five regular courses.

The thought that occurred to her back then wasn't that she might not have been working hard enough but that she froze on exams. So, shortly after receiving her first semester grades, she went to see the Business School psychologist for help with that problem. For weeks in his office on the second floor of the little gray career development office, she dutifully practiced a series of exercises—one set for her face, another for her feet—that he said would help her relax. "What does one do when one wants to relax? One relaxes!" he thundered. And as she spoke about the experience now, in the quiet of her little study in Belmont, the thought occurred to me that the man's suggestions were absurd.

"Wait a minute," I said, cutting her off and asking her to demonstrate one of the exercises. As blindly as she had followed his orders, she followed mine. She stuck out her big toe and began wiggling it back and forth, until finally we both burst out laughing and couldn't stop, the first visible sign that Tess was about to confront the reality of what had happened back then.

"Can you imagine being so confused that you don't know which end is up and having this turkey tell you that what you really need to do is to exercise your feet?" she said, wiping tears from the corners of her eyes. "Can you imagine saying that to someone who feels she's drowning?"

Her slide at the Business School worsened after that. By mid March, she began cutting classes, sometimes weeks at a time. Then, one memorable morning in April, she woke up and discovered that what she really wanted to do was to plant pachysandra, the ground cover for her garden.

"I think I planted a thousand pachysandra plants that spring," she exclaimed. "Do you know what a sense of accomplishment you have when you take something out of the plot, and you put it into the ground, and it's there! When you started in the morning, there was nothing, and now there's something. It's measurable, definable. . . . I was outside in the sunshine, and it was spring, and all my tulip bulbs were coming up. And the trees were coming into bloom, and the birds were singing, and I thought, 'There is life, God! There really is!' " The following month, she drove into Boston to tell the dean she was dropping out.

The year she dropped out of the Business School was an especially difficult one, Tess continued. Her first inclination was to return to the minicomputer maker where she had had her first taste of success. But once there, she discovered that it wasn't the same. So she went to work for another computer company and was fired five weeks later, after a tiff with her boss. "I had a chip on my shoulder," she confessed. "Things weren't right there because things weren't right with me." Then she went to work for a much smaller company, a maker of software—packages of instructions that enable computers to do specific tasks. She stayed until the following summer, when the firm went bankrupt and for the second time in the short span of a year, she was let go.

But it wasn't strictly this series of events that led her back to the Business School. Rather, it was her decision to become pregnant. The decision wasn't one that she made on a strictly voluntary basis, she began, when we delved into that subject. That spring, when she was failing at the career she professed to want, her husband, Kevin, felt it was time to have a child. They had been married five years, after all. But Tess's response was indecision, as it always had been when she had thought from time to time in the past about having a child. It was a thought she had always pushed to the back of her mind.

But now that time was clicking away—she was, after all, almost thirty—and Kevin was pressuring her, and she was failing at what she had set out to do, she felt vulnerable in a way that she hadn't in the past. So without really agreeing with Kevin, she quietly went off the Pill and refused to use any other method of birth control; she argued that she didn't want her body "messed with." The day she found out she was pregnant, at perhaps her most vulnerable moment that year—three days after she was fired from the software concern—she made an appointment for an abortion. At the very same time, she told Kevin. And when she did, the tension between them erupted into a full-fledged crisis. "Kevin said to me, 'You're robbing me of my child,' " Tess explained. "He said, 'It's my child, and I want it.' "

Perhaps because she felt she would lose her husband if she chose otherwise, she explained, she canceled her appointment for the abortion. In the process, however, she came to yet another decision: She would return to the Business School that very year, the year she would be pregnant.

From the perspective of six years, Tess could see that this event had been the turning point in her life. It gave her the resolve to do something that she hadn't ever been able to do in the past: She was able to put herself first. In the past, she had accomplished what she had strictly within the confines of the rigid code she had lived by ever since her girlhood in Pawtucket: that she fit her need to achieve around the needs of the men in her life.

"So I was playing a game, that's what I was doing," Tess said of her confrontation with Kevin. "I was saying to him, 'I will give you this, but in return I will feel justified in taking.' It was really a striking back when I think about it. But it was the best thing I ever did. It may have been done in anger at that point, but it forced me to say, 'I am going to do something I want to do.'

"You see, I had always felt grateful to be, quote, unquote, allowed to work. I really felt like I had escaped, put something over on the world. That was one part of it. The other part was that I had always wanted to be a wife—that was not offensive to me. I was interested in domestic things. I was interested in my home, in cooking, in entertaining. All of the things you do when you have time. And that was also consistent with what the world expected me to do. That was okay. It was okay to work. It was even okay to work on a professional level. It was just not okay, in my value system, to put my needs, my wants, first."

With her pregnancy as the justification, she was able during her second year to make that leap. The very fact that her pregnancy was so tangible—as planting pachysandra had been the year before when it became the catalyst enabling her to drop out—made it possible for her to deal with the problem of getting through the Business School in a concrete, step-by-step way. Aware of her limitations as a scholar, for example, she arranged her schedule to make up for that lack with hard work. She divided her day into fifteen minute segments and relegated each of the tasks she had to accomplish into one of those segments. She gave herself fifteen minutes for her shower, fifteen minutes for breakfast, fifteen minutes for scanning the front page of the newspaper. "I realized that I had responsibilities and under constraints." She explained, "Either I was going to do what had to be done within a limited period of time or—guess what, folks?—I wasn't going to do it at all!"

She had hired Chris's baby nurse by October, six months before he was even born. Over Christmas vacation, she fixed up the nursery. And on the day of his birth, a beautiful Wednesday in April, she refused to go into the hospital until the very last moment, when the labor pains had become excruciating.

In Tess's response to her son's birth, I could see a hint of the defensiveness that I had spotted when she first spoke about her pregnancy in the continental restaurant and had made the comment that had caused me to wince: "Is this all there is?" she had told me she said when the doctor laid him in her arms. But within the context of how her pregnancy had been the lever enabling her to achieve what she hadn't been able to achieve the year before, I began to see how much more complicated the issue really was.

The day before Chris was born, when the labor pains began, for example, Tess stayed home from school, did her nails, and called the doctor. When he asked her what was happening, she replied angrily that nothing was, and that furthermore, she was angry. She had missed a whole day of school, and she had a paper due on Monday. The following day, when the contractions finally began coming so hard that she conceded to go into the hospital, she remembers being directed into an X-ray room. She was dripping blood, no one seemed to care, and she thought to herself, "What a revolting development! Doesn't everyone know I'm not Earth Mother? C'mon, give me a break! Maybe I'll die."

Then she remembers being wheeled into a delivery room filled with people: her doctor and a backup for him; the anesthesiologist and a backup for him; the pediatrician and his backup; and hordes of nurses, interns, and medical students. She remembers her doctor telling her that the baby was breech—that was why so many people had come to witness the birth—and mentioning a cesarean section. Then she remembers shouting, "No, no!"—she had a paper due on Monday—and her doctor saying, "If you can cope with it, we're going to try to deliver this child." Finally she remembers the anesthesiologist approaching her and she accepting the painkiller of which she had been so afraid—because, she explained, the nurse who had taught the childbirth classes that she and Kevin had taken had said that what happens with painkillers "is that you get spacey, and you lose control."

So within the context of Tess's whole story, I was to come to believe that what had really been propelling her was her fear of being out of control as a pregnant woman. Should she fail to make it through the Business School this time, she would be forever out of control of her life. As the mother of a small child, she would be forever relegated to a subordinate role in her marriage.

Going back to the Business School as a pregnant woman "was the hardest thing I've ever done, probably the hardest thing I'll ever do," Tess said. "But I think I may have needed to be pregnant that year. I think I really needed to stretch for the long yardage, if you will. The challenge of the Business School alone wouldn't have been enough to shock me out of my past modus operandi. With the pregnancy, it may have been seventy hours a week, but it was finite. In control!"

That Tess had seized control of her life was to figure prominently in the way she approached her post Business School career. After graduation, she worked for four years as a salesperson for a big Boston-based computer manufacturer and did so well that she began earning more money than Kevin. Then she set her sights on the type of company where she could make even bigger money—the kind of money that she would never be able to make in an established firm.

She wanted to find an entrepreneurial concern where she would have a piece of the action, and for weeks she sat in the Career Resources Room at the Business School, pouring over dozens of trade magazines with names such as *Byte* and *Datamation,* until she zeroed in on just the company for her. It was the little company that was thought to have the product that would take the decade by storm, the personal computer that would sell for about five hundred dollars.

"Why a start-up company?" she asked in her typical question-and-answer style, beginning to rattle off the reasons why she joined the personal-computer company. "Start-up because I'd have a better opportunity to do something I wanted to do. Set my own imprint on what was happening. Wear more hats. Make more decisions. All the reasons one goes to a small company."

The decision to go with that particular start-up company had been predicated on the product, with which she was enamored. It wasn't a cut-and-dried, nuts-and-bolts product that would sell itself. Because it was so new, few people knew anything about it. She would have to do what a salesperson should do, which was to sell, rather than just take orders. "I really wanted an opportunity to sell sizzle," she began, and when I didn't quite understand and asked her to repeat what she had said, she threw back her head and said it loud and clear.

"Sizzle!" The word rang through the stillness of that warm September evening. "Sex!" she added, presumably her own synonym for "sizzle."

"When you sell bananas, you sell bananas! They're long, thin things with yellow skins, and you can describe the characteristic of the banana. But it's still a banana. When you sell a personal computer with software that does wild and woolly things, that's something different. People can't touch software. They can't feel software. It never does all of the things you tell them it's going to do. Never! I don't care who you are. You always embellish on it. And you talk about all of the benefits, all of the things you can do with this wonderful stuff. It's just a lot more fun."

She got the title she wanted, which was sales manager, right off the bat, she said, because she knew enough to tussle with the man who hired her and who would become her boss. His name was Jerry Blake, and he had first offered her the job of salesperson for the New England region, which she had immediately turned down.

She wanted to hold out for the managerial job, she explained, and when Jerry told her he couldn't conceive of a woman in such a position, she had an answer for him. "There are a lot of people who feel the same way you do, and there are more people in your camp than in mine," she had said to him, and I could almost hear her as she spoke those words to Jerry, hustling hard to convince him that she was every inch the salesperson she knew she was. "But I don't consider it an issue whether I'm male, female, black, or blue. I think that what you'll find is, one, I can do your job, and two, you'll feel comfortable with me and that other people will too. So tell me again why you don't want to hire me?"

The pace had been every bit as frenetic as she would have expected and then some, she said. The summer she joined the company, which had been the year before we spoke, the company hadn't had a sales force, hadn't done a marketing plan, and hadn't even rolled its product off the assembly line, although Jerry had indicated before she took the job that all of that spade work had been done. When I let out a short gasp of surprise, Tess shook her head and laughed. All of that was to be expected in a start-up concern, she said.

"Products are a year late, and when they're out, they don't work as well as they should," she said. "Reality just isn't as nice as we'd all like it to be." And then she laughed again, shortly this time. "I used to tell people that we had absolutely no unsatisfied customers, because we had absolutely no customers."

Tess's biggest problem over the previous year, however, had been getting along with founder Kip Karlin and the three engineers he had recruited from some of the best computer companies in the Boston area. The four were rebels all, as perhaps she herself was, men who would have headed west a century earlier, men who certainly didn't feel comfortable in established organizations today. All four, in fact, had come from companies that had been turned over to professional managers once the founders had gotten them off the ground. The companies had turned into, according to their way of looking at things, impossible places to work. Two of the four, Jerry Blake included, were about to be fired when they left.

As the ringleader, Kip was the most mercurial of all. His biggest flaw, even according to his closest associates, was that he wanted absolute control over everything and didn't know how to differentiate between what was important and what was not. "He'll win the battles but lose the war," Tess said, ever so slightly dismissing him. "I treat him like my five-year-old son."

When I asked her for an example of his penchant for control, she gave me a you-won't-believe-what-I'm-about-to-say-next look and said with a flourish, "Colors!" Then she explained that Kip was so fond of the color pink that he insisted that everything in his company be pink. The walls in the lobby were painted pink. The company's stationery was pink. Kip himself drove a pink car and wore a pink raincoat. But when he had insisted recently that the personal computer upon which they had pinned their hopes for the future had to be pink, he had locked horns with Jerry. As marketing vice-president, Jerry had insisted that it be yellow. And the two had become embroiled in a power struggle that was still going on.

But Tess's current concern was her rapport with her own boss, Jerry Blake, and when she began to tell me about him toward the end of one of our last evenings together, I remember feeling for the first time that she sounded uneasy. The fact was that she wasn't getting along well with Jerry. She had tried until she was blue in the face to do things his way, and now she just didn't know where to turn. A lot of the problems were built into his personality, she said, painting a picture of an egotistical man in his mid-forties who had made so much money at the last company he was with that he would never have to work again.

The only reason he was working was for fun, she explained. He enjoyed being the man to whom people would turn when all around them was chaos. He enjoyed being the man who set things straight, and, most especially, he liked being recognized for doing that.

"Jerry's a thunder stealer," Tess said, easing into the problem, which was that he wasn't above taking credit away from his subordinates and blaming them when things went wrong, all of which he had been doing to her. His latest tactic was to let her subordinates know that they could come directly to him with their problems. A clearer way of undermining her authority couldn't be found, she said.

The classic case had been his suggestion that the company start making personal computers for the diesel industry, Tess continued. At one of his previous jobs, he had done particularly well selling to that industry. "We need to develop a product for the diesel industry, so I can work my magic," he had said, with nary a comment about whether the industry would need and buy such a product. Tess's eyes were opened with amazement even as she related this story, and when she saw my look of disbelief, she held up her right hand boy scout style. "Honest," she said.

Then a grave expression crossed her face. "I really don't believe much of what Jerry says," she said. "I don't care how many good things he says about me. I don't want a bagful of jelly beans. I want my own checking account."

For a moment, sitting there in the corner of the leather sofa in her study, Tess looked so somber that I was touched. I wanted to reach out and tell her that things would be all right. I remember casually asking her whether she would do it all over again and expecting her to say never. Instead, she seemed to snap out of it, the grave expression all but faded from her face. "I'd do it again," she said emphatically. "If Kip Karlin left the personal-computer company to start another one, I'd follow him."

The reason she would do that, she said, was that men like Kip were where the action was, and that was where she wanted to be. That they were sometimes impossible was beside the point. "My theory is that only neurotics accomplish things," she said. "The world is full of wackos. Unfortunately, there are some very smart wackos who are very successful. You've got to be prepared for a certain amount of that."

I remember studying Tess intensely for a long moment. Then I posed a question in a format I knew she would appreciate. "Tell me something," I said, asking her to tally up the score on her job. "How would you rate your happiness at the personal-computer company on a scale from one to ten?"

"Seven," she said, without a bit of hesitation.

"That's not bad," I replied.

And Tess agreed.

But what was the price of control? If I were to suggest to Tess, as I did from time to time in not so many words, that the price had been her marriage, she would have shaken her head back and forth in that deliberate and persistent way of hers and vehemently denied it.

One of the major things she wanted to get across, she made a point of telling me from the very first time we spoke, was that her family meant an awful lot to her. And indeed, from a lot of what she said and from what I was to come to observe, I couldn't help but agree.

She laughed when she told me about how she and Kevin had met; how she had disliked him so much when she worked for him at the minicomputer company that she specifically requested a transfer when she became aware of an opening in the department of the executive who eventually nurtured her career. She told me about how she had always known that Kevin wanted to ask her out; about how she accepted when she left his department and he finally did ask her, because she was so impressed that an executive of his stature would want to date her.

The dates continued until she agreed not only to marry him, but to leave the company in which she had worked so hard to advance and follow him to Springfield, Massachusetts, where he was sent to oversee the branch office.

The following year, when he was transferred back to Westboro and she entered the Business School, Tess told me that they bought their first house, which she said they "loved like a child." It was a little Cape that needed to be painted and stained but which didn't matter. They loved doing that type of work, because they saw it as a way to relax and be together.

They also loved to entertain, and even though Tess was knee deep in the rigors of her first year at the Business School, she still found time to throw little dinner parties for six or eight, or big Sunday afternoon get-togethers "to introduce our neighbors to the right to our neighbors to the left."

That interest was something that had continued even to this day, in their new home in Belmont, she said when we talked about her family life, and I was to get a first-hand feel for her flair for entertaining the following New Year's Eve, in 1981, when she invited my husband and me to a formal supper party.

For that event, Tess and Kevin had prepared the food them-selves. There was a sumptuous assortment of hors d'oeuvres, each one a picture and so memorable that the main course was almost an indulgence. They invited just the right mix of people: two men from the minicomputer company (where Kevin still worked) and their wives, a couple who were old friends, and us, presumably people they wanted to know better.

Tess's fondness for her family, was to become even more apparent as she continued to talk about the other things she and Kevin shared. There was the way she would come crashing home after four or five days on the road, refusing dinner on the airplane even though she was hungry and utterly exhausted, so that she could eat popcorn with Kevin. "Whenever I'm exhausted—popcorn!" she declared.

Then there were the vacations they loved to take, to the islands in the winter, just the two of them, and in the summer with Chris to the home they were building on the Cape. She had softened from the moment she mentioned her son at our first interview. "I think you learn so much being a parent," she had sighed.

Then she had said that Chris would be entering kindergarten that fall at an exclusive private boys' school that she and Kevin had taken pains to select. She had rolled her eyes when she discussed the tuition and fees but I could tell that she didn't mind. They had just gone to buy his uniform, she continued affectionately, a royal blue blazer and tie, such proper attire for so little a boy.

But even as Tess spoke about her family with an affection that seemed genuine, I couldn't help but sense that undercurrent of defensiveness that had cut like a knife through both of our interviews. And I couldn't help but see in it another side of the truth about her feelings for Kevin in particular.

There was the way she had told me, no sooner than our first few moments together at the restaurant, that she wanted to make two or three million. She had uttered those words with a haughty little lift of her chin, and shortly thereafter, she had made a point of telling me about how her goals differed from Kevin's.

In the confession that had astonished me, she had explained that he had failed so miserably on the assignment in Springfield that he just "never surfaced again" at the computer company; that she on the other hand, had begun earning more money than he as early as two years into her first post–Business School job.

That was difficult for both of them to deal with, she continued, her eyes downcast and worrisome, until they both learned to accept the fact that her career had taken off while his had plateaued, and to revel in the good points of such a marriage.

As she described what she meant by the good points, she seemed to click into gear. She spoke as if she were reading from a script and in a tone of voice that struck me as superior, as a parent might sound when talking about a child, a teacher when discussing a student. "Kevin's goals are partly within himself," she began. "He is interested in seeing our son develop emotionally, intellectually. He is interested in supporting me in my career. In other words, his goals are sixty percent personal, forty percent professional"—and a bit too hastily, she added—"and I don't mean to make that eighty-twenty."

For a long while she talked about how Kevin had assumed the role of what she called the "primary" parent. It was he who brought the boy to and from the babysitter's; he who washed and fed and dressed Chris for the three-, four-, five-day stretches that she was on the road. After all, she emphasized, Kevin didn't travel —he didn't travel well at all! she exclaimed—and she traveled all of the time on her job.

The point that was to emerge from the way Tess talked about her husband, however, wasn't to become apparent to me until I interviewed Kevin midway through my six sessions with Tess in late September. She had to break for a business trip after our fourth night together and Kevin was going to be available, so it was agreed that I should talk to him before completing my interview with Tess.

The point, moreover, was to emerge quite by surprise, and only at the very end of my evening with Kevin. Throughout most of our time together, he had spoken rather aimlessly and in excruciating detail about his childhood and adolescence, his career at the minicomputer maker, and his life with Tess and Chris, and I remember beginning to grow more than a touch restless. But toward the end of the evening, in the same little study where I had been interviewing Tess and as much in an effort to bring my conversation with Kevin to a close as to elicit information, I remember casually asking whether he thought there were any problems in his marriage.

"Sure, every marriage has problems," Kevin replied, and when he spotted the look of astonishment on my face, he laughed softly. Then he explained, very calmly and evenly, that their biggest problem was the virtual lack of any sex life, and for a split second I thought he was joking until I began to put together the pieces. The problem had started in earnest the year Tess returned to the Business School, he said. The very year, I found myself thinking, that she had taken that huge psychological leap—from being in constant conflict about which came first in her life, her work or her marriage, to knowing without question that her work did.

Nor had the situation ever gotten better, Kevin continued, and at that point, he seemed terribly sad and a touch more resigned than he may have wanted to let on. "Periodically, I do things to rekindle her interest," he said. "I'm sensitive to the clothes she likes on me, to the right hairstyles. I've suggested that we send Chris away for a weekend. The ideal solution would be more private time. Shut out the world! I'd love for us to get lost in each other!"

Tess's response was that such solutions were impractical—she didn't see Chris enough as it was, Kevin said, which was only to be expected. The problem was inherent in the way they had chosen to live their lives, he explained, as a couple with two careers, hers an especially high-powered one with her twelve-hour days and days at a stretch on the road. There weren't even little slivers of time to sandwich between all of that. "It's hard for any woman in business to do anything but turn off thoughts of sex," Kevin said. "The highs and lows come from the job, not from personal relationships!"

Then he sighed, stretched out as he was on the black leather sofa in almost a semitrance, and I was speechless. With one simple comment, he had identified the problem that had hovered menacingly around all of the comments Tess had made about her marriage.

I remember asking Tess, the next night we talked, about what Kevin had said to me, pinning her to the wall when she tried to downplay the issue and insist that it didn't matter, as she did try to do.

"First, let's talk about available time," she began, quickly marshaling her defenses as she slowly began to realize what I now knew and what she hadn't wanted me to know. There was no time for sex. She was just going, going, going all of the time; putting in sixteen-hour days, eighteen-hour days.

When I made the obvious point that people make time for what they want, she conceded that perhaps she just wasn't interested in sex to the extent that it is assumed most people are. As for those assumptions, she added with a barely perceptible little snicker, "Where, pray tell, is it written that three point two times a week is normal?"

But as I had during her conversations about her husband, I felt as if this comment wasn't the full extent of her feelings about the matter. I remember pushing her further about her lack of interest, pushing her to such a degree that finally it was I who lost control of the exchange. She refused to capitulate. In no uncertain terms and in a slow and measured tone of voice, she wanted to make clear to me what she considered to be the most important aspect of her life.

"Work is the most fundamental, most basic thing in life," she said. Then with a flourish she added, "It can be the greatest impetus, the greatest facilitator of personal growth!"

So for the time being, it was Kevin to whom I had to turn for the truth about Tess's life. As he lay there that evening in a semitrance, he became silent for a long moment. Then he made one last comment. "I'd love to have the time to know how to really please her," he said. "Maybe someday we will."

Four weeks after I talked with Tess, on a Saturday night in late October, she called to tell me that she had been fired from the personal-computer company. She wanted to know whether I knew, from my contacts at the newspaper, what other computer companies in the area were looking for sales managers.

My first reaction was surprise that she had thought to follow up with me. None of the other five women I had interviewed for a second time ever had. My second was to feel sorry for her, knowing as I alone could the premium she placed on her work. "Sure, sure, Tess," I said as I scrambled to run down my list of contacts.

As she continued to speak, however, pouring out the story of what had happened in big bursts of narrative, I began to believe that my sympathy was ill-placed. Things like this happen from time to time in business, she was saying. She understood that they were more likely to happen in the type of environment she had chosen —an entrepreneurial venture that by definition had to be volatile and run by highly unpredictable people.

What had happened over the previous several weeks, she explained, was that the three vice-presidents whom Kip had recruited finally had gotten so fed up with his attempts to control everything that they had decided to band together against him. They spent their afternoons in long lunches plotting his overthrow. And in the course of doing that, her boss decided to fire her, Tess explained, if only to have someone to blame for the marketing plan he never wrote while otherwise occupied.

Then she said that she had gone over to Kip's house just that morning to find out from his perspective why she had been fired, and at that point, she began to laugh. She wanted me to picture the scene. There was Kip in a pair of bermuda shorts, standing over a chopping block in his kitchen. "He cooked me breakfast," Tess said with a little giggle.

Kip told her that he couldn't tell her why she had been fired. That had been her boss's decision, and he had no right to interfere. But then he posed a question that took her completely by surprise, because it showed how unaware he was of what was going on. "Can you give me any advice?" he asked.

"So I said to him, 'Kip, you may be the rich kid on the block, but it's a street-corner society. You've got three vice-presidents sitting there with their arms crossed saying, "Pass the salt!" You need to do something to break up that cartel.'"

She was speaking with such enthusiasm by that point in our telephone conversation that I knew I could do nothing but sit back and enjoy the show, as she so obviously was, and as she so obviously had at every point in her career. No, my sympathy for Tess was best reserved for that other aspect of her life, which we were to discuss again over lunch the following February, in 1982.

The lunch was Tess's idea. She had called right after the first of the year to suggest it, and to tell me that she was going back to work. She had gotten nine job offers and had chosen a medium-sized maker of computerized medical equipment.

There was an unmistakable hint of spring in the air as we made our way over to the Magic Pan at the Faneuil Hall marketplace. The freshness in the air seemed to complement the way Tess was feeling about her life those days. Her new job wasn't the step up to vice-president that she had been hoping for, she explained. But she was directing a much larger sales force and the money was at least as good: a base of $60,000, plus a much bigger commission, which meant that she could easily top $100,000 that year.

Then, too, there was the fact that she had decided to go into therapy, she said. She had begun seeing a psychiatrist the previous fall, just after we had completed our interviews, partly because she had decided that she wanted to work on a number of issues that I had raised about her life. But the real trigger had been that she had met a man during the course of her job search, a corporate recruiter. He had helped her find her job, so there were a lot of things about him that appealed to her.

"Including," she said, slowing the pace of her voice deliberately, as if to signal that I should pay special attention to what she was about to say next, "a strong physical attraction."

I felt a rush as Tess made that comment, and I was speechless. So I had been right after all, I found myself thinking. No matter how much she had tried to convince me to the contrary, the loss of her sexual self, the price that she ultimately had had to pay for control of her life, did matter to her. "I guess I wasn't willing to admit the truth of what you brought up," she continued, a touch hesitantly.

"I can understand that," I replied, cutting her short. Then I explained that I had always felt that we shared a special rapport. We had both come from dying northeastern factory towns, for example, and we had had to make it out by sheer persistence, for what else did we have? Certainly not wealth or an exceptional degree of beauty or brains.

I caught Tess's look of anxious empathy. "But we aren't alike in all ways," I added hastily, knowing that I wouldn't have been able to pay the price she had paid for control of her life. Yet as I thought about what she had done, I couldn't bring myself to criticize her either. I had interviewed far too many women in the class who had lost that fight, and they, too, seemed to have paid a price. My next step was to determine what the price had been for a woman who seemed to have lost control over her career—Martha Davis.

7.

MARTHA: Femininity, Overexpectations, and the Loss of Control

Over the course of my research for this project, one finding that struck me as among the most surprising was that such a large percentage of the women of the class of 1975 appeared to be ambivalent about their careers, or had actually made the decision to cut back, tone down, or, in some cases, leave the work force entirely. I began noticing this pattern as early as the fall of 1980, when I was conducting my first interviews, and by the time I completed my investigation a year later, I was shocked to have to conclude that fully two fifths of the group fit this pattern.

This finding came as a shock primarily because it ran counter to what is presumed about graduates of the Harvard Business School: that they are hard-charging go-getters intent on nothing less than the "fast track" to the top. While this image could be said to be trite and stereotypical, it is also one that is buttressed with objective evidence from the Business School itself. A greater percentage of its graduates achieve senior positions in major corporations than alumni of most other schools, according to the Business School's own statistics. And judged by the growing interest in courses about small business and entrepreneurship, another large segment of its students aim for a stake in smaller concerns or expect to start their own companies.

Like the women who were ambitious for their careers, those who were ambivalent or frankly not ambitious didn't appear to have anything tangible in common. They were just as likely to have come from a poor or lower-middle-class background as they were to have come from an upper-middle-class or wealthy one. They were just as likely to be single or divorced as married or married with children; just as likely to be working for a corporation as a nonprofit concern, to be earning a six-figure salary as a more modest sum.

In one of the cases I found to be most remarkable, for example, a lovely young woman with long red hair that swept to her waist held the impressive-sounding title of director of financial strategy for a major midwestern bank. She worked directly for the executive vice-president, the third man in line for the top, and he thought so highly of her work that he had been trying for years to convince her to accept a job with line responsibility for a small segment of the business. That would put her in the running for senior positions at the bank in the years ahead, he had said.

But whenever he approached her with such an offer, she would refuse, she said during our interview. She explained that she didn't want a job in which she would have to run something, in which she would have responsibility for the bottom line. She didn't want to be a "king," she said, which is what a person has to want if he or she wants to run something. Rather she preferred the type of job she currently had, the staff position of writing research reports for her boss. She preferred being, as she put it, "an 'assistant to' some powerful man."

This woman intrigued me to such an extent that I had hoped to make her one of the major characters in this book, and I had even gone to her suburban home to begin my second interview. But that day, a cloudy Saturday afternoon in the fall of 1981, the man she was living with greeted me at the door with the pronouncement that he wouldn't cooperate. Then he said that I would have to leave by 4:00 P.M. At precisely 4:00 P.M., even though she and I hadn't finished, he took me by the elbow and ushered me out of the door, while she stood by helplessly, not uttering a word.

A feeling of helplessness, a sense that they could do little to control their lives, did indeed seem to characterize the women who fit this pattern. While it wasn't always apparent from their stories per se, I would often spot it in the way they chose to tell those stories. There was the way Alexis Drake, the Baker Scholar whom Phoebe Holstrom had scorned for having dropped out of the work force, had tried to rationalize her decision, for example. It didn't do any good to strive in a career, she had said with a shake of her great mane of chestnut-brown hair, because business wasn't about to accept women in anything but menial staff jobs. Then there was the way Tess Beckett's two friends had spoken about their lives—the lack of joy in Maureen Graham's voice when she talked about her infant daughter, the distinct edge in Polly Drascovitch's throughout our entire interview.

To be fair, a certain segment of the women who fit this pattern had chosen very deliberately to deemphasize their careers and to live primarily through and for their families, and they seemed happy with their choice. But despite their overall satisfaction, I couldn't help but detect an ever-so-slight touch of envy when they spoke about their more ambitious classmates. In one instance, a short, chunky woman who had just relocated from New York to Ann Arbor, Michigan, so that her husband could accept a top post at the University of Michigan, had exclaimed during our interview, "That kind of ambition! Where does it come from?" She was referring to Mary Pat Horner, who had been in her section at the Business School and who she felt was among the most ambitious.

The woman had shaken her head as she spoke. She herself couldn't be that way, she said. She had always known that she would put her husband's career first, as she had done recently when she had relocated with nary a question in her mind. She had quit her job with a nonprofit concern back east, easily landed another in Ann Arbor, and there she expected to remain. She saw her career as something to fit around the needs of her husband and the two children she wanted to have. And while she sometimes wished she were as ambitious as women like Mary Pat, she told me that she suspected she'd be happier in the long run. "What does one do it all for anyway?" she said, turning to face me as she summed up, her plain-as-a-peanut face oddly in synch with the hustle and bustle of the Italian restaurant she had chosen for our meeting. "For family! For friends!"

The feeling on the part of these women, even those who were among the happiest with their choice, that they had somehow given up stemmed in part from the expectations the Business School had for its graduates, I have come to believe. In a more compelling way, however, it also stemmed from the expectations the women themselves had for their careers. The majority of the women in the class of 1975 had first gone to work prior to entering the Business School, in the early part of the 1970's, when barriers to women's entry into management and the professions had begun to crumble. They hadn't known the kind of discrimination faced by past generations of women. By the time they graduated from the Business School, armed with a few years of on-the-job experience and their new degrees, they assumed that access meant acceptance and had expectations for their careers that were unrealistic at best, damaging at worst. And nowhere were such expectations more evident than during my first interview with Martha Davis, the woman who had, in the Palm Court of the Plaza in New York, uttered a phrase that would haunt me as few had throughout the entire course of my research: "Bleak . . . so bleak."

That Martha's expectations were out of line with reality wasn't something that she herself could believe, or indeed, even acknowledge. She would speak, as she did sometime later, of "unrealized expectations," goals for her career that she would have to forfeit to devote her energies to the other aspects of her life— her marriage, for example, and the child she was about to adopt. And that her expectations were excessive wasn't something that I was able to accept upon first meeting her either, my broader perspective of being able to see her in relation to the others in the class notwithstanding.

For on the surface, she seemed to be the epitome of today's successful young businesswoman—she with her career at the prestigious venture-capital group of the major national bank, her marriage to a rising young cardiologist, and her prospective role of mother. Then there was the way she had just assumed that all of this was her due, rather than anything for which she need be grateful. Her attitude was perhaps indicative of her background, one in which both daughters were expected to become professionals; her older sister, for example, was just completing her residency in pediatrics. But it also could have stemmed from her own academic orientation: graduation from one of the finest universities in the country—Brandeis—with a double major in two demanding subjects, and her degree from the Business School, where she had done very well.

The circumstances surrounding Martha's marriage to Luke Davis were equally remarkable. For no other woman in the class was able, it appeared to me, to establish a relationship of such emotional intensity at such a young age. She and Luke had met during her senior year at Brandeis on a blind date arranged by her roommate. They dated off and on over the next several years and were married in 1973, the year Luke graduated from medical school. They survived the rigors of being married during Luke's residency and her tenure at the Business School, to say nothing of their early years in two demanding careers.

Their emotional bond was so intense that neither would have considered even the briefest affair. There had been a look of hurt in Martha's eyes when I had posed that specific question, even though she was the first to admit that given their extensive periods apart, they both had had ample opportunity. During her first year at the Business School, for example, Luke had spent six weeks in Chicago, working with the cardiology group he would eventually join on a type of treatment that wasn't being offered at Mass General. Martha could have joined him for a few weeks over semester break. But she had insisted on staying on in Boston just to prove she could be independent, she said with a soft smile, admitting that all she had proven was that she missed Luke. Then there was the two-month period she spent in Boston, several years into her career with the venture-capital group at the bank, which was something else entirely, because the opportunity had been one that she couldn't pass up.

From Luke's perspective, the marriage was equally unique, although not without some problems, which became apparent when we spoke over breakfast at The Ritz-Carlton in Chicago, the day after my second interview with Martha in January 1982. At our interview, Luke underscored a characteristic about his wife that had also come to my attention. That was what I perceived to be Martha's indecisiveness, which in turn, Luke noted, led to a discontent that had permeated many of the stages of her life. At Brandeis, for example, when offers from the top forecasting firms began pouring in and she wasn't even sure she wanted a career in economics, she decided to work for a few years instead, doing market research for the advertising agency. Then, four years later, she decided to enroll at the Business School, which meant that she wouldn't have to make a decision about her career for another two years. Once she graduated and the offers again began pouring in, however, she was so confused that, she could now admit, she was almost relieved to have had to accept the position in Chicago because of Luke's career.

When Luke first spoke about his wife's discontent, he attributed the problem to stress. He reminded me that what they were trying to do, which was the almost-impossible task of building two careers, a marriage, and a family, was so inherently difficult that stress was inevitable. But when I asked him if such problems had ever made him want to cheat on his wife, he was as hurt as Martha had been when I had asked the same of her. His straight blond hair fell soberly across his brow, making him look like a young Dennis Wilson during the early days of the Beach Boys. "We got married for emotional reasons," he said quietly. "It's kind of romantic to have married the way we did, when you're young and not jaded, and to your first real sweetheart . . . that was good."

The contradiction between image and reality in Martha's life was to persist throughout our second interview in January 1982, a year after we had first spoken at the Plaza. I flew out to Chicago in a blizzard, and when I first spotted Martha walking through the door of the dramatic modern hotel where I was staying and where we had agreed to meet, I was once again taken by her. She appeared to be a foil for the weather I had left behind. She looked even more stunning than I remembered from the year before. She was wearing a beaver-brown coat with a fox collar that swept around her neck like a statement, a broad-brimmed hat, and high leather boots with little buttons up the sides.

She smiled when she spotted me sitting on the couch in the far corner, and with a flick of her wrist, she gave me a cheery wave. But from the moment she began to speak, I could sense the undercurrent of discouragement. The first point she made was that she and Luke had, in fact, adopted a baby boy, whom they named Ben, and that she had taken the leave the bank had offered. She supposed she wanted to do that all along, she said. "And the one thing I absolutely refused to do," she added nervously, bringing up the subject of her career without my even having had to ask, "was to think about my future." Then she laughed shortly. "Didn't want to get anxious."

One decision she did come to during her time off, however, was to leave the venture-capital group, and for the next several minutes we talked about why she hadn't ever liked it. She hadn't ever been perceived as outstanding, she began, which wouldn't have been so bad had it not been for the fact that she was bored with the job and didn't even like the people she worked with. She was assigned at first to an executive who made it clear that he didn't want to work with a woman, and she had neither the confidence nor the experience to handle the rebuff as well as she might have. Once she became an assistant vice-president, she did most of the research on a new industry the group was considering investing in, which meant endless hours in the library poring over reams of statistics. She was working for an executive who was superb, and she did exceptionally well. But still she wasn't happy. "All systems were go, and I didn't like it. I hated to go to work in the morning. I was miserable."

That confused her to such an extent that she took six weeks off in 1979 to think about her future and probably would have left then had it not been for the assignment in Boston. That assignment involved working with the senior executives of some of the biggest companies in Boston and the top executives of the bank itself to determine the feasibility of investing in joint ventures between Fortune 500 companies and fledglings in the high-tech industry. It was just the type of work she wanted to do. "It was far reaching! Big stuff! Interesting stuff!" she explained, hitting each of those phrases with a burst of delight in her voice. She was in Boston, of course, where she had wanted to be ever since the Business School, and she was able to meet all of her friends for dinner and the theater. "I have more friends in Boston than in any other city," she chimed. The firm let her take her two-week vacation two months into the assignment, and she was able to meet Luke for a wonderful vacation on the Maine coast.

She leaned back in her chair as she savored her memories. "The Boston project was fun. I was managing it. I was master of my own time. I liked the people in the Boston office, and I was away from the Chicago executives. I just don't like them very much. They wouldn't laugh, which made me nervous. I mean, I really loved working in Boston with people who were funny and knew how to be irreverent. I was working with the top executives in the firm, and they would laugh and make fun of themselves. One of them forgot the name of one of our client's most important executives, and in the cab coming back, the other said, 'Jake, you screwed it up again!' Well, you'd be embarrassed to say that to someone in Chicago."

The decision she made during her time off, she continued, as we sat catercorner from each other in the lobby of the hotel, was to leave not only the venture-capital group but the banking field altogether. Not only was the career impractical for a woman with a small child, she explained, but she had pretty much decided that she wanted to work only part time. So she decided to make use of her background in economics and try for a career with an economics-forecasting firm, which she suspected would be more flexible about hours.

That fall, she began talking to all of the forecasting firms in Chicago and had already received several job offers, including one from a prestigious group affiliated with the University of Chicago. The firms were delighted with a candidate who had banking experience plus credentials from top schools.

But the more Martha spoke about her decision to change careers—in big gulps of narrative, lowering her voice to such an extent whenever she came to a point she considered important that I could barely hear her—the more I began to accept the reality of her life. The first point she made was that her decision wouldn't in any way alter what she hoped to be doing—and at this point, she used a phrase that was one of her staples—long-term. That had always been and still was "foreign economic structure," she said.

As I tried to figure out how juggling data for a forecasting firm would relate to work that somehow involved international economics, Martha began to explain. As an economist, she'd be working with exporting companies that had to adhere to government regulations when doing business abroad. "So the economics work will be on those issues where foreign economic structure comes to bear," she said with utmost seriousness. When I cut in and said I didn't understand, she was flustered for a brief moment before regaining her composure and reiterating essentially the same point. "When a company wants to do business overseas, there are certain regulations about currency transactions," she said. "You have to make all sorts of disclosures and, you know, adhere to regulations. As an economist, I'll be able to see how those regulations affect decision making in the company."

When I suggested, as I knew I had to, that as an economist working with those currency transactions, she would be making very few decisions about them or about how a company could best use that information, she replied, "No, but I'll be watching the international situation."

Then a dreamlike expression crossed her face, one that I was to see from time to time when she talked about her career. "And I'll be writing articles for economics journals. That's part of the economics profession. Then I can build a reputation as an individual and develop a career that allows me to make recommendations on the international level."

I remember asking her, at one point, where she saw herself at the end of her career. She leaned back in her chair, a look of contentment on her face. "Where would I like to be at age sixty?" she said, rephrasing my question. "I would like to have had a long career in international trade, culminating as an adviser to the president of a multinational corporation, someone who was having a real impact on international economic structure, formulation of the decisions that control trade relations. That's what interests me, really foreign trade. So my pie-in-the-sky dream has always been to have a career that allows me to make those kind of contributions."

Finally, I asked her which of the three forecasting firms she planned to join. She replied that she had been all set to make her decision that fall, but over Thanksgiving vacation with her family, she began to worry about the effect working full time might have on her young son. That was when she decided that she didn't want anything more than a part-time job.

So she went back to the firms, and to her surprise, two of the three agreed, including the group at the University of Chicago. The principals explained that they had to make such concessions to get the top people they wanted, since more and more were apt to be women with family responsibilities.

For a brief moment, I suppose I thought all had fallen in place for Martha. She would have her new career, in a prestigious organization if she so chose, and the scheduling would even permit ample time with her family. But at that point, she seemed to become discouraged in the way that she first had when we had talked at the Plaza about relocation. The fact was that she hadn't decided which firm to join, she confessed, clearly bewildered now, which she said was so funny for "someone who was so good at making decisions."

I remember teasing her gently at that point. "You mean I'll have to go back to Boston without knowing which firm you're going to join?" I asked. But I saw no reason to puncture what I was beginning to believe were fantasies on her part. So it wasn't until the following morning, during my breakfast with Luke, that I finally let my own opinion be known. It came in the form of a rhetorical question to Luke that caused him to shake his head knowingly. "Tell me something," I said. "What is it precisely that Martha wants?"

The reason for Martha's ambivalence came together at one particularly illuminating moment toward the end of my conversation with Luke that morning. We had been talking, for the better part of our time together, about the decision that lay ahead for Martha in the next year —which forecasting firm she should join —and the major point Luke wanted to make was that this time he wasn't going to tell her what he thought she should do.

The last time he did, in 1975, the year she graduated from the Business School and he completed his residency at Mass General, and he suggested that she take the job in the Chicago office of the bank so that he could work for the cardiology group there, the price had been considerable discontent on Martha's part. As Luke talked about this period in their lives, I began to see that this was the chief way in which he differed from his wife. He brought a rational dimension to the decisions he made in a way that she could not, or at least not to the same degree, I found myself thinking. Whereas he had joined the cardiology group not only because he was emotionally committed to practicing there but also because he felt confident that he could do what had to be done, which was to pioneer a new type of treatment for cardiac patients, she hadn't ever felt confident about her abilities in business.

That thought shocked me for a brief moment, until Luke began to explain. The fact was that she had always needed constant reassurance and approval. "She always rises to the occasion," Luke added hastily, tempering what might have otherwise sounded like criticism, but she couldn't operate as autonomously as he had always done. Which was probably why she hadn't really been able to make any headway in the career she said she wanted. There wasn't any well-defined career ladder when it came to jobs that in some way involved "foreign economic structures." Rather, one gropes toward such goals by taking advantage of opportunities that don't seem like opportunities, which was what he had been trying to tell her to do for the past several years. If she wanted to be considered for a post that involved international trade, she should get herself a job in the international department of a major company or bank and get to know people in the field, he had been saying. "But she always gets back to the fact that that's small time, and the people there deal with mundane issues while her interest is in economics on the international level."

The fact was that Martha put a much greater premium than he ever had on the importance of patrons and sponsors and mentors in one's career, Luke continued, on a slightly different tack now, which he said had enabled her to flourish at Brandeis. "In all of her life, I'm sure that was her happiest time," he said, explaining that at Brandeis "a lot of high-level people responded to her and thought highly of her and had her doing all these things on projects." When he said that, I was struck by how closely her experience at Brandeis seemed to parallel that only other time in her life during which she had been happy, the two months she spent working on the assignment in Boston. What had been so seductive about that assignment, she had said again and again, not always in so many words, was that she was working with the "top people": the senior officers of the biggest companies.

"She has always gone at every point in her life for the prestige route," Luke explained. Then he told me he suspected she'd join the nationally renowned forecasting group affiliated with the university rather than the other firm.

The bottom line was that she didn't know what she wanted, even at this juncture in her career, Luke said, summing up now, and this point was to become even more evident the more he talked about his position on the issue that she felt was holding her back: relocation. In fact, he had meant what he said about moving for her when she finished Business School and he his residency, he began. He had been all set to go three years into their careers if she had gotten a job in Boston that she really wanted. But they had never gotten to the point of discussing the matter because she had decided to stay with the venture-capital group to work on the Boston-based job, which was considered a temporary assignment. They were at another juncture now, and he would be willing to go. The cardiology group had finished its work on the project that had interested Luke, he was becoming known in the field, and there were plenty of opportunities for him in Boston.

"So periodically, when this Boston issue reaches a crescendo, I think, Hell, let's go to Boston," he said with pique in his voice. "It's not that big an issue. I can start over in Boston. I mean, there are nice things about Boston."

Only she wouldn't ever ask him to do that, he added, this time with softness rather than exasperation. For that was another thing he understood about his wife. She wasn't one to put her needs ahead of those of the people she loved. Luke's expression broadened into a smile as he mentioned that just the previous Thanksgiving, for example, when they had been scheduled to leave for a long weekend in New York and her sister had developed a problem that he considered quite minor, Martha had been all in a tizzy. She wouldn't leave Chicago until she was assured that her sister was going to be fine.

In the same vein, she wouldn't leave Chicago for a job in Boston unless she was assured that he, too, would be fine, Luke continued. And that was what she couldn't be sure of. She saw Chicago as the city that was his, the place where he had begun to make a name for himself in his career. "She wants me to say, 'Let's move,' " he continued. "She wants me to force the issue, and I haven't done that."

As Luke made this point, I was struck by the way he seemed to switch moods, from pique to warmth and back to pique again. And it occurred to me that the reason for Martha's ambivalence cut deeper than the insecurity to which Luke had alluded. It cut so deep that it was the very factor that made her like many of the other women in her class with whom she ultimately had so much in common, all of those women—two fifths of the class, to be precise—most of whom had neither her sophistication nor her style.

The reason for her ambivalence could be found in what she really thought her husband was saying, I found myself thinking. To be sure, he was telling her in words that he would relocate for her, but his gestures were saying something else entirely. His smile of approval came when he spoke of the way in which she would sacrifice for others, presumably he being one of those people for whom she would.

I remember telling Luke at that point in our interview that Martha would find it far more difficult to ask him to move than he had ever had in asking the same of her, for an even more fundamental reason than the one he had outlined. In making the request of her, he would be perceived as merely doing what any man should do: making the best possible decision about the work he would be doing to support a family. Should she make the same request of him, however, she would be taking an extraordinary risk. She would be taking a step that involved going against what was expected of her as a woman—crossing a sex barrier, if you will.

I told Luke that one of the women I planned to include in my book had done just that, and that the consequences had been enormous. "Unlike Martha, she has no sexual interest in her husband," I said, as the face of Tess Beckett flashed across my mind. Then I explained that for Tess, that had led to a loss of respect for her husband.

My point stopped Luke cold. "Well, that's it," he said, in a tone that suggested both relief and sudden recognition. As he began to comment, I, too, found myself coming to a better understanding of Martha's ambivalence. I could see now that what was at stake for her was nothing less than what had brought her together with Luke so long ago and had kept them committed throughout all of those many years: the intensity of their emotional bond.

"I think that is fundamental to why she hasn't called the chips and gone to Boston," Luke said. "She is concerned that if we got into a situation in which there wasn't some reasonable balance between my status and her status, my level and her level, our marriage would start to deteriorate. She doesn't want to lose esteem for me, to become the 'man' in the family. I think she's worried that if she went to Boston she would flourish and star, and I would be kind of lost, and eventually that would lead to the loss of respect for me and the end of our marriage."

In the weeks and months after I had interviewed Martha Davis in Chicago, I began to wonder if I was being too hard on her. Being objective, I had to admit that there were times during our conversation that she appeared to be delighted with her life and happy—or happier at least than many of the women in the class who were single-minded about their careers. That Friday in Chicago, for example, when we were talking in the lobby of the hotel, Martha had alluded to a luncheon she had to attend, so we agreed to continue our interview later in the afternoon at her condominium. When we did, she appeared to be the picture of contentment as she settled across from me in her living room.

The condominium had been Luke's idea, Martha said. It was located on the top floor of a sleek new high rise in one of Chicago's best downtown neighborhoods, and Luke had insisted that they buy it the year they moved to Chicago, which had appalled her at the time. They were going to be in Chicago for only a few years, and at work she was having enormous problems with the officer who headed her first project.

But Luke had fallen in love with the condominium and felt it would be a good investment, and looked at from that point of view, she couldn't disagree. "For a doctor, my husband is very good with investments," she said with obvious pride in her voice. She giggled a little when she told me that story, leaning back on her sleek cream-colored couch as she surveyed her living room, a look of approval on her face. The living room, with its chrome and glass and the dramatic piece of modern sculpture she had just purchased, was the site of a recent dinner party that she and Luke had given for her parents, a family reunion that she had planned in honor of a visit from her mother's sister who lived in Canada and hadn't been to Chicago in years. Martha recalled that event warmly and gestured to the door that led to the ultramodern kitchen. She and Luke had cooked the meal themselves, even though it would have been so much easier to have it catered, just to show how much they cared.

Little Ben crawled about as Martha and I talked that afternoon. Not quite eight months old, he already had begun to crawl and seemed delighted with his newfound skill. He scampered blithely over piles of toys strewn about. And whenever Martha would glance at her child or hold out her arms to intercept him, I was reminded of how she had spoken about her time with her son the previous summer.

She hadn't expected to enjoy child-rearing as much as she had, Martha said, especially since the pace was so different from what she had been used to for the previous five years. But there she was, spending day in and day out at home alone with an infant, doing things like shopping for groceries, cooking dinner for Luke every night ("I don't think we ever had regular dinners before," she said, that fact apparently striking her as curious for a brief moment), and having casual lunches with her friends, many of whom were also at home with their first babies. The time had passed far more quickly than she would have expected, what with family and friends coming to see the baby for the first several months and staying overnight. "You know how it is when you have house-guests," she said.

Then there was little Ben himself. Watching her son grow and develop had become more fascinating as the months went on, she said. "Just the other day, for example," she exclaimed with a little lilt in her voice that said as much as her words, "we were practicing all of the words that began with *B*—baby, bottle, bird—and he knew!"

Later that afternoon, when Martha began talking about the women who had been her classmates at the Business School, I got a sense of her contentment from another perspective. The major point she wanted to make was that she couldn't see herself at age thirty-five with no husband, no children, as was the case for so many of the others, even if that would have meant that she had gone further in her career.

As Martha spoke, I thought about Elizabeth Connor, who fit that description, and I remember thinking how different Elizabeth appeared to be when I viewed her from Martha's perspective than she had when I viewed her from, say, Suzanne Sheehan's. I had always felt that Suzanne's admiration for Elizabeth—subliminally at least, for she hadn't ever made the point—stemmed from her perception of Elizabeth as the feminine woman she would never be. Yet when I compared her with Martha, a woman who had chosen, in the final analysis, to live primarily through and for her family, Elizabeth appeared to be anything but feminine. She appeared to be curiously sexless.

I had to smile when I thought about that, because there had been a time during my interview with Elizabeth in Philadelphia when the frosty woman who had tried to stand me up for our meeting had broken down and begun to talk about the way she really felt about her life. "Sometimes I think I'm a neuter," she had said, softly and sadly, catching me by surprise when she mouthed those words, for that very thought had crossed my mind briefly at one point during our interview. For my own perception of Elizabeth, from the moment she had dashed into the lobby of the hotel where we had met for brunch, was that she wasn't so much a woman who was interested in the personal gratification of the corporate climb. Rather, I saw her as a brilliant idealist who worked in an effort to help humanity, a woman who might have been a nun in a past generation.

But much later in our conversation, even Elizabeth Conner had spoken with emotion about what she considered to be the central problem in her life. What with all of the time she spent on the road, she had said, there wasn't any chance to develop what she thought she might like to have at this stage of her life, which was a relationship. All of her friends who were single felt the same way, she had added, although none would admit it, as she herself would not. They would lie and say they were staying single for the sake of their careers. And then she had made a comment that moved me in a way that few had during the entire course of my research for this book. "Sometimes I think of myself as a wonderful surprise package," she said with a burst of enthusiasm that seemed to be the verbal equivalent of her ripping off her dowdy clothes. "There's the way I seem to be on the outside. But there's the way I could be if someone dared untie me. . . ."

The comment said as much about Martha as it did about Elizabeth, I suppose. And for a moment, as Martha and I spoke in the living room of her condominium, I found myself thinking, Is there anything so bad about the life she has chosen, centered as it is around her husband and child? Yet I couldn't accept that line of thinking unequivocally, because I sensed that her decision hadn't been an entirely joyful—or free—one.

The decision to adopt a child had been primarily hers, Martha explained, which was precisely the opposite of the way her decision to marry Luke had evolved. When they discovered that they couldn't have children of their own, Luke concluded it might be just as well, given their careers. But Martha was determined and took the lead in filing the papers.

At that time, she was just finishing the assignment in Boston, and she had once again been at a juncture in her career. Just like all of the other times in the past, she was getting more offers than she knew what to do with, so many offers that she felt as if they were pressing in on her. The assignment in Boston had been such a success that the venture-capital group wanted her to handle a similar assignment in Atlanta, which would have meant several months in that city. She was six to twelve months away from being promoted to vice-president at the venture-capital group, which would give her her choice of assignments in Chicago. Finally, there was the standing offer from the bank, which had pretty much existed ever since her graduation from the Business School, to work at headquarters in Boston rather than in the regional office in Chicago.

Yet, for all of these options, she knew in her heart that she really didn't have any options at all. For she had to pay a price for what mattered most to her, which was her marriage to Luke, and that price was a loss of control over her own career. She had known that, down deep, ever since they had moved to Chicago and bought the condominium that Luke had argued was just a good investment.

"I was depressed and down on myself and down on, well, the situation at the venture-capital group. And I was trying to figure some things out. I don't know if I could blame it in part on the decision to move here. But really I'd lost control over certain things. I'd moved, hadn't any control over that. We bought the condominium somewhat over my objections, although I'd also agreed to it at the same time. But I was feeling more and more trapped in Chicago. . . ."

The same thing was happening in the fall of 1979, when she was finishing work on the assignment she had so enjoyed in Boston and saw herself going back once again to the city that stood, as Luke had observed during our breakfast, as a symbol of all she had lost.

Luke had smiled a little as he came to that part of his analysis of his wife's modus operandi. For the previous year, he had sometimes wondered why she had gotten so upset whenever he tried to do what he saw as necessary for facilitating their new status as working parents. In addition to their housekeeper, for example, he had hired a secretary to do their books and had arranged standing reservations for them every Thursday night at a comfortable neighborhood restaurant, all in an effort to eliminate as many tedious tasks as possible so that they would have time for their careers, their child, and each other. But Martha had protested. "She told me she thought I wanted to be 'Lord of the Manor,' " Luke said with a laugh.

So in the fall of 1979, when she knew she would have to return once again to Chicago, Martha had turned to the only aspect of her life over which she felt she had any mastery, I began to realize.

And in doing what she did, for the reason she chose to do it, she was acting in concert with what women had done for generations, and with what such a significant portion of the women in her own class at Harvard had done, their M.B.A. degrees and all that stood for notwithstanding. Speaking about it, she slipped here and there into the use of the pronoun *we,* but it was clear she was speaking from the perspective of her own feelings.

"I started realizing that all variables were fluid. Do we adopt a baby? Do we go to Boston? Do we go to Atlanta for me to work on another project? Do we stay in Chicago? Everything was getting so balled up that, finally, I said, 'Well, I really think the most important thing is adopting a child.' Frankly, I said, 'Once we have a child, things will fall in place. At least there's a given.'

"I kind of liked the idea that I could adapt the other things. Because Luke and I both agreed that when we did adopt a child, the child was going to be first. If I had a child who needed a great deal of emotional support, I would quit working for it. Since that was how we viewed having a child, I really didn't want to adopt a baby and start a new assignment two months later. I didn't want to go to Boston, bring Luke there, uproot him from his job, just for me to adopt a baby and then go part time somewhere. Finally, I just said, 'Screw it!' It really was a sense of, Well, there's one thing that I can control and that's when I adopt the baby. So let's just do it."

I never saw Martha Davis again after that Friday in Chicago. I remember thinking at one point that day, as afternoon slipped into evening and she kept talking as if she were beginning to enjoy herself, that perhaps we had begun to develop a rapport. But as we wound up the conversation, there was an awkward moment. I sensed that she thought I wanted to be invited to dinner, which she wasn't prepared to do. And so I reconsidered what was going on between us.

The thought occurred to me during my discussion with Luke at breakfast the following morning that the hiring of the housekeepers and the arranging for dinners out to ease the burdens of their hectic lives wasn't going to resolve the issues in this couple's lives. The thought occurred to me that perhaps there weren't any solutions at all, at least not with a woman who was as ambivalent as

Martha was about her career. For Luke had been especially attentive when I spoke about one of the women in Martha's class who had both a marriage she cared about as well as a full-fledged career. The reason that that woman had been able to have both had fascinated Luke. He had been skeptical at first and had challenged many of the points I made about her.

By the time we finished breakfast and parted in front of The Ritz in Chicago, however, it was clear that he had begun to understand the points I was trying to make and that we had achieved a certain rapport. Convinced, therefore, that I was on the right track, I thought back to my second interview a month before, over the Christmas holidays, with one of the few women in the class who had indeed managed both a marriage in which she was emotionally involved and an upwardly mobile career—Holly Lane Pfeiffer.

8.

HOLLY:
Unspoken
Perceptions

Whenever I would tell anyone about Holly Lane Pfeiffer, the woman who had been Suzanne Sheehan's roommate at the Business School and whom I had interviewed on that memorable evening at The Ritz-Carlton in Chicago, the individual invariably would ask whether or not she had any children. When I would reply that she had three, he or she would ask how old the children were. With smug satisfaction, for I knew what would happen next, I would say something like, "Oh, they're all small; they're all under five."

The comment would be enough to silence the inquirer. I could almost see the person visibly retreat into the sofa or chair, wherever he or she was sitting, hard pressed for anything further to say. As for myself, I would once again review the details of Holly's story, like a craftsman examining a piece of work one last time, just to make sure. I would check for the stone yet unturned, the loose end untied. Finding none, I would breathe a figurative sigh of relief. I had once again confirmed that Holly was for real and that her story, or at least my perception of it, was all that I found it to be when we first spoke at The Ritz.

For the most extraordinary thing about Holly, the woman who had rushed up to me in the thirteenth-floor lobby and stood squarely in front of me, her gesture the first little clue that she would have something significant to say, was that she, more than any of the others, had, to use that overworked and weary phrase, "it all." Not only did she have her three beautiful children, but she had her husband, Chuck, whom she was still, as Suzanne had put it, "crazy in love with," and her upwardly mobile career at the Dallas-based subsidiary of one of the biggest Fortune 100 companies in the country.

No one could appreciate more than I how truly extraordinary that was. I had spent the better part of a year and a half crisscrossing the country and elbowing my way into the hearts and souls of a group of women who, I had thought when I began my research, would have been able to provide insights into how precisely to do "it all," only to wonder whether any woman actually was. For the bottom line and one of the big surprises of my research was that very, very few, perhaps no more than a handful, had managed to coordinate all three facets of life in a way I would consider "meaningful." There were some who appeared to be doing that, of course, until one delved beneath the surface: the Tess Becketts of the class whose marriages were shams; the Martha Davises whose careers were less than they could have been.

The particulars of Holly's story were so extraordinary, in fact, that I came to regard that fact as one reason for people's skepticism whenever I spoke about her. Less idealistic perhaps than I had been when I began my research, people *knew*. They knew it wasn't as easy to combine a career and a family as I may have wanted to believe, and perhaps therefore had made it out to be.

Yet there appeared to be another reason for people's disbelief. The more I spoke with the women in the class, the more I came to believe that many wanted to cling to a set of assumptions about the married woman with children—a quagmire of, in the memorable words of one woman, "unspoken perceptions" about what she would or wouldn't do when she added a career to her traditional roles of wife and mother. Always, the assumptions boiled down to the belief that the married woman couldn't be as committed to her career, no matter what she said or did to the contrary, and as a result, wouldn't get as far as those whose energies weren't split.

This set of assumptions, I suppose, was comforting for women who had chosen, for whatever reason, to abandon the quest. No matter how they may have felt about the choice they made, they could take comfort in the belief that it would have been impossible to have had a full-fledged career with a family anyway. "You're not going to find many women who are striving in their careers the way men do," Maureen Graham had said to me during the first few moments of our first telephone conversation. "The women I know don't want to give up husbands and children."

This set of assumptions also was a favorite of people responsible for advancing women in management and the professions: specifically, the male managers who dominate the upper echelons of virtually every corporation and professional association in the country; but even more disturbingly, women who themselves had begun to approach those levels. The men could rationalize that there wasn't any need to develop women whose commitment obviously couldn't be as great as it need be, I theorized, whereas the women could see themselves as superior to their counterparts with husbands and children. The image of Suzanne Sheehan disparaging the woman who had pleaded for improved benefits for working parents and questioning Holly's commitment to her career because of her parallel concern about her family was one I couldn't easily forget.

Suzanne's doubt about her friend's commitment to her career was to occur to me whenever I thought back to my first interview with Holly that night at The Ritz. From the moment she slid across the table from me in the café, in a far corner of the spacious and inviting lobby, and so confidently ordered a filet mignon—as if there were no question that she was deserving of the best on the menu—I saw her as a breed apart from most of the women in her class at Harvard.

The first clue came when she jumped immediately into a discussion of her career as if it were an entity apart from her life as wife and mother. She had decided to go to work for the powerful vice-president for finance in New York right after the Business School, she began, because she felt that job would be the best first step toward her ultimate goal—which at the time had been to run her own company but which she had since modified. The dream now was to run a major division of a big company. She had been recommended for the financial job very specifically by one of her professors at the Business School. The company was committed to advancing women, and, very early on, she was given the opportunity to work for bosses who were highly regarded and thus could pull her along.

While it was true that she had quit not quite a year after she joined that company to go to Dallas and marry Chuck—she seemed only the slightest bit disturbed when I mentioned at our second interview that Suzanne had taken that as a sign of a less-than-total commitment to her career—she had landed her materials-management job in Dallas six weeks after she began her search. That was about as long as it would take to find such a job, she said. And if the truth be known, that she was Chuck Pfeiffer's wife hadn't done anything but help her cause, she added with a delightful little smile.

The day she went for her interview and mentioned that her husband had gone to the University of Pennsylvania, one of the executives said, "You're not married to Chuck Pfeiffer, are you? His reputation runs far and wide." When she said that she was, the executive "jumped up and ran up to another guy and said, 'I just met so-and-so, and she's married to Chuck Pfeiffer!' " Holly said.

Then there was the way she had survived at the company when all around her was chaos, and even though she had been one of the first women to have done the unthinkable, which was to have had her three children in the throes of her corporate climb. The year her first child was born, 1977, had been particularly difficult. The division was in the midst of a change from one whose top executives managed functions such as accounting and finance to one in which they oversaw specific product lines, and three of her bosses were fired. One, two, three, right in a row, which certainly didn't help her career any, for who would be waving the banner for her to the higher-ups if the executives most familiar with her work were themselves discredited? As an aside, I asked her why she felt she survived, and she replied that her boss's boss had noticed and thought highly of her work even though he apparently hadn't thought much of the work of her three immediate supervisors.

The concept of Holly's being noticed and respected by the senior managers of the division was to emerge as the chief reason for her rapid rise, comparatively speaking at least, through the ranks of the division and ultimately into her job at headquarters in New York. From our first moments together, she had emphasized the necessity of bosses pushing for subordinates if the latter were ever to advance. "Because business is built on personal relationships," she said. "Your future in a company is built on your personal relationship with your boss and your boss's boss."

When I mentioned that it sounded as if otherwise capable individuals who didn't have that kind of support were doomed, she shook her head, big swings back and forth, to underscore her point. "They'll never make it, I've seen it *happen*," she said.

She herself paid at least as much attention to that aspect of her career as she did to getting her work done. The one time she had been in an impossible situation, for example, the only time she thought about leaving the company, she simply had gotten herself out from under. The problem had occurred when her third boss was fired and she found herself working for a senior operating man who in her view didn't think women belonged in executive positions. She could see that from the way he treated his secretary, to take just one tiny example, calling her "honey" and being overly solicitous of her. As for his treatment of Holly, she said he would do things such as refuse to see her, which was especially troublesome in the field of materials management, because managers had to act quickly if offered a special price on an item. Then there were times she did get to see him, only to be subjected to his fits. "He would yell at me, throw me out of his office," she said, and for the first time that evening, I detected a note of sadness, an uncharacteristic what's-the-use tone in her voice.

So she quietly made it known around the company that she was available and was quickly snapped up by the man who had been championing her cause all along, her boss's boss, whose title was vice-president for administration. She did so well under him that she became a part of the tight little cadre of executives whom he and his boss, the division president, considered confidantes. And when her boss was promoted to headquarters in New York, she told me a year later when we spoke at a restaurant by the commuter rail stop near her new home in New Jersey, it was he who had insisted that she go with him as director of materials management for the whole corporation.

That evening in December, at the restaurant by the rail stop, we talked about what she had done to ingratiate herself to her bosses. One of the most important things she had accomplished for her boss, and indeed for the president of the division, was to make herself an expert on the personalities of their superiors at headquarters, she said. Unlike many of her colleagues, she would soak up all of the gossip, so that if her bosses, say, wanted to build a new factory, and their superiors couldn't see why the division should, "I would have already asked so many questions of them and been sort of a mirror for them at all angles that they could easily get through any intellectual hurdle with their superiors."

The point I had to remember about business was that decisions aren't ever black or white, Holly continued. What was best for the division wasn't necessarily top priority for the corporation. The game therefore became for division executives to convince their superiors of a project's value to the corporation, and the way to do that was to sell the project to each superior individually. "Take the president of the company," Holly said. "If you talk to him about strategy and competitive advantage, he will always be sold. Then take the chairman. If you talk to him about sales and growth, he will always be sold. . . ."

It was perhaps ironic, therefore, that to sell herself as a candidate for promotion to headquarters Holly had to resort to a tactic she had taken pains to avoid throughout her career. She had to lay out the particulars of her personal situation to convince her bosses that she could transfer, and that was the topic that had dominated our first interview at The Ritz, when the possibility of a promotion to headquarters recently had surfaced.

The thought that her bosses apparently had assumed she couldn't move because of Chuck had shocked her at first, if only because the issue of relocation hadn't been uppermost in her mind. With all of the turmoil at the company and her three maternity leaves—six weeks for her first child in 1977, then three weeks each for her second and third, in 1979 and 1980—she had all she could do to keep her career on track at the division.

But by then, when she had come to the point at which she would have to transfer to continue on the "fast track," she was to discover that her bosses made precisely the opposite presumption about her than they would have made about a man in her position. They knew she had come to Dallas to marry Chuck, of course, and they figured that with family ties to the area and three young children, she wouldn't be able to relocate.

The presumption came up in the course of a discussion with her boss the previous month, she began. It was he who had broached the topic. "What do you want to be when you grow up?" he had asked. When she told him she wanted to go to headquarters, he had hemmed and hawed, and she could tell from his reticence that something was awry. The problem was that like any suitor he didn't want to ask unless there was a reasonable chance she'd say yes, she explained. And when I retorted that her bosses should have known she meant what she said—she had always come back after her maternity leaves, for example—she threw back her head and laughed that infectious laugh of hers. Her commitment was still in doubt, she said. "They're still afraid you'll"—and then with a sweep of her arm—*"do it again!"*

In the wake of our laughter, she turned abruptly serious. "At first I felt reluctant to say, 'Hey, I can move!' Because I don't consider myself an appendage of my husband. I felt embarrassed about the need to reveal all of the details of my husband's career in order to be considered for a job. I felt . . . 'Wait a minute! In order to get a job in New York, I don't feel that you have to know what his job is, whether he's a winner or a loser.' They're thinking that if I can move, does that mean I've got a better job than my husband and therefore he's some pantywaist who hangs around at home and just follows me? Or does that mean I'm getting a divorce?"

In the midst of her growing pique, however, a stronger emotion prevailed. And that was her almost innate sense for the way organizations work, which had characterized every facet of her career, no matter what people's perceptions to the contrary. The simple fact was that she would have to do what she found distasteful if she were to be considered for the job she wanted in New York. What finally drove the point home was a comment made by the president of the corporation at a luncheon for female managers. His belief was that women weren't getting opportunities because they weren't mobile. That the president felt that way told her that the presumption was grounded deep in the fabric of the organization.

"I finally said, 'Holly, you're kidding yourself. You're crazy! Just spill the beans, and tell them what the situation is . . . get it all out on the table, and let them handle it. The fact is that you can move, and if you have to compromise your privacy, that's . . . then do it!' "

Which was precisely what she did, and which was precisely why her boss finally asked her to follow him to headquarters in New York.

The concept of unspoken perceptions—presumptions about Holly that didn't turn out as people had supposed—was to figure prominently in my assessment of why she had been able to make an equal commitment to her career and her family. One of my first images of Holly had been Suzanne's perception of her, for example, when they had met the first day at the Business School and Holly had walked into the dorm in her blue jeans, her frizzy hair unkempt and nothing in her knapsack but a rug, after having spent the previous five years traveling throughout Asia.

Yet while all of that was true, the way Holly told the story of her background, somewhat methodically at the end of our first interview at The Ritz, put it in a far different light. She told me about growing up in the country town of Manchester, Vermont, in an upper-middle-class family that valued culture and education. But the thing that struck me most of all about her early years was that she had so admired her mother.

Her mother didn't work when Holly, her older brother, and her younger sister were small, because her father hadn't wanted his wife to work. "But she was a highly motivated, highly competent, and intellectual woman," Holly said with warmth and respect in her voice. "She spent a lot of time doing volunteer work and eventually became president of the P.T.A. and a girl scout leader and then, you know, head of the regional girl scout board, and I mean she was just working full-time. She was always successful, she was always the president of this and, 'Oh my gosh, now they've made me president of that,' and eventually she did return to work. She got her master's degree and worked as a guidance counselor, a high school guidance counselor."

Holly's admiration for her mother struck me primarily because none of the other women I interviewed for a second time had talked that way about their mothers. As I thought back to my conversations with Suzanne, Phoebe, Mary Pat, and Tess, I recalled that they had spoken about their mothers as women who lived in the shadows of their husbands, submissive women to be disregarded and pitied.

"Father was director of personnel for a local company," Holly continued. "He never really knocked the lights out in business or in his job, but he became active in local politics and became a selectman of our town. And he was the one who, in fact, in the end—"

She paused as she considered her father, and again her feeling for him struck me as being far different from the way some of the other women had perceived their fathers. While acknowledging that her father hadn't been particularly successful in his career, she spoke with none of the vengeance or resentment or actual dislike that permeated some of the other women's characterizations. I remembered how both Suzanne and Phoebe had recoiled from their fathers, whom they regarded as domineering, how both Mary Pat and Tess saw their fathers as weaklings. "I can't count on Lloyd, I can't count on my father, and I can't count on myself anymore because I am exhausted," Mary Pat had cried toward the end of our evening at Zapata's when she was explaining why she had turned to God. And I remember being shocked that she had mentioned her father at that point in our interview, because it had been hours since we had talked about her background.

The year after she graduated from Wellesley, in 1968, Holly convinced two male friends from Wesleyan to start a nightclub with her in Singapore, which had been her girlhood fantasy. "An adolescent dream, queen of the hop," she said, laughing and catching me by surprise as she always did when she mentioned her fondness for pop culture. She liked best-sellers, memoirs of movie stars, I recalled.

She majored in sociology at Wellesley and did quite well, although she wasn't an academic superstar. Her real strength was her ability to put her ideas across to people who could act on them. At a time when campuses across the country were becoming more liberal, and Wellesley was no exception, she led the fight for the end of curfews and parietals. A more radical faction on campus had wanted to stage a demonstration, but Holly's strategy was to give the administration a chance to address student concerns first, which was why those changes came peaceably at Wellesley.

Her idea for the nightclub came with a hefty dose of confidence that she could pull it off. "I gave *them* the confidence to do it," she said of her two male friends. She and her two friends dug deep into their savings for the financing, and for two years—until they got tired of the venture and wanted to go on to other things—they ran the business. "And it was a great success. We ran a little bar, served liquor, and had bands and dancing and everything. It was just tremendously exciting."

The year after they closed the club, Holly traveled throughout Asia with the man she had been seeing since college, a moody painter who professed to need solitude and open spaces to work. He was the love of her life back then. At one point during their travels, when he wanted to move to the country and she insisted on staying in Hong Kong, he just up and left her. Then he must have reconsidered, because he wired her from the fishing village where he had settled. "Come join me," he said, and Holly agonized for weeks before she wired back. No, she didn't want to come, she said. She had found a job in Hong Kong, a job doing the books for a small local textile company. She didn't know anything about accounting, but she was learning as she worked and she was making money, all of which felt good. "I had to make a choice between doing what my mother would have done, which would have been to follow him, and doing what I wanted to do," she explained.

After about nine months in the accounting job, when she started getting itchy again and began thinking about what she wanted to do next, she got a letter from her father—"my dad," she said fondly. Her father mentioned that she probably had a flair for business since she had run the nightclub so successfully and that she should go to business school.

The suggestion made a lot of sense to her. "The time had come to . . ." she said, and then she paused, breaking off in mid-thought. "Youth doesn't go on forever, and you can't be doing this when you're thirty-five years old, cruising around Asia, looking over the next mountain." Which was why she decided to take her father's advice. He was telling her to come home, home to where she belonged, home to the Harvard Business School.

The same unspoken perceptions that were to cloud people's judgment of Holly the adolescent were to do the same with Holly the adult, and this time the focal point became Holly's marriage to Chuck Pfeiffer. Again my first image came from Suzanne, who told me that Holly had met Chuck in her section at the Business School and had kept their relationship a secret, even from her. Although she and Holly were roommates, she explained that Chuck had wanted it that way. He felt it wouldn't be good for either of their reputations if anyone knew they were dating.

Suzanne had talked about Chuck during our first interview at Il Monello as if she didn't have an opinion of him, regarding him merely as the man with whom her roommate was infatuated. His notorious pranks were a facet of his personality that she appeared to accept, as did everyone else, acknowledging them with a shake of her head and a half smile on her face. But the second time we talked, in her apartment in New York, her real opinion of Chuck had bubbled to the surface. Gone was her tolerance of him as, as she had put it, a "big, overgrown teddy-bear type." The fact was that his pranks weren't all that funny, and he had a lot to learn when it came to treating Holly as well as he should.

His mistreatment of Holly began as far back as the Business School, Suzanne had said. The spring of their second year, for example, when Holly was all set to follow him, take a job in Dallas if necessary, even though her best offer came from the company in New York, it was he who had broken off their relationship. He did it quite abruptly and, to Suzanne's way of looking at it, cruelly. The last day of school, when she went to his apartment to help him pack his van—he was driving to Dallas with all of his stuff—he had left her standing on the curb as he pulled away. He hadn't even had the decency to drive her back to her apartment.

That type of treatment continued to the present, at least as far as Suzanne could tell from her visit to Holly's home the previous fall. The children were crammed into the smallest of the three bedrooms so that Chuck could have the bigger bedroom for his study. He needed the space for his grasshoppers. I had raised my eyebrow when Suzanne had said that. But she didn't alter the flat and angry expression on her face. Didn't I know? she had said. Chuck raised grasshoppers.

The point was that Holly "has no voice" in her marriage, Suzanne had continued. And then she had added, as if to sum up, "Let's put it this way. I'd hate to wake up one Saturday morning and have three children and know that this was my husband."

The story of her marriage from Holly's point of view was quite another matter, however. The more she talked about it, the more I came to the curious conclusion that it was precisely because of Chuck that she was able to be as committed to her career as she was to her family. He brought a dimension to her life that she wouldn't have otherwise had: His tendency to poke fun at convention and to live by his wits was perhaps what made her, the disciplined and organized one, realize that it was okay to live in an unorthodox way, to buck the expectations of society.

She began by admitting that it had been Chuck who had broken up with her at the end of their second year at the Business School, just as Suzanne had said. Yet he did it because he could see that she was just a little bit too eager to compromise her own objectives for him, she explained at our second interview. "He's a strong personality," she said, adding that he didn't want to be bothered with women who weren't equally strong. When women would become dependent on him, he would lose interest.

Holly's assessment of her husband was to come to mind the following evening, the night before New Year's Eve, when I interviewed Chuck Pfeiffer at the Harvard Club in New York. At first glance, he didn't appear to be the type of man who would be, in the parlance of the day, "supportive." He was well over six feet tall, not quite stocky but certainly solidly built, and he paid no heed to convention. Even for dinner at the Harvard Club, where couples sauntered into the lobby in their holiday finery, the young men neatly put together in jackets and ties, he wore a V-neck sweater and a shirt that was open at the neck. He spoke just as plainly, in a challenging tone of voice that both irritated and intimidated me.

The moment we sat down across the table from each other in the spacious main dining room, for example, he tried to put me on the defensive. When I flicked on my recorder and asked him a bit too meekly if I could tape the interview, he told me gruffly to shut it off. "You're a reporter," he said. "You can remember what I said." He had spotted my intimidation and had already begun to lose interest.

Then he asked me if I were married and if I had any children. When I replied that I was both a wife and a mother and that my daughter was but six months old, it was his turn to be shown up. He hadn't expected that of me, but seemed to respect me for it. We were back on an even keel. I sensed that he felt that if I were a wife and mother, plus a full-time newspaper reporter and aspiring writer, I was woman enough for him.

The same could be said about his wife, which was what he found so attractive about her, he seemed to be intimating as our interview progressed. "You're talking about a woman who dropped a baby on a Saturday afternoon," he said, referring to the birth of their third child in the spring of 1980, "and showed up at the company two weeks later for her mail. She didn't miss a step in a man's job in a man's company."

His eyes narrowed into hard little slits that I would come to see as a gesture of approval on his part, and he didn't smile. He continued to speak matter-of-factly, in that gruff tone of voice that struck me as Hemingwayesque. "Materials management! It's a cigar-smoking, name-calling, deal-making, rough-and-tumble man's business," he said, adding, "but she's an unusual person. For all of that, she's an incredible mother. She runs a home life that is very traditional."

And yet even more than she, I found myself thinking as he spoke, it was he who was incredible, an incredible man. For what came out in my interview with him was that here was a man who meant what he said when he declared that he wouldn't expect his wife to accept a job that was her second or third choice just to accommodate his career. He wouldn't expect his wife to—in a word that was a favorite of Holly's—*suboptimize.*

From this perspective, I could see that there was another way of looking at the fact that he had left Holly years before at the Business School. By leaving her, he had given her the encouragement to take the job that was best for her. Likewise, just that year, when she was wrestling with the decision to transfer to New York, it was because of him that she was able to go to her bosses and state so assuredly that she was able to move. "She came to me and said, 'Will you go?' " Chuck said. "And I said, 'Geography doesn't make a difference. Is it the right opportunity? If it is, go for it!' "

The point was, of course, that he had been able to say that to her on both of those occasions, even though it was he who would be inconvenienced. It was he who would have to go to New York six months after Holly had taken her first job, with the diamond ring he had wanted to give her all along. It was he who would now have to pull up stakes and go to New York for her.

I remember regarding Chuck with admiration, because unlike most men, he had let his wife go when she most needed to do that: right after the Business School when she had to establish an independent professional identity, and just that year, when she had to take that critical next step to stay on the "fast track" in her company. When I asked him why he had done that, he looked at me curiously, as if to say there shouldn't be any need to explain something so basic. The simple fact was, he said, snuffing out his cigar in the ashtray on the table, that "relocation isn't a permission granted of me—it's a decision made because of combined opportunity."

The advantages of being married to a man like Chuck were

clear to me as Holly and I spoke that Tuesday before New Year's Eve, in 1981, at the restaurant by the rail stop in New Jersey. Still basking in the glory of her recent promotion, she sat tall and confidently across the table from me. The move had been difficult, she explained, what with selling the house in Dallas and uprooting the family, buying another house and finding another house-keeper. She shook her head when she came to that point in her litany. The housekeeper she had hired when she first came to New Jersey a month earlier hadn't worked out, so she had had to find yet another.

"But I can tell you that it's worth it," she continued, in that even and emphatic way of hers. And as I studied her, I could tell that it was. She had her big job at corporate headquarters, a job that paid $70,000 a year and came with perks such as a company car. She had her husband and her children, whom she loved. But most of all, she had swung the door wide open for her future. The division vice-presidency she hoped for someday was at least a possibility for Holly Lane Pfeiffer.

The advantages of such a wife for Chuck were less obvious, however. When I made a point of asking him what they were, that night at the Harvard Club, I remember very distinctly how he had leaned back in his chair, his eyes narrowing into those hard little slits. "I like winning football teams," he said, "and I like successful women."

The thought that there were problems in Holly's marriage was to occur to me only gradually, perhaps because I had become so comfortable with the pleasant reality that lay behind people's unspoken perceptions of her. By the time she began to allude to such problems toward the very end of our first interview, I sup-pose I wasn't willing to pursue the topic for fear of having to alter my own perceptions.

It wasn't until the following year, therefore, during our inter-view in the curiously pretentious rail-stop restaurant, that I began to ask her about the matters she had hinted at the year before. There was the "potential for affairs," for example, because Chuck was spending so much time away from home.

The fact was that ever since he had left the Dallas-based company he had joined after the Business School to start his own consulting firm, he had been spending about twenty-four days a month away from home, Holly confessed. The problem began in the spring of 1980, the day after the birth of her third child, when Chuck left for the Middle East for a week and a half. The trips became lengthier and more frequent as the year progressed, so that by the middle of 1981, Holly considered a divorce for the first time in her marriage. "There was a lot of tension, and we were fighting," she began, trying to explain what she herself didn't fully understand.

At first, the only thing she sensed was that she didn't need Chuck as much as she had in the past, she said. She felt more independent. That was what she had been referring to when she cited the "potential for affairs."

When I asked if she had actually considered an affair, she turned away from me and hung her head, confessing that she had. "Oh, with my boss," she said softly, and then she added quickly that it was only to be expected in an environment such as the one in which they worked. There they were, working so closely together on matters of heady importance at one of the biggest companies in the country. "And I know he felt the same way about me," she added. "There was just a great deal of mutual respect and admiration."

Her infatuation lasted for about a month before fading, she continued, and she knew she had been right to resist. Not that there had been any scenes, of course. That generally doesn't happen unless both parties allow it to, she explained. And she certainly hadn't, especially after considering what such an affair would mean for her career.

But in the wake of her infatuation with her boss, when Chuck's trips became more frequent and more extensive, the problems in her marriage intensified. The final straw occurred in August, when Chuck came back from weeks on the road and declared that he was going on a ten-day fishing trip with a group of friends. "And I thought that was just outrageous," Holly said, looking uncharacteristically vulnerable in her black turtleneck and paisley scarf, as she leaned back in her chair across the table from me. "I mean, I could accept it if it were business. But to have been away for so long and then to have taken a trip with a bunch of guys struck me as inexcusable. I mean, where does the family fit? Where do we win?''

Their problems notwithstanding, she said she had decided not to ask Chuck for a divorce. "I have three young ones," she began, explaining that her first instinct had been to "preserve the family" and to assure her children of a stable home life. "And then there's the fact that I still adore Chuck. I have a great deal of respect for him, and I think he's the right man for me.''

The major reason she backed off, however, was that their marriage had begun to improve since they had moved east, and that brought me face-to-face with the final unspoken perception people had of her. Her comment brought to mind Suzanne's perception that she had transferred more to save her marriage than to promote her career. But when I put that thesis to Holly, she was once again taken aback.

The fact was that she had begun to push for her promotion the year before, long before she began to realize that her marriage was in trouble, she said. Chuck had just set up his consulting business and had just begun to travel. Nor had she foreseen what would happen, the way his travel would become oppressive, the way communication would all but break down between them, as it had the following summer.

When I queried her against my better judgment from a theoretical perspective, she backed off a bit. She said she supposed that if Chuck were really tied to Dallas she would not have moved, and I had stopped her at that point. That was perhaps the only way in which even the most ambitious women who also cared about their families differed from men, I suggested to her. "You mean in trying to sort and fit the family pieces together, rather than just one's own personal pieces?" she asked, and I nodded.

The fact that she seemed to stop just short of the kind of commitment expected of the country's most ambitious men didn't surprise me. But it didn't trouble me either. I had posed that question from a perspective that had always troubled me. The fact was that she *had* married someone like Chuck Pfeiffer, she *was* mobile, and she *had* made the decision to go to New York for her career, and I couldn't help but feel that that said it all about Holly.

When we finished our dinner, a rich northern Italian pasta served in the dark and less-than-inviting atmosphere of the restaurant by the whistle stop, she accompanied me to the platform where I was to wait for my train back to New York. Standing tall and erect beside me, her head held high and her eyes focused straight ahead, she wanted to make one last point. "I think being married to Chuck has been nothing but a plus for my career," she said. "It has done nothing but help me."

In the weeks and months after I interviewed Holly, I often thought about why she was able to commit to both her family and her career, and the point I kept coming back to was that, first and foremost, she had always wanted a career. Her facility for what she called "the integration of the technical and the social," which she felt lay at the heart of success in business, had been a part of her from the very beginning.

It went back to her roots, I suppose. She had come from a family whose members moved with ease within their own milieu. There was the way her father had been able to accept himself for what he was; the way her mother had always been accepted among her peers, the woman they'd make, "Oh my gosh, president of this or that." Then there was the fact that her mother had been successful, from the standpoint of what was expected of her in her day, without having had to forfeit a marriage or a family. That had to have had a profound affect on her daughter, I thought.

Yet in the final analysis, I had to make the ironic admission that it was primarily because of the men in her life that Holly hadn't strayed from the straight and narrow when it came to her career. It had been her father who had convinced her to go for what she excelled at, specifically, the conventional world of business. And it had been her husband who had held her on course when she became a wife and mother, and indeed, at least had given some thought to, as she would put it, "suboptimizing." For it was Chuck Pfeiffer who ultimately had realized the importance of doing what they were trying to do, which was to build a marriage in which both partners were equally strong. That he had, brought to-mind my interview with Luke Davis, Martha's husband, on that Saturday morning at The Ritz.

In the heated moments that had followed Luke's admission that his wife hadn't been able to call the shots and go to Boston because she feared for the deterioration of their marriage, he suddenly had turned calm and rational. In carefully measured cadence and with utmost sincerity, he had questioned whether the problem between them could be that Martha hadn't been willing to plan as carefully as couples with two careers should plan for their future, and as he was always suggesting they should do.

"Do you want to know what I really think it is?" I had said, cutting him short and dismissing his thesis. Then I had told him about Holly. I told him that I felt she was able to make a commitment to both her career and her family because hers was a marriage of equals, one of the very few in the class. As had so many other people, Luke had appeared doubtful. He had asked me whether Holly had any children, and when I said that she had three and all were preschoolers, he had seemed to reconsider.

Then he said he thought he knew what I meant. There were times in his career, he said, that he would win a point with a colleague whom he didn't consider his equal. "And I often wonder whether the decision that resulted was the best that could have been made for the patient, given the fact that I wasn't sparring with an equal," he said. The same could be said of his marriage, Luke continued, and that was when our rapport seemed to solidify. The fact that he wasn't sparring with a spouse willing to fight with equal vigor for what she wanted in her career could mean that their decisions weren't always the best.

I never felt as if I had the kind of rapport with Chuck Pfeiffer that I had with Luke Davis. Despite Chuck's apparent admiration for me, at least at that point during our interview when I had shown him up, and my admiration for what he stood for, I was no match for him. The intimidation I felt from the moment we sat down across the table from each other at the Harvard Club was to continue for the rest of our evening together. And whenever I thought about that, I couldn't help but think that my intimidation was indicative of something else that could be said about the women of the class of 1975 at the Harvard Business School: that unlike Holly, very few really wanted a man such as Chuck. Something held them back from really wanting a union of equals, and whatever that something was, I could feel it myself. I could sense it from the way I *allowed* myself to be intimidated by him.

As we walked out of the Harvard Club and parted on the corner of Fifth Avenue and Forty-fourth Street, the night before I was to attend Tess Beckett's New Year's Eve party, I remember being somewhat at a loss for what to say to Chuck. "How about the business cards that read 'Texas Treetops Inc.'?" I said, referring to one of his more notorious pranks—that of passing out fake business cards to all of his professors at the Business School. I just wanted to show him that I knew more about him than he realized. And as the taxi I had hailed screeched to the curb to pick me up, Chuck Pfeiffer laughed, a heartfelt laugh that was every bit as genuine and infectious as Holly's own.

How Ambitious
Would You
Say You Are?

It is 1984, three years after I talked to the women of the class of 1975 at the Harvard Business School, and not a day goes by that I don't think about them. Sometimes, when I'd be walking across Boston's broad Government Center Plaza on my way to work, considering the problems of the day or, more broadly, my career and my family, my plans for the future, I would find myself comparing my feelings and concerns to theirs. This is a problem Tess might have faced, or this is how Martha would have felt, I might think to myself. Or Mary Pat. Or Phoebe.

In the months after I interviewed the women of the class, I made a deliberate decision not to keep in touch with them. I wanted to remember them as they were in 1981, their problems and pressures, their special pleasures, their dreams for the future, all frozen in time, all as they were the year I talked to them.

I made only one deliberate exception to this rule. In May 1983, when I was in Chicago for a week-long business trip, I decided to call Martha Davis. I don't have any friends in the Chicago area, so I thought it would be fun to spend an evening with Martha and Luke. I was also curious. I still didn't know whether Martha had joined the small local economics firm or, as Luke had predicted, the big nationally acclaimed group affiliated with the University of Chicago.

I didn't call Martha until I was comfortably settled in The Ritz-Carlton Hotel. I knew that I should have called earlier to reserve a place on her busy calendar, but old intimidations die hard. I was still put off by her style and sophistication and the advantages she had had, even now that I had come to believe that she was far more ambivalent than those quailties would have led me to believe.

"Oh, hi, Liz," she said breezily when she picked up the telephone, cutting short the formal and stilted introduction I felt the need to make, even though there wasn't any reason to believe she would have forgotten me. We talked briefly about the book, Martha wondering when I would finish it, I giving her an approximate timetable.

Then I asked her, a bit too quickly into the conversation, about what she had decided to do. "I've been wondering about that ever since we talked a year ago," I said. Martha replied that she had decided to join the group at the university and that she suspected she'd be very happy. Much happier working on economic issues of importance to multinational corporations than on mundane financing problems for little firms, she said in a tone that suggested relief rather than satisfaction.

When I extended my dinner invitation, she said she would check with Luke and call back within a few days. And when she did, she said they had decided to decline. Time was so short for them, a professional couple. They wanted to spend as much of it as possible with each other and with Ben.

We chatted briefly about our children, and when it became apparent that Ben was wresting the telephone from his mother, I suggested that Martha invest in a Fisher-Price toy model. In that tone of mock superiority mothers sometimes assume, Martha replied that she already had and that Ben had lost interest within minutes.

Then the conversation came to an abrupt halt. It was obvious that we had nothing else to say to each other. I bade Martha a hasty good-bye, satisfied that I now knew what I had come to find out and that I had been right about what I felt she would do.

In the spring of that year, I made an impromptu decision to place a call to Mary Pat Horner. I had resisted the temptation to do so ever since we parted after the church service that Sunday in October 1981. I suspected that she had left the bank, and I didn't want to know for sure. The thought of what might have become of her was too frightening.

Then I stumbled across an item in a Business School publication, asking for help in locating several people in the class of 1975 "who have dropped off the radar screen." Hers was one of the names. So that morning, I dialed the switchboard number for the bank, and, sure enough, I was told there was no one by that name at the bank. A year later, I called her home in Larchmont, and an unrelated individual answered. She had been gone so long that her number had been given to someone else. I thought it curious that we had come full circle. I wasn't able to locate her just as I hadn't been four years earlier when I began my research for the project.

Although I haven't contacted any of the others, I do hear occasionally from Phoebe Holstrom. Every so often, after a lapse of a few months—there doesn't seem to be any pattern—she calls me out of the blue, catching me by surprise. There never seems to be a purpose for her calls; rather, I am left feeling that I have to pry a reason out of her.

The first time she called was in the spring of 1982, six months after I had interviewed her in her apartment in New York. I remember being surprised—and flattered—to hear from her. But after a few minutes, as she continued to talk without coming to the point, I became confused. Feeling that I had to give the conversation a purpose, I found myself suggesting lunch. She promptly agreed, noting that she would be in Boston within a few weeks. I suggested the Magic Pan in the Faneuil Hall marketplace, a restaurant I reserve for friends rather than business associates. I suppose even then I clung to the notion that we could be friends.

We met on a brilliantly sunny Friday afternoon in late April. Phoebe was dressed in tattered jeans and a voluminous wool poncho. It encircled her like a toreador's cape, dwarfing her beneath its folds. Her long hair fell in wisps down her back, just as I remembered from our first meeting at the Berkshire Place. There were traces of youth in her face, traces of the waif. But in the piercing sunlight of that beautiful spring day, she appeared more old than young. The lines in her face were clearly visible, and she appeared to be tired, weary to the bone.

At the restaurant, Phoebe did all of the talking. She seemed to be trying so hard to be enthusiastic that she came across as perfunctory. She told me about her latest project for the consulting firm. She had been hired by one of the biggest Canadian energy companies to do a major study, so she had spent the previous several months in, of all places, St. John, Newfoundland, her father's birthplace. She shut her eyes briefly, as if preparing to make a speech. A soft expression came across her face. I knew she was about to cast her spell on her audience of one, namely me.

She told me that the best part of the assignment was that she was able to get a feel for the town where her father had grown up. One day, she said, she made a pilgrimage to her grandmother's house in the country a few dozen miles from St. John, and spent the day peering through the windows and walking the grounds. As she rambled on about this experience, I found myself growing impatient. Why was she telling me this? Why was I listening?

We made our way out of the restaurant and across the Government Center Plaza to the subway station, where I had to catch a train for a conference, and she brought up a completely unrelated topic. "Do you ever see Karen Muller?" she asked, a bit too casually, as if she didn't want to let on how badly she wanted to hear about her former friend. I replied that I hadn't seen Karen since the previous fall. Then Phoebe stopped at the entrance to the subway and turned to face me, a sad and serious expression on her face. "A nice girl," she said. "A really nice girl."

She called again that summer and in December, the latter time cutting me off as abruptly as she had begun. She was at work, someone was paging her, and she had to go. Then she called in March 1983, and this time she said she was calling for two reasons: She wanted to find out how I was doing on the book, and she wanted to mention that she had heard from a friend who was also writing a book about women. She had given her friend my name, and she asked me if I would help her if she called. I told Phoebe that I would be happy to help her friend, but I was smiling to myself. I could almost hear Phoebe telling her friend about me, dowdy old me, whom she now included in her circle of "friends."

I have become friends with only one of the women in the class of 1975, Tess Beckett. The month after we talked in the fall of 1981, I remember being surprised and pleased to hear from her. I was touched that she thought enough of me to tell me about being fired from the computer company and then, four months later, in February 1982, to tell me about her new job at the medical-instruments firm.

That summer, she and Kevin and Chris joined Paul and me and our year-old daughter for a day in Kennebunkport, Maine, where we were vacationing. The day was sunny but cool, so we lay on the beach wrapped in blankets. I remember suspecting that Tess was sticking it out on the beach only because I was, and she wanted to measure up. She appeared at times to regard me with a bit of awe, as if there were aspects of my personality she wanted to emulate but knew she could not. I got the same feeling when I went out on a catamaran with a friend, and she, shivering and even less athletic than I, watched from the shore, her gray eyes downcast and wistful.

I also remember that she brought presents for us that day, which made me think she had begun to care. There was a bottle of fine white wine for Paul and me, and a set of plastic figurines for my daughter.

In the weeks ahead, therefore, when she would call and talk about her problems as if we were still subject and interviewer, I would stop myself from cutting her off. I was witnessing the awkward but sincere metamorphosis of a friendship that I wanted to let develop.

One evening that fall, when she telephoned, there was a sense of urgency and desperation in her voice. She wanted to talk about her psychiatrist, whom she had just stopped seeing. They had both agreed he couldn't do anything else for her. She was fine. But if the truth be known, she hadn't wanted the sessions to end. Her attraction to the corporate recruiter who had helped her find her job hadn't subsided, and she wanted to continue to discuss that with her psychiatrist. She wanted to seduce the recruiter, she said flatly, and she wanted to know how she should make that overture.

The tone of her voice made me nervous. I wanted to believe that this was a career woman's idea of a joke, pretending to care about seducing a man when everyone knew it was her career that really counted. But knowing that she wasn't kidding, I was embarrassed for her and tried to make light of it. "Be a reporter," I said. "Tell him you're working on a story about corporate recruiting and want to interview him."

"I really do think an affair could be the solution for some people," she replied, interrupting me and explaining that even Kevin had told her to go ahead. He would look the other way if only she wouldn't leave, as she had intimated she might do. Then she laughed shortly. "Matinees, I think they call them."

I didn't have an answer for Tess. But I was beginning to have a feel for the enormity of her problem. I was beginning to see how trapped she felt, married to a good and decent man who simply didn't interest her now that she had gone as far as she had in the world.

Paul and I went to the Becketts' dinner party that New Year's Eve, 1982, just as we had the year before. Then, in February 1983, I had dinner with Tess at her home in Belmont. She was more sanguine that evening, showing me pictures of Virgin Gorda, where she and Kevin had taken their winter vacation the month before. In her kitchen, as she gently tossed an assortment of vegetables in her electric wok, she brought up the subject of the recruiter, not with the intensity I remembered from the previous fall, but in a detached sort of way. "You know that headhunter I had a crush on," she began, referring to him in the past tense, a slight smile on her face. She seemed to be trying to say she had been foolish and was relieved to be done with her infatuation. But then she came to her point. It didn't have to be him, she said, "just someone like him."

In April, Tess and I had dinner at a small Mexican restaurant down the street from where I used to live in Brookline. Having arrived after I had been seated, she walked toward me with a smile that matched the brilliance of her brand-new red suit. We talked about many things that evening, and as is often the case with people I have come to know through interviews for stories, I found myself easily picking up on the nuances.

We talked about children, for example, and Tess told me that she would love to have another child someday. "But not with Kevin," she said, quickly turning away, as if she didn't want to discuss the subject with someone who knew as much as I did.

She talked about her career at the medical-instruments company. And I wasn't as surprised as I suppose I should have been, when she spoke not with the enthusiasm I remembered from two years before but with a touch of ennui. She was doing well. There was about to be a shake-up in the managerial ranks, and she had every reason to believe she would get her boss's job. Vice-president for sales for one of the biggest regions of the country.

She was pleased, of course, but she had to confess that it wasn't like those heady days two years earlier, when she was scrambling to sell a product that hadn't even come off the assembly line for a company that was barely out of its infancy. Something was missing, she said, her gray eyes fixed steadfastly on my own— piercing, as if she felt that if she could convince me, I would have an answer for her, as if she finally had to face the truth about something she had said to me in one of our many conversations: "There is no holy grail!"

One of the last times I saw Tess was on a Saturday afternoon very early in October 1983. We met for lunch at a little café in Harvard Square, and she appeared to be tense. She had called on the spur of the moment that morning suggesting the impromptu get-together because she wanted to tell me about a few things.

The main thing she wanted to tell me was that she had decided to make a play for the recruiter. She meant what she said this time; she wanted to have an affair with him and she was going to do it. She wasn't afraid of the risk. She took risks every day on her job in sales.

She told me she came to her decision as the result of a series of recent developments in her life. The first was that she had gotten her promotion. The promotion hadn't been as assured as she had made it seem the previous spring, she could now confess.

As recently as a few weeks before, a new man had been brought in to replace her boss and had told her he was going to hire someone else for the job. "And all of a sudden, you know how it is, a rubber band just snapped," she said.

She had ranted and raved until the new man had no choice but to promote her. He hadn't expected a woman to fight so hard for her career. And that must have appealed to him, she said with triumph and an unmistakable touch of pride in her voice. For what happened next was that he took her out to dinner, and as they were walking back to the parking lot, he grabbed her and said, "My God! I've just got to sleep with you tonight!"

Tess's euphoria metamorphosed into concern when she saw the look of disbelief and weariness on my face. She hadn't slept with him, of course, she added hastily. She had told him she makes it a rule never to mix business and pleasure, and she even had called the next day to assure him that it had all been a very human mistake. They both had had just a little too much to drink. The only point she wanted to make to me, she said, "is that I am no longer willing to deny that part of myself."

During the course of our conversation that afternoon, the subject of her marriage surfaced from time to time. She had reached a watershed when it came to that aspect of her life too, she said. She could now admit that she had nothing but a marriage that was convenient for her. "It may sound selfish, it may sound crass," she said at one point, "but the reason I'm staying with Kevin is because he is a 'wife.' "

The edginess I sensed whenever we broached the subject of her marriage erupted at one point when one or the other of us—I cannot remember which—alluded to her sex life. "I absolutely refuse to sleep with that man," she said of her husband, blurting out those words in a fit of anger and desperation. "I mean, we sleep in the same bed. But I've decided I'll never have sex with him again."

As she spoke about this and other aspects of her life, she seemed to be turning to me for advice and counsel, and I found myself reluctant to be thrust into that role. So throughout the course of our conversation that afternoon, I brought up the points I had made about the six women whose stories form the backbone of this book. I wanted Tess to see her dilemma not as an isolated incident but in relation to the ways the others felt about their careers and their families.

I began by telling her about Suzanne Sheehan, and I wasn't surprised to watch her lose a bit of interest when I mentioned that Suzanne cared about nothing but her career. That was the major reason she stood the best chance of becoming a chief executive, I explained. I sensed that Tess didn't understand a woman like Suzanne and didn't particularly want to. She seemed bored by a woman who cared so little about her personal life, especially now that she had been awakened to the passion in her own self.

I brushed lightly over Phoebe Holstrom. I mentioned that she was as impersonal as Suzanne but nowhere near as ordinary. She was the very antithesis of that, in fact, a maverick who couldn't fit within the structure of any established organization. Tess nodded as if she knew what I meant, but wasn't particularly interested in pursuing the issue, and had it not been for the fact that I was to hear from Phoebe once again, in December 1983, I probably would have all but forgotten Tess's reaction.

That day on the phone, Phoebe called, as she had in the past, to tell me about this friend and that one. She also mentioned that she had finally left the consulting firm to start her own business, a company that would be making one of the most exciting new products of the decade. That Phoebe had made me think about Tess, because I had felt for a long while that of the six, Tess would have been the most likely to start her own company.

In talking to Phoebe that day, however, I found myself reconsidering. Tess was rebellious enough to want to strike out against established organizations, to be sure, having gone to the start-up maker of personal computers three years earlier. But she was far from the type of person who would form her own company. Her rebelliousness was born of anger and of fear; beneath the surface, there lay a personality that was every bit as prosaic as Suzanne's. Phoebe's rebelliousness, on the other hand, was the product of an interesting and esoteric personality.

I remember mentioning to Phoebe that she had stayed with the consulting firm for a long time, nine years, far longer than most people who didn't want to make partner. She laughed when I said that. She was different from all of the others, she said. They leave because they tire of the travel, of the pace, but she reveled in that and, I was to recall, the work itself—her client work. Then she laughed again. The reason she left now must have been because she had worked in all but one country in which the firm had clients; she would soon run out of new places to go to, interesting projects to handle.

That Tess was too prosaic to have been interested in Phoebe struck me as self-evident, therefore. Whether Phoebe was the self-confident individual she professed to be or the person with virtually no self-confidence at all as Karen Muller had theorized (and I was beginning to believe there was a fine line between the two), I felt that Karen's major observation was proving itself once again: For all of her idiosyncrasies, Phoebe was the person most likely to do something interesting and innovative in the world.

Continuing my litany with Tess, I pushed on to Mary Pat Horner, the first of the four women who were "personal" individuals, in that they cared about relationships on a personal level. Tess perked up; Mary Pat was more the type of woman she could understand. "Then there is you," I said to Tess. "You've certainly done well in your career, and you are married. But because you are far more ambitious than your husband, the price has been the lack of an emotional attachment."

I caught her look of unease and self-pity. She asked me, somewhat self-consciously, whether I could have told she felt that way about her husband. I told her that I could not have. She and Kevin appeared to be a model couple—with their two careers, their marriage of a decade's duration, their handsome young son. "Good," she said with relief in her voice. "Because I don't want anyone to know."

I moved quickly on to Martha Davis. The point I wanted to get across to Tess was that forfeiting a commitment to one's career isn't necessarily the solution either. I told her about the advantages Martha had had: her style, her sophistication, the credentials that had brought opportunities at every stage of her career. Then I told Tess about the ambivalence that characterized every chapter of Martha's career.

Finally, I told Tess about Holly Lane Pfeiffer, who had managed to have an upwardly mobile career, a marriage in which she was emotionally involved, and three young children. I wanted to make the point that women needn't sacrifice any of these aspects of life. Tess raised an eyebrow when I mentioned Holly's children, as had so many of the others who had heard Holly's story. But I pressed on. I mentioned Holly's transfer to New York for the promotion, the intensity of her feeling for Chuck.

"But there are problems in that kind of relationship too," I added hastily, because I didn't want Holly to come across as a paragon. I mentioned the time Chuck spent away from home, and the fact that Holly had considered a divorce. "I mean, she doesn't have a 'wife,' " I said. "When he wants to go, he goes, and she has to put up with that."

Listening to me speak, Tess seemed to be comparing herself with Holly. She asked me how Holly had avoided marrying someone like Kevin a decade earlier, when she was young and vulnerable. I replied that Holly had come from the upper middle class and was perhaps more sophisticated than she had been back then.

Then Tess asked me if Chuck had had affairs, and I replied that I didn't know but suspected that he had not. "I mean, he doesn't seem to have the time," I said. "And then, they still seem genuinely attracted to each other."

The point I was trying to get across, I said to Tess, was that the key to having both a full-fledged career and a marriage in which one is emotionally involved seems to be choosing a man who is equally ambitious. That isn't a widely accepted thesis, I added. Though women tend to marry men who are their equals when it comes to level of education or degree of physical attractiveness, they tend for the most part to want men who are more ambitious.

Tess considered what I said for a long moment. "That is a very controversial thesis," she said. Then she told me that her second year at the Business School, when she was pregnant and just beginning to come to terms with what she would have to do to have both an upwardly mobile career and a family, she had taken a seminar designed to help couples coordinate careers and families. The major point that emerged had been that the best marriages were those in which "one partner was pulling ahead and the other staying in the background."

"I know," I said to Tess. "But I am telling you what I actually saw out there among the women of your class."

Driving me back to Brookline in her big company car, Tess asked how I was doing since I had left *The Wall Street Journal.* A month earlier, when she had called, I had told her I had left over the summer. We hadn't had a chance to talk about it at the time, so I suspected she would ask.

There were a number of things I could have told Tess about my decision. I could have told her that it could be traced back six years to the time I had turned down the transfer to New York. I could have told her how confused I had been back then, how depressed I became in the weeks and months that followed.

I could have told her that from the perspective of six years, I felt that I had made the wrong decision, that in fact, it had been one of the worst decisions I ever made. In saying no, I had slammed the door shut on my future with that company. No matter how I had tried to rationalize to the contrary, the fact remained that in today's corporations, an individual, and most particularly, a woman, got one shot, two at the most. "That was your chance!" hissed the career counselor I spoke with in New York, nearly four years after the fact, seeking to untangle the mess I had woven for myself. "Why didn't you *go?* Why didn't you tell your husband any old thing?"

Why indeed! That is something else I could have discussed with Tess. For after having spent the better part of six years talking to a group of women who had been just as confused as I, I had a better grasp of the reasons why. The reasons boiled down to the fact that in many ways I was handling my career as a woman might have.

Like Tess, I had been persistent enough about my career, of course. But as she had been and as women are more likely to be, aliens as they are in the business world, I hadn't been confident that I would have a place in that world. "I'm insecure about everything!" Tess had cried toward the end of one of our last evenings together, her honesty ringing through the stillness of the warm September evening.

Like Martha, on the other hand, I had been ambivalent about what I wanted from my career for a reason that seems to plague many women. I couldn't bring myself to put my needs, my wants, first—ahead of those of my husband, ahead of those of the child we hoped to have.

On another level, I had cared too much and in the wrong way. Like Mary Pat, I had cared in a way that was sharply personal and so inappropriate in the impersonal milieu of business.

Then, too, I could see in myself a touch of the maverick. While I was by no means in Phoebe's league, I had tended to stand at arm's length in my company. I never had dared trust the organization, for fear that my trust would be betrayed, as I suspected it would be.

There was something else I could have told Tess. I could have told her about the ultimate irony, that I left *The Journal* primarily because of a personality conflict with, of all things, a female boss —the first woman, in fact, to be named a bureau chief for the paper. The details of our personality conflict wouldn't have been important, of course. But what would have mattered was the way in which my boss and I differed.

I could see that she had been handling her career as a man would. She was single and in her mid-thirties. She had transferred three times in the short span of her four years with the paper, each time for the next step on her climb up the ladder. At one point, in trying to understand why she and I seemed to clash so often, I had sought the advice of an attorney, herself a woman in business. "Your boss is very threatened by you," the attorney had said. "By your multiple roles—worker, wife, mother." As Suzanne Sheehan had been by Holly, I thought. And so, in many respects, my boss reminded me of Suzanne, with whom I had never had a rapport. I hadn't ever been able to see even the least little piece of myself in her.

The thought of what had happened to Suzanne in the years since we talked had crossed my mind from time to time, but it wasn't until I was writing the final draft of this book that I felt obliged to find out. I called the Fortune 100 company she had been working for three years earlier, and there she was, on the line—still at the same company, still director of planning for the North American Group.

The fact that she hadn't advanced didn't alter my opinion of her as the woman most likely to make it in a large corporation, especially when I considered the awesome problems for women advancing into senior positions. But she seemed a bit edgy about the fact. She hadn't gotten the line job she had wanted three years earlier, she said hastily, because both she and her boss agreed that it wasn't the right job for her. It wouldn't have given her the chance to show her stuff as well as she could. She also seemed an ever-so-slight touch more willing to concede that the problem might be simply that she was a woman. The thought occurred to her, for example, that she might support a Democrat in the 1984 election, something she wouldn't have done before. Women would be appointed to positions of power in such an administration and be seen as models for what they could attain in business, she explained.

The tension between us eased when we talked about her personal life. She was still single, and she was seeing a new man, she began, the ennui I would note whenever she spoke about her relationships already making its way into her tone of voice. Then she made another comment about her career. She was still as hopeful as ever about her future at the company. She had to be, she explained; otherwise, what was the point of being there? And what else would there be in her life?

I glanced at the backseat of Tess's car, where my daughter was sleeping, her head cocked gently to the right and such a sweet expression on her little face—sweeter than I would have ever imagined three years earlier when I was pregnant with her. She had come to the café with us that afternoon, because I hadn't even tried to get a baby-sitter; Tess had called on such short notice.

Looking at my two-year-old now, I knew there was another point I could have made to Tess. I could have told her that there were some good things about the decision I had made six years before. I had a child. I still had a marriage. Whether I would have, had I gone to New York, was doubtful at best, unlikely at worst.

And that would have been as unbearable as the loss of my career, at least to my way of looking at things.

In the final analysis, I chose not to tell Tess what I was thinking. I suppose I didn't want to reveal as much of myself to her as she had to me, for our friendship had long been grounded on the premise that she was the subject, me the confidante, and hadn't yet evolved into a truly mutual friendship.

Then, too, I wasn't sure that Tess would understand. The conflict between career and family, central in the lives of so many women in the class of 1975, was something she had come to terms with, as she so often made a point of telling me, years earlier. And no matter what the consequences, even those of which she was just becoming painfully aware, she had always chosen not to compromise.

Nearly a year before I met Tess, I talked to another woman in the class who was to become in my mind the archetype of the ambivalent women of my generation. The interview hadn't been unusual, except for the way she had responded to my question about her plans for the future: She had erupted in a curious fit of pique.

She was an international banker who had crisscrossed the globe for five years. She had said no to every man in her life, from the law student she had left behind at Harvard to the lawyer she had stopped seeing weeks earlier. Only now she was tired, she said, sinking down into her makeshift couch in her sparsely furnished apartment. She thought she might want a family. She thought she might want a different career, another job— something with the government or a corporation. The life of an international banker was just "too unreasonable," she said. And perhaps because by then I had heard one woman too many collapse into confusion, I blurted out, "Well, how ambitious would you say you are?"

The question stopped her cold. She got up from the couch, slung her hands into her pockets, and swiveled around to face me. "Well, I don't know," she said. "That's the other question. That's the other obvious question. Because as I'm starting to look around, I'm beginning to wonder now. I always thought I was very ambitious, and I *seem* to be very ambitious. But I wonder how much I would be willing to compromise. Maybe more than I thought.''

The tug of compromise had been a reality for all but a few of the women in the class of 1975 at the Harvard Business School. Among those who were torn, fewer still chose not to compromise. Tess was among those very few.

So in answer to Tess's question about my future, I talked about the new housekeeper Paul and I had just hired to care for our daughter. I talked about the house we were planning to buy. And I talked about my career. I told her I was hoping to strike out in a new direction, writing books full-time perhaps, or, maybe as an interim step, going to work for a magazine. I was being purposely vague about my plans because I wasn't sure myself. The only point I wanted to get across was that I was ready for a second chance should it choose to come my way. I had discovered the woman I wanted to be, and like Holly herself, I was no longer afraid to face the future.

Epilogue:

The Score

A friend of mine who read several drafts of this book suggested at one point that she would like to read a chapter about all of the women in the class. She wanted to know how the group as a whole compared with the six women I chose to make the central characters.

Whenever I considered this task, I found myself coming back to sets of numbers which for me helped put the group into perspective. The first set showed that the eighty-two women I interviewed came from a range of backgrounds that fell a cut above the bell curve for American society as a whole. More than half came from the upper middle class, another third from the middle class or from wealth. Put another way, only a fifth came from a background that could be considered "disadvantaged," from the lower middle class or from poverty. All but one—Tess Beckett—had graduated from college, and in 1981, they ranged in age from twenty-nine to forty.

There were only three black women in the class, and only one other minority woman, an American Indian. These minority women didn't fare well at the Business School. Two dropped out, specifically one of the black women and the American Indian. The two black women who graduated appeared to have had some special advantages. One came from an aristocratic family, the other from a family that had emphasized education as the route to success.

The high dropout rate for minority women puzzled me until I talked with the American Indian woman. She was an affable thirty-eight-year-old who had five children from two marriages and was already a grandmother. But she seemed younger than she was old. She spoke with enthusiasm about subjects such as day care for her two preschoolers and the legal clinic she hoped to start someday for her people.

She made a point of mentioning that she hadn't failed at any-thing else in her life. She had made it through college, even though she had entered in her late twenties, eight years into a marriage that eventually broke up. She made it through a master's program in education at Harvard, and she was currently making it through a midwestern law school, one of the best in the country.

But the Business School was different, she said. And when she tried to analyze her failure, she tossed aside all the conventional explanations: that her first marriage was breaking up that year, that she was having problems with her teen-age daughter. She said that another American Indian recruited the same year as she also dropped out, even though he had had the support of his family.

The reason for her failure was rather that she couldn't assimilate to the degree demanded by the Business School, she explained. She hadn't been prepared for that aspect of the school, for it was unheard of at any other school or college she had attended, nor had she felt comfortable with it. She never expected to assimilate into society at large. Her dream was to go back to her people, start the legal clinic for them.

In terms of professional accomplishments, the women as a group appear to have assimilated, at least to a certain extent, however. All but eight were working full-time in 1981, and of the eight who weren't, five had part-time jobs. The remaining three were unemployed, but two of the three spoke about returning to work in the near future. About a third of the group were working for corporations; another fifth were working for banks, insurance companies, and real-estate firms. Fourteen were consultants. Nine were working for nonprofit concerns. Six were entrepreneurs. Three were teaching at the college level. Three were pursuing graduate degrees.

Of those working full-time, the majority were earning between $30,000 and $60,000 (in 1981 dollars). Four were earning more than $100,000 and only three were earning less than $20,000. Their titles were also impressive. Those in corporations were middle to upper middle managers. Those in banking were at or near the level of vice-president; those in consulting were at the edge of partnership.

Another set of figures suggested, however, that the group paid a price for whatever assimilation they achieved. Well into the fourth decade of their lives, fewer than three fifths of the group were married, and fully one third were still single. Another thirteen had been divorced; four had remarried. Of the married and divorced women, only twenty-four had children: fifteen had one child, seven had two, one had three. Only the American Indian, with her five children, had more than three.

Then, too, of the eighty-two women I interviewed, thirty-five had been in therapy, twenty of them for an extended period of time. Four had allowed themselves to be beaten by their husbands. Two had been anorectic. Two sought refuge in Christian fundamentalism. One had been the victim of bulimia. Two were lesbians.

The various sets of numbers don't tell the whole story for the women of the class of 1975, however. From the personal conversations in which they revealed bits and pieces of their hearts and souls, I was to come to a far different conclusion about their progress in management and the professions. At a time when the doors seemed to have swung open for women, and most especially for this specific group—indeed, an "elite"—the women in the class hadn't for the most part assimilated to the degree necessary to make it to the top. Fully two fifths of the group were ambivalent or frankly not ambitious for their careers. And even the most ambitious—the Suzanne Sheehans of the class who had patterned themselves after the men who had made it—seemed to pull back from whatever one has to do or be to make it that far. Witness

Suzanne sitting in the shadows of her New York apartment, its guilded decor a monument to the femininity she didn't have or had to deny, discussing the contradictions in her personality: her desire for power cut by a humility that was virtually unknown to her powerful male superiors.

That perhaps these women were just part of a generation, men as well as women, that had eschewed the traditional definition of managerial and professional success was a theory I considered but ultimately abandoned. While I didn't do a comparative study of the men in the class of 1975, recent studies of business school graduates show that women fall behind the men who are their contemporaries in the race up the corporate ladder.

In a recent study of graduates of the classes of 1969 through 1972 at Columbia University's Graduate School of Business, for example, forty men and forty women were paired so that their social, economic, and academic backgrounds were identical. When they began working, men and women had nearly equal salaries: an average of $13,692 and $12,414, respectively. By 1979, however, the men had outpaced the women by more than two fifths: an average of $48,000 compared with $34,036. Likewise, a study of men and women in the classes of 1973, 1974, and 1975 at Stanford University's Graduate School of Business showed that the gap between men's and women's salaries had widened significantly five years into their careers. The Stanford study, moreover, pointed up that women had lower salary expectations than men, and tended more often to choose (or be chosen for) staff jobs, which are less powerful and remunerative than the line jobs men more frequently choose.

The reason for women's tendency to pull back is as fundamental as the difference between women and men, I have come to believe. The gains of the past decade notwithstanding, nothing much has changed in the country's corporations and professional associations: Business and most especially, management, is still very much a male milieu. Small wonder then why women who succeed are most often those who choose to live their lives as men in a man's world; small wonder why these women are such a select few.

In many respects, however, the fact that women pull back is a good sign. For there seems to be, in women's retrenchment, a reluctance to forfeit what is uniquely theirs, their femininity. When I first started my research for this book, I made an assumption about the women in the class of 1975. I assumed they would be representative of a very unique and select group of women, those who expected to have careers in management and the professions—women like us. In their reluctance to make themselves into men in a man's world, in their concern about retaining their femininity, however, I could see that they weren't as select a group as I had assumed. Indeed, they had a great deal in common with women in general, that massive pool of women living as wives of men, as mothers of children, as workers of one sort or another, teachers and secretaries as well as professionals and managers.

The women's reluctance to forfeit their entire selves for the sake of their careers, moreover, strikes me as a particularly thoughtful and intelligent attitude. For no matter how often a particular woman may choose to deny the feminine side of herself, the fact remains that women as a group are society's childbearers, and that is something else that will not change. While the choice to have a child is an individual one for each woman, there is no choice for the female sex as a whole, and to deny that is short-sighted at best, sheer stupidity at worst.

Ironically, the women's reluctance also strikes me as savvy from a business point of view. One of the major findings of my study, in fact, is that it isn't enough to talk about women as a homogeneous group. There are different *types* of women, and the types break down along attitudinal lines. The good news is that women don't necessarily *have to* fashion themselves totally in the male image to be successful in business—for every Suzanne Sheehan there is a Holly Lane Pfeiffer. Indeed, another one of my major findings pointed up that women who *were* ambitious for their careers were just as likely to be married, and just as likely to have children, as they were to be single or divorced.

While some of those married women admittedly had marriages they weren't committed to on an emotional level—Tess Beckett comes immediately to mind—the best part of the truth could be found in the stories of those for whom that wasn't the case. Holly's is such a story. In Holly, we see a capsule of the world of the 1980's as it pertains to professional and managerial women. Femininity notwithstanding, the women of the class of 1975 had come of age at a time when they were permitted to assimilate, at least to a certain extent. They couldn't ignore that profound change.

Indeed, Holly had not. Hers was the story of the search for a way to accommodate that change while preserving the best of what was innately hers as a woman. Hers was a story of the search for realistic solutions—not to the surface problems of who does the housework in a two-career family and who transfers for whose career—but rather to the real issues that lay deep beneath the surface. Hers was the search for the courage to decide within her own heart and mind what she really wanted to do; for the willingness to come to terms with certain realities about forming a career in today's business world—that one must put that career first, before husbands, even before children, however harsh that may sound; for the savvy to marry a man who, for all of his unwillingness to play the "supportive" role, help with the housework or care for the children, made it possible for her to be the individual she had to be in order to be a successful businesswoman.

In the final analysis, hers was the search for the wisdom to realize that she couldn't have done otherwise in today's changing world for women. As a whole, the women of the class of 1975 seemed to have realized that too. For all of their problems, they appeared as a group to be satisfied that they had gone to the Harvard Business School, that they had taken the risk to reach for their dreams. The happiest seemed to be those who were still reaching, still risking.